COMMON SENSING

Spector Books   CRA Press

Editors: Riccardo Badano, Tomas Percival,
and Susan Schuppli
Associate editor: Aslı Uludağ

CASE STUDIES

FIELD NOTES

This book series situates you, the reader, at our roundtable in the Centre for Research Architecture on the third floor of the aptly named Richard Hoggart building at Goldsmiths, University of London. Gathered 'around' this table you will find yourself amongst a group of emergent but also established spatial practitioners and researchers who convene to work together, sharing their projects and insights. These assemblies have produced a space of critical encounter and pedagogical experimentation with the aim of developing new investigative methods and speculative insights aimed at responding to and intervening into the urgent political conditions of our time. Students work collaboratively with their peers as well as with the affected communities in which their research projects are embedded. Staff and guests bring critical ideas and key works into this context.

This roundtable—which we now seek to re-animate through a series of written reflections, investigative accounts, and documented fieldworks, as well as transcribed conversations and glossaries—is both the spatial form that organises our encounters non-hierarchically and the material surface upon which projects are laid out and ideas debated. As this book series unfolds across its thematic issues we invite you to become a part of this lively environment that has nourished us intellectually and shaped us politically.

Across the series we have sought to foreground the distinctive pedagogy and field of research that distinguishes the Centre for Research Architecture. Since its founding in 2005, the Centre has brought together a diverse group of architects, artists, urbanists, geographers, lawyers, scientists, journalists, and activists to work on expanded notions of space. Projects in the Centre address contemporary struggles and conflicts as they register themselves in the transformation of environments: shifting scales and intensities from the architectural and urban to that of territorial and planetary processes, from the micro-scale of buildings and infrastructure to the macro-scale of borders and global flows. In the Centre, space is analysed as an elastic medium that is constantly reshaped by political and mediatic forces. To address such complex interrelations, our researchers have necessarily developed diverse creative and practical approaches for conducting their fieldwork and developing their conceptual frameworks. The book series explores these spatial entanglements by drawing upon contributions from current as well as former graduate students and staff, many of whom have gone on to establish investigative agencies and teach in programmes directly inspired by our work. It also includes the research of collaborators, friends, and thinkers who have informed and motivated our interventions.

Alongside spatial reformulations, the Centre has also developed specific aesthetic considerations. In conceptualising the books and laying out contributions, we have tried to retain the inventiveness of these methods and practices. Images, audio recordings, videos, maps, and other media take on specific roles within each of the projects presented. In particular, many audio-visual materials become fields of investigation in and of themselves. Alongside their means of production, their modes of circulation and their networks of exchange, such media are treated as sites of research that open areas of investigation and intervention. The quality of a photograph, the metadata of a file, the resolution of a satellite image, the frequency of an audio recording, all become registers of the complex politics of events. To transform this mode of 'investigative aesthetics' into book format, we worked with Ariadna Serrahima, to develop a number of design strategies to help readers identify the different roles that materials play throughout its pages. These highlight the interrogation of media that 'do not speak for themselves' but rather need to be patiently studied and carefully narrated in order to make their specific political claims.

Each book in the thematic series brings together a heterogeneous range of materials and contributions, with a particular attention to collective modes of knowledge production. As stated, our aim is to invite the reader into this ever-evolving pedagogical context. For those of us studying and working in the Centre for Research Architecture, the book series offers another iteration of this generative assembly in which knowledge is co-produced, shared, and mobilised. Publishing is, for us, an extension of our Roundtable forums. In this regard, each book is a collection that engages with current spatial processes and research practices and the series is a critical reflection on how these act and are acted upon in the world. Here, we must thank Spector Books for providing the framework and context for this endeavour and for their guidance and expertise on translating these projects into book form.

Situated Testimony with DG, December 2020. Source: Forensic Architecture and the Colombian Truth (2021).

A farmer indicates where his fields were fumigated, detailing how the soil became sterile and how agriculture is no longer possible in the fields. Source: Film still from *La Tierra Proscrita* (The Outlawed Earth), ongoing film project, Hannah Meszaros Martin (November 2022).

12 DECEMBER 2024

Transcription of a Roundtable discussion that took place between the editors of *Common Sensing*—Riccardo Badano, Tomas Percival, Susan Schuppli, Asli Uludağ—and researchers Hannah Meszaros Martin and Godofredo Enes Pereira

SUSAN With every book in this series, we've attempted to situate the reader in the conceptual space of the Centre for Research Architecture (CRA); welcoming them into the kinds of conversations that unfold quite literally around our roundtable. The books thus operate as proxies for these encounters, which have shaped the pedagogy, politics, and practices that take place in the Centre and which continue to thrive as graduates move out into the world to continue their research and, in some cases, to even set up their own research agencies and educational programmes. This is the case for the two guests and former PhD students, Hannah Meszaros Martin and Godofredo Enes Pereira, who join us today for a discussion around *common sensing*.

Their voices are prominent in this discussion with us, the editorial team, because both have engaged with affected communities and have also worked with different technological modes of sensing; a dynamic that mirrors the book as it moves between accounts of embodied experiences, situated knowledges, communal perspectives on the ground, and those of more automated systems of environmental monitoring such as satellite platforms and distributed sensor technologies. This shift in register between the strata of remote sensing and everyday, 'common sense' practices conditioned by their critical proximity to the ground informs and guides our discussion today.

HANNAH I think for those of us who were students at the Centre, a lot of the techniques and concepts that we work with began when we were all sitting together around this roundtable. I like this format for having a conversation around a CRA book, as it lets everyone else in on the seven-hour, never-ending discussions that we typically had—which I have to say I miss.

My project, which began in the CRA—actually during my Master's and then continued into the PhD—was about the detection and sensing of the coca plant, primarily in Colombia, as it related to its forced eradication despite the plant's spiritual and cultural importance to indigenous communities. I studied the imaging technologies that captured coca, and how these imaging technologies were used for the analysis, justification, and legitimacy of the forced eradication campaign. And because of the way that we approach things at the CRA, it wasn't just a study of these technologies, it was also about the politics of these technologies: how these technologies are mediated in different forums, what they capture, what they don't capture... and the issue of detection, which is present throughout many projects that have crossed the doors of the CRA and the Forensic Architecture (FA) agency, also based in the Centre.

I started to engage in many different collaborations while looking into the various ways in which coca and coca's destruction were being registered. This led me to investigate on multiple scales. Scalar analysis enables us to cross these different realms of sensing. It's not just from above or just from the ground. It enables us to cross-pollinate different materials with different perspectives and different forms of expertise—forms of expertise that are predominantly negated when approaching issues such as the creation of legitimate data, which then gets sanctioned by governments, circulated, and used for legal mandates, policies etc. So, my scalar analysis led me to work predominantly with farmers who had experienced forced eradication with herbicides from planes flying over their coca crops.

ASLI Can you describe for us what this scalar research involves? I'd be interested to hear in detail about some of your collaborations and engagements with farmers in relation to sensing.

HANNAH The first form of sensing I did with the farmers who I worked with was a form of what we call *situated testimony*, a method of gathering testimony that occurs in-situ, developed in documentary practices over the decades, and more recently, by Forensic Architecture, involving a participatory digital reconstruction of the event in question. My variation of situated testimony was more ethnographic, occuring in the space of their farm and engaging directly with their situated practices, modes of knowledge and expertise of the ecologies they inhabited. We walked together as they narrated how their agricultural spaces were deteriorating and changing as practices of aerial fumigation transformed them. This method led to modes of seeing that were definitely not picked up by remote sensing technologies, aerial photographs, or the different forms of seeing that are typically used to justify the practice of eradication. These other sensibilities resulted in us talking about things such as the quality of life that is in the soil, in the water, or even in their own bodies—how they were embodying and feeling the toxins that were being sprayed.

RICCARDO Did these in-situ forms of testimony produce new and different forms of environmental evidence? As I would imagine this was one of the objectives in developing your hybrid research methods.

HANNAH People often approach victims of war—in Colombia's case a decades-long internal armed conflict, combined with the US War on Drugs—simply as victims who have experienced *something*. Rarely do they see them as experts who can also have a critical lens into a situation and who can offer a form of analysis and testimony in an evidentiary manner.

Yet engaging with farmers as experts of the Earth who work with earth, plants, water, and air, and not just as victims who are solely defined by their suffering—as this definition neutralizes their expertise and knowledge and reduces their political agency to their pain—led to new modes of engagement. It led people to narrate situations of violence in ways that weren't just a repetition of what they had said to the human rights NGOs about their experiences of conflict. The people I worked with felt a sense of ownership over the stories they narrated and their participation in the research. This method of working with farmers informed the collaboration between Forensic Architecture and the Colombian Truth Commission between 2019 and 2021 that I went on to lead, in which we developed an investigation around land dispossession. This enabled me to further develop the technique I had been working with during my PhD—engaging with farmers in a way that honoured and highlighted their expertise in reading the Earth. Using the resources and technologies of Forensic Architecture, such as 3D modelling, we conducted extensive situated testimonies and used the platform Unreal to reconstruct agricultural spaces they had built but lost through years of land dispossession.

So, when thinking through a scalar analysis, it's not about negating the aerial or remote view due to its conflation with state power; it's about putting the remote view into conversation with other viewpoints. The expertise of farmers and the Earth's memory—embodied in the soil, plants, and water—should be placed alongside the work of biologists, remote sensing scientists, and others. This creates a kind of common epistemological ground, a commons that we can construct together by placing these materials into a shared field. No matter the fields a project might bring together, this is what the approach *common sensing* in the CRA does in a different way for each student.

TOMAS

I have a couple of thoughts in response to this, which relate to how, within your collaborations, you are interrogating the technology itself and its positioning as the primary means of detection. Which, as you suggest, appears to rest on a conception of legitimacy that marginalises or even negates the expertise of farmers. It strikes me that you have pointed to a central concern of this book: how to construct and sustain relationships between fundamentally different registers of information, data, and expertise within a project.

You address modes of remote sensing, but also ground-truthing, situated testimony, and diverse forms of image-making alongside narrative and storytelling practices. These scalar dynamics and the challenges posed by heterogeneous forms of evidence come up in many of the projects in this book. This leads me to wonder about the practices and methodologies you develop in your work in order to integrate these registers or, alternatively, how to read across them and cultivate a poly-perspectival view. How do these distinct forms of knowledge and representation interact and operate across the various scales of your work?

HANNAH

That definitely is an issue because, as multidisciplinary artists and practitioners, we often collect different things like sound files, videos, and photographs. And then we start making cartographies, and you end up with this very diverse range of materials, but these materials don't always speak to each other. I think the formats that do work are often like the written format, where you can narrate through different materials and across different contexts. I've been working predominantly in the space of film, in particular the experimental documentary form, which enables me to narrate different materials in the same space. I think that's why a lot of people in the CRA work in film or video in some respect.

TOMAS I have another slightly abstract question that stems from some terms that Hannah was using at the beginning: expert and expertise. And it made me think about the framework for the book more generally around the notion of 'common sense' and the role of so-called disinterested experts. There's something about the way expertise can end up humiliating or alienating people. I was also thinking about the status of facts in making claims: facts of different kinds, facts of different registers, and facts that appear as facts in particular contexts but not others. For instance, as activist and philosopher of science Isabelle Stengers reminds us, a scientific fact borne out of laboratory experimentation might not hold up as a fact out in the wild. She gives us the example of GMOs, where people have risen up against the imposition of a certain kind of technoscientific knowledge. She wants to intervene here not to take sides in this contestation but to find new and generative ways of "making sense in common"—to propagate the scene with more protagonists and avoid the bifurcation between scientific expertise on one side, and people with practical and lived experiences on the other. So, I have two questions here. First, how should we think about such forms of refusal of scientific knowledge by publics? Second, how do we reconcile a plurality of perspectives while still valuing the scientific method for determining information? A kind of multiplication of the figures involved who get to claim certain kinds of facts, such that those facts get mobilised in different ways for different kinds of commons.

SUSAN Just to add that, within the context of Forensic Architecture, it's precisely the production of collective knowledge by the agency that has, time and time again, troubled institutional frameworks like courts and served various attempts at invalidating their political and evidential claims. Expertise that is held in common, or arises out of collective forms of practice that are aggregated from across multiple disciplinary contexts, is sometimes viewed with suspicion since it's much more difficult to cross-examine the credentials of a community than an individual.

GODOFREDO Maybe I can connect to these points around this question of expertise. In the work that we (the Lithium Triangle Research Studio at the RCA) developed with Indigenous communities in the Atacama Desert, Chile, one of the things that was crucial for us was to recognise our situatedness and the contexts we speak from. This is to understand that the work we do must enter and work in composition with investigations and with knowledge produced in other situations. Both across different disciplinary positions, between academic and non-academic collaborators, between agricultural knowledge and militant groups in the area, etc. Knowledge is always situated. So how do knowledges enter in composition with each other?

And so, for us, more than expertise, we were interested in commitment and in militancy—what I call militancy as presence. The idea of militancy as presence speaks to the point that Tomas was raising about the disinterested expert. This is a massive problem that we encounter constantly. The difference between knowledge produced out of presence, out of care about something in the world, care about the consequences and the impacts of knowledge production itself, versus knowledge that is disinterested.

There was this farmer, Don Raul Chinchilla, with whom we had collaborated for a few years. Our work with legal and archaeological teams at the time was trying to understand the different types of impacts of lithium extraction in the desert. On an immediate level the impacts were very legible, it being a visibly drier environment; but at the same time, it was not so clear how these compounded with the afterlives of genocide and the different histories of extraction in that same ground.
Don Raul was fantastic in his capacity of sensing the surrounding environment, and in doing so, unleashing new lines of research for us. I remember this conversation in which he was looking at the angle of a leaf of corn. So, imagine a corn stalk with its long thin leaves growing outwards, and Don Raul raising the fact that the leaf angle wasn't as good as it used to be, that the angle was wrong for that time of year. The leaves were not as expressive as they should be, he said. His expertise was corn, he was a farmer, and he was there every day caring for it, watering it. He'd pay attention to its smell, to its colour, to its transparency, to its shine. He had substantial expert knowledge around the expected behaviour of a corn stalk. This observation eventually led us to identify that a mining company was doing unauthorised water extraction in the area. While we used remote sensing to evidence the impacts of water extraction on vegetation—we were looking at immense tracts of land—the catalyst for that discovery was Don Raul's analysis of a stalk of corn.

This speaks to the composition of different forms of expertise, in the sense of a commitment to knowledge production, because you care about something in the world. People affected by mining are researchers on a daily basis, accumulating information about the environments in which they live. You are investigating every day; that's your life. Your entire body is traversed by a kind of investigative drive, ultimately. And so, for us, it was quite natural how everyday knowledge entered into composition with our sometimes more technical knowledge. It was a common struggle.

RICCARDO I wanted to kind of reverse this question because your experience is guided by working with affected communities or constituencies that are already organised around a struggle, around a set of political languages, and around a specific socio-political context. So, I was wondering, what is the effect of this encounter with the language of design, with the production of visual materials? What does it mean to access other forms of visualisation and narration that are not necessarily the same ones that are proper to their context? What effect is the encounter having, not on you as one of the researchers, but on the community itself? I realise you've made the point that communities living in proximity to situations of harm are already researchers, but I mean in terms of rearticulating their demands or expressing these conditions in their own language. How does this kind of engagement with academia, with spatial design, and image-making techniques impact them?

HANNAH I'm pretty careful around the use of the word 'community' in my work, just because there are many different kinds of communities. Communities are very complicated structures with their own inner politics and inner desires. So, first of all, my technique has been predominantly to work with individuals situated within different communities. This approach allows for a clearer understanding of their own politics and guarantees a degree of safety, security, and a common understanding with those people.

It's also important to keep in mind that the issues these communities are still facing remain unresolved. The people I work with are deeply interested in telling and narrating a history that has been almost entirely erased from the national memory of the war. There's a strong interest in highlighting not just their voices but also the elements of their experiences and perspectives that have been negated.

It remains to be seen what the transformative quality of this work will ultimately be. It's important to be clear with people when you're working with them about the limitations of what different forms of media can achieve—films operate in one way, maps in another, and investigations in yet another.

That said, we know that these forms circulate in other ways. For example, the work I'm doing also engages with legal cases. Legal cases are often seen as mechanisms for change, but they're also problematic in many ways.

I think the real transformative quality comes at the meeting point—the process of actually making the thing, whatever that might be. Bringing together researchers and people who wouldn't ordinarily be in the same space to discuss these issues has a transformative quality. Then, what happens in the aftermath—how the work circulates, how the legal case unfolds, or how the transitional justice process progresses—is still an open question.

ASLI I'm very interested in how you would both define the 'commons' in *common sensing*. We talk a lot about the ways in which we synchronise different forms of sense, but it is still an open question, as the commons is composed of a whole variety of things: commonwealth, community, commoner, commoning. It's a combination of all of these things, and linked to social practices and organisational forms, natural resources, knowledge systems, modes of production, governance, individual subjectivities etc. From a Marxist perspective, the commons would be an autonomous body that is self-governed, where resources are shared equally in certain ways, and 'commoning' is the way to get there.

So then, could we conceptualise *common sensing* as a way of commoning—would that work for both of you? If so, how do we engage with the term 'commons' and all of its expansive meanings when we're talking about common sensing? For instance, Hannah, you said that you choose not to use the term community in your work, but Silvia Federici would say there would be no commons without community. Godofredo, what composition of the Commons are we talking about?

GODOFREDO I think we first need to think about the types of questions we pose and the kind of trouble we put ourselves through. Concepts are pragmatic, and processes of sensing or semiotisation are both pragmatic and existential. We could describe the type of work and the conversations that emerge from the CRA as emblematic of this condition. The academic expectations of a certain performance of concepts get constantly unsettled by the work that emerges in these types of practices—ones which we all, more or less, engage with. That expectation is constantly being undone.

For example, there's a kind of transversal, investigative aesthetic practice at stake in much of the sensing work that emerges through the CRA and FA. But if we think about it in terms of the question of the commons, which is where we're trying to get, it's something very simple: this mode of work has spread and is being replicated throughout the world. There are of course limitations that need to be considered, and asymmetries in terms of access to different types of technologies and different types of practices, etc. And yet, it's something that has transformed the field, or better, that has led to the creation of a new field of practice, first and foremost.

I just came back from a trip to areas affected by lithium mining in Brazil, and community organisations were very interested in understanding certain FA approaches and techniques and in learning how to put them to use. A commons was produced—in the sense of modes of knowledge production that were not privatised, and that were shared and made shareable, able to be used and modified in different situations.

We can think of the work that emerges out of the CRA as oriented towards a commons, in the sense of being oriented towards the possibility of being replicated, reappropriated, reinvented, and re-transformed throughout the world—and that has been happening with all sorts of different nuances.

ASLI Would you say, then—if we are to stay with concepts—that this connects to the notion of collective modes of sense-making we talked about earlier?

GODOFREDO It means that we don't just produce drawings and maps together, we also produce the words that are used to narrate events. Even if we use the same word, its political, affective, and existential resonances will change to a point where certain struggles will find it very important to speak in terms of community, and other struggles will not. There's no possible academic resolution to that problem and it's not simply a recognition that words exist in situated contexts. Images, 3D renderings, point cloud datasets, words—none of these things exist *only* as technologies out in the world. We always exist in assemblages, in compositions, and technologies are as much part of the analysis as the words that we use with each other are. I think the question of the commons, for me, is productive not as a conceptual problem that elicits some sort of resolution but as a tracing of something operative. The possibility that methodologies coming out of the CRA allow, for example, to hold the smell of corn and the gradient of a pixel together, such that those two things are not kept separate by notions of incommensurability, but instead can come together within a process of creating meaning and insights.

SUSAN There's certainly a lot of technical writing on sensing practices, but when it comes to sensing as a process for building a commons across seemingly incommensurate realities on the ground with widely divergent political stakes and cultural attachments, I think there is still much space for further theoretical reflection and critical work to be done, which is in part what motivated this book. And so I've found this conversation with everyone here today to have been incredibly enriching and enlivening in contributing to this much-needed work.

GODOFREDO I suppose it's particularly hard to grapple with the term *common sensing*, especially because it's closely tied to the history—and political history—of 'common sense'. From the phenomenological or affective dimensions of sense to the broader notion of common sense and the commons itself. These layers are quite challenging to navigate. The work of Margarida Mendes (a former PhD in the CRA and one of the contributors to this book) on sensorial ecologies adds to the techno-scientific literature on sensing, which often focuses on the precision of human and non-human sensing technologies and how they interact, by bringing to the table a bodily and expanded sensorium. This is something we see in ecological struggles, where sensing plays a key role in understanding environmental issues.

This also relates to the question of the unconscious—how subjectivities are shaped by the material, ideological, and machinic forces that traverse them—and has a significant bearing on how we engage with sensing, particularly when it's instrumentalised. Whether in the context of legal struggles or public campaigns, how do our senses and our shared ways of understanding play into these processes?

Sensing is not just about gathering data about something 'out there', it's about the collective analytical processes (in the psychoanalytical sense), it's about the ways in which we understand and relate to each other, and the larger forces that shape how we act. I think that *common sensing* is to engage in a collective analytical process. And I think it is crucial that we remind ourselves of this, when we are part of environmental, ecological, and human rights struggles. These questions need to be part of our systematic thinking about investigative practices from the outset. The collective analytical processes at stake in investigations aren't just instrumental; they're connected to our own modes of existence.

HANNAH I agree, but it's also crucial to take stock of what has been accomplished thus far in this field, especially when reflecting on the evolution of practices and the reception of unconventional expertise. One thing that stands out to me, particularly with organisations like Forensic Architecture, is the ongoing questioning of expertise, especially in more traditional forums like the law. There's often a tension when unconventional methods, such as using films or creative media in investigations, are brought into highly structured, professional spaces. It's as if these practices are seen as out of place or inappropriate for certain contexts. It's not uncommon to hear questions like "what are you doing?" or "what exactly can you bring to this field?".

Perhaps, in a sense, we're all brought together in the Centre through this shared experience of not fully fitting into neatly-defined roles that are expected in more conventional academic or professional settings. There's something profoundly generative about being in a space where you don't necessarily have a predefined role or set of expectations placed upon you. And it's precisely this experience that brings people into this kind of space—a space that thrives on its own ambiguities, where things don't have to be fully understood or fully categorised to have value.

RICCARDO May I ask then, given the interdisciplinary nature of both of your work, how do you approach decisions regarding visual materials? Specifically, how do you determine what kinds of materials and evidence are incorporated into your work and what roles they play? How do you assess their relative value?

GODOFREDO I remember, at one point, there were many exhibitions using remote sensing images. Spectacular, large-scale images, data visualisations, this sort of thing. Of course, the nitty-gritty of remote sensing, counting pixels and putting them into graphs, is not glamorous. But these dramatic visual representations seemed to dominate, rather than the actual practice and labour of remote sensing. But here's the thing: we don't do this work merely as computers. We're not simply making decisions regarding visual materials in an instrumental way. There's a whole range of human aspects—desire, sensibilities—that shape how we relate to images. These aren't just static visual representations.

Even when we don't always have a clear, instrumental reason for deploying these tools, they form part of an ecology of practices. They are how we become accustomed to certain ways of working and, eventually, certain ways of seeing and interacting with the world. These practices, these images, they have a social dimension. If we reduce it all to a purely instrumental capacity, we lose something essential—something that is both personal and collective, something that shapes how we imagine and feel the world.

TOMAS I have a question about the decision to use certain kinds of materials and certain kinds of visualisations derived from sensory systems. Specifically, I'm curious about the decision to use these visual materials not necessarily against but in parallel with the ways in which they are typically understood to be produced and the forms of evidence they represent. Godofredo mentioned the sensibility of these materials, so I wonder if we could explore further the aesthetic register of the sensory. Here, I am thinking about the aesthetic dimension not solely in terms of formal qualities but also as a sense-making practice. This leads me to think about what has been termed the *sensory turn* in certain fields of social research: attempts to theorise sensing while also valuing the unique capacities of non-textual and aesthetic materials. I wonder how your engagements with the multiplicity of sensory materials produce distinct kinds of encounters and experiences. How do you approach such materials in what might seem like opposing ways—both as evidence, functioning as indexical registrations of events on the ground (for instance, counting pixels in a satellite image), and as sensory tools that convince, compose new lines of thought, generate affects, and, perhaps, speculatively mobilise.

HANNAH My decision to include remote sensing technologies in my work is because remote sensing is operationalised to justify the forced eradication of the coca plant. Therefore, the politics and technological specificities of that form of sensing became relevant and crucial to understanding the conflicts produced by it. In our field, when you're investigating a topic, you need to look at the different technologies that are mobilised to perpetuate a form of violence and the kinds of systems and strategies employed for its dissemination, each of which has its own histories of research, development, and use. This we inherited from filmmaker Harun Farocki through his concept of the *operational image*. Thus, as practitioners, we have to decide whether to work with them or to somehow subvert and work against them.

For example, I have been working with remote sensing scientists Jamon Van Den Hoek of the Conflict Ecology Lab at Oregon State University and Paulo Murillo Sandoval from the University of Tolima to understand the methodologies employed by the United Nations Office on Drugs and Crime to analyse coca cultivation using medium resolution Landsat satellite images. This is a long-term collaboration—which started as a counter-cartographic experiment—engaging with the technical limitations of the Landsat images, which cannot see through clouds. Coca cultivation is mostly concentrated in the areas of the country with the highest frequency of cloud cover, leading us to question the results of the methodology.

In the counter-cartography, we decided to focus on the clouds instead of the ground, amassing all of the cloudy images over one location over the course of the aerial fumigation campaign. This was an attempt to see *into* the gap of information, instead of through it. Now, our collaboration has grown and is looking at detecting—using SPOT imagery—transformations of the forest where we know there was an eradication event. But I think these decisions about how to engage with a particular material are ultimately guided by what tangible forms of engagement we want to have beyond spaces of academia, and how we want our own work to be operationalised.

GODOFREDO And if I can add to that, of course our work needs to be aware of the negative impacts that it might have in bringing forth certain forms of representation that carry all sorts of hegemonic capacities when deployed by the state. So, it needs to be understood in terms of the political ecology into which our work is entering into. I remember this film that we made with GIT about lithium mining in Covas do Barroso, and we had a lot of conversations about the need to address impacts that cannot be captured by colonial forms of representation, such as spiritual impacts. And yet, those issues were already part of the struggle. The thing that was not there was someone who could produce 3D simulations of the environmental impact assessment and analyse them technically in the most technical way possible. This is precisely what was lacking, and what was urgently needed by those communities so that they could anchor claims to spiritual relationships with the mountain on the back of such a technical document.

RICCARDO I wanted to ask about the end goal of all these collective practices of *common sensing*. It seems that a lot of the research practices we are describing are kind of an endpoint, rather than a departure for defining a better way of organising together in order to respond to social-political struggles. Maybe it's just a different distribution of agency, but I would like to hear your thoughts on this.

GODOFREDO The state did not invent research; research is a basic component of being alive. It is dedicating continuous attention to something to produce shareable knowledge. You find instances of research everywhere. It was not only the relationship of intellectuals in the factory that developed the tradition of mutualist education, in which a worker teaches a worker, a brother teaches a younger sister, and so on. There's a broader genealogy. We should expand the spectrum of what constitutes research vis-à-vis the multiplicity of lines of struggle that we're trying to grapple with.

Through the work of research, you make contact with different struggles. Our environmental struggles around extractivism in Portugal take place in contact with similar struggles that are happening in Brazil or Chile. So, we're constantly thinking these avenues of militant research together, at the same time, which is structurally very interesting because you immediately see the limits of the concepts and practices that you deploy, since they never work everywhere.

SUSAN Thank you to everyone for joining us around the table today and trying to make sense of what we've come to hold in common, it's been an inspiring conversation with which to open this book.

CASE

STUDIES

SENSING A PLANET ON FIRE AND LISTENING WITH FORESTS

Jennifer Gabrys

Wildfires are increasingly consuming forests, grasslands, and peatlands around the world. One view of fires can be found on the NASA web platform for the Fire Information for Resource Management System (or FIRMS), which is used primarily in North America to monitor wildfires, but has also been used to spot conflagrations during the Ukraine War. The site shows red dots flickering against a Blue Marble static background of the planet. These geospatial points amass into thick red conglomerations across the Brazilian Amazon, as well as the forests and grasslands of Eastern Africa, and the diverse landscapes of western North America. Remote sensing satellites provide observations and data on "thermal anomalies" to signal where fires could be occurring in near real-time (NRT). Aqua and Terra satellites send data from the Moderate Resolution Imaging Spectroradiometer (MODIS), while the S-NPP, NOAA 20, and NOAA 21 satellites transmit Visible Infrared Imaging Radiometer Suite (VIIRS) imagery.[1] Satellites positioned 700 to 800 kilometres from Earth send Earth systems data for monitoring not just fires but also water and carbon cycles, among other variables. Here, fires materialise within sensory infrastructures through multiple modes of detection, alert and action. Yet many other ways of sensing fire are materialising, or being re-encountered or transforming, as fire events grow and spread worldwide.

Forest fires point to the changing sensory ecologies or milieus that could be required to detect and respond to planetary transformations. They can spark and remake collective sensing practices.[2] This focus on collective sensing practices considers sensing not from the perspective of a pre-formed universal human subject with fixed sensory apparatuses acting on a relatively inert world 'out there', but rather through the distinct distributions of sense and sensation that materialise across entities and environments.[3] These are

1 The FIRMS website, along with multiple datasets and imagery options, can be found at https://firms.modaps.eosdis.nasa.gov.

2 For a more extended discussion of different approaches to "collectivising sense", see Jennifer Gabrys, *Citizens of Worlds: Open-Air Toolkits for Environmental Struggle* (University of Minnesota Press, 2022).

3 This is a concept I develop in more depth in Jennifer Gabrys, *Program Earth: Environmental Sensing and the Making of a Computational Planet* (University of Minnesota Press, 2016).

changing compositions. Environments are now transforming, often irrevocably, through the force of climate change, biodiversity loss, and land-use change. Humans and more-than-humans affect and are affected by these transformations, where the possibilities of sensing, signalling, and acting are composed together in distinct worlds of experience. Forest fires and post-fire landscapes summon different ways of sensing, experiencing, and acting within these altered ecologies. How does fire erupt into or transform sensory worlds? And how do different modes of sensing fire enable practices of collectivising sense? Through a more extended engagement with a post-fire landscape in Chile, this essay considers these questions by moving through locations where fire, forests, technologies, humans, and more-than-humans differently materialise and collectivise sense in a time when the planet is on fire.

LISTENING WITH FORESTS

This investigation into forest fires and technologies is situated within the context of an ongoing research project, Smart Forests, which examines how digital technologies, forest environments, and social life are being reworked in this time of planetary change. In the Smart Forests project, we are investigating carbon markets, biodiversity credits, participatory mapping for land rights, and forest fires at sites in Indonesia, Holland, India, Chile, and the United Kingdom, among other places.[4] We ask how digital technologies help to tune into forests, how they potentially limit sensory engagements, and what the consequences of these eco-social formations could be, especially in relation to democratic environmental engagements. A key focus of the Smart Forests research is to consider the "cosmopolitics of socio-technical worlds", where forest engagements are necessarily plural, extending across understandings, experiences, and transformations of forests.[5] The politics of forest worlds, in other words, incorporate diverse ways of living with and in relation to these environments, as well as with the technologies used to observe and care for them. By researching the different technologies that are proliferating alongside forest environments, Smart Forests keeps in mind these plural inhabitations and the many ways in which environmental politics can materialise.

Forests are now affected by heat, drought, insects, and invasive species, as well as disturbance in the form of deforestation, fragmentation, development, fires, and more. Forests have signalled multiple alerts, yet their warnings have not been sufficiently heeded or acted upon. While wildfires can be integral to the regeneration of some environments, they are also increasing in severity, frequency, and extent due to climate change, especially but not limited to the wildlands-urban interface. Forest fires can indicate environments under stress, signalling different conditions of environmental change and sounding multiple alerts within and across ecological relations. Forests can be more prone to fires, especially megafires, because of the ecological stresses they endure. Climate change is often rendered as

4 More information on the Smart Forests project can be found at https://smartforests.net.

5 Jennifer Gabrys et al., "Reworking the Political in Digital Forests: The Cosmopolitics of Socio-technical Worlds", *Progress in Environmental Geography* 1, no. 1-4 (2022): 58-83.

an imminent event, with the warning that there are only a set number of years left to avert catastrophe. In common discourse, it is also often said that "our house is on fire", and we need to find an adequate way to respond to the current emergency. But many catastrophic fires have already occurred, and environments have been significantly altered. Signals of environmental change, such as fires, will continue to ignite environments into increasingly destructive conflagrations. There is no shortage of sites where the 'house' has burned down, the environment has changed, and transformed ecologies are taking hold. As anthropologist Adriana Petryna notes, the "runaway change" of warming climates and burning environments creates "perceptual divergence", where unpredictable and uncontrollable fires destroy usual ways of understanding and managing them.[6] Yet uncertainty and ambiguity can be integral to the very conditions of sensory infrastructures, as Rahul Mukherjee has shown through his research into nuclear power plants and mobile phone masts.[7]

Conaf Boldo 1 fire headquarters with a view of geospatial tools used to track fires in the region in relative real-time. Source: Image by author (2023).

Conaf Boldo 1 fire headquarters with a view of a map for tracking the severity of fire incidents in the region. Source: Image by author (2023).

6 Adriana Petryna, "Wildfires at the Edges of Science: Horizoning Work amid Runaway Change", *Cultural Anthropology* 33, no. 4 (2018): 570-595.

7 Rahul Mukherjee, *Radiant Infrastructures: Media, Environment, and Cultures of Uncertainty* (Duke University Press, 2020).

Perhaps in part due to its perceptual unruliness, fire is a paradigmatic example of an event that is at once changing forests while also becoming the focus of an increasing range of technological systems to manage it.

Remote sensing is a key tool for monitoring fires, and numerous platforms track blazes. Yet fire is more than the moment of the blaze: it extends to how land is managed and how or whether regeneration occurs. Satellite monitoring can help avert fires before they occur and identify potential for regeneration after the fire. Monitoring and alerting infrastructures span remote sensing satellites, watchtowers increasingly equipped with AI-powered cameras, and geospatial dashboards for mapping, modelling, and gauging risk about near real-time fire events.[8] Yet the use of these tools, and the responses to them, depend upon social-political responsiveness and resources to address changing environments. As researchers working on "critical remote sensing", "machinic vision", and pluralities of planet sensing suggest, power and politics suffuse observations that come to make the most sense, while also raising questions of what is left out of these prevailing perspectives.[9]

While an extensive range of FireTech is now being developed to monitor, detect, and manage fires, no amount of technological infrastructure can operate separately from the eco-social sensory practices and relations that detect and respond to fire worlds. Indigenous land practices engage with fire as an ancestral technology, rather than an event to be entirely suppressed.[10] With fire as a relational, seasonal, and ecological technique for cultivating and shaping environments, a different eco-technical configuration of how to listen, sense, respond, and act in relation to changing environments materialises. Different modes of sensing, whether through Indigenous attunements to land and water, land conflict, or environmental change, can generate different inhabitations and modes of action that counter prevailing modes of common sense, while also creating new or transformed sensory worlds.[11]

8 For just a few examples of emerging FireTech projects and practices, which include attending to the social-cultural aspects of fire management, see the Smart Forests Atlas Radio, including Shefali Juneja Lakhina & Jennifer Gabrys, "Shefali Lakhina: Innovating FireTech with Frontline Communities", Smart Forests Atlas (2024), https://atlas.smartforests.net/en/radio/shefali-lakhina; and Waleed Haddad & Jennifer Gabrys, "BurnBot: Mitigating Wildfire Risks through Prescribed Burns", Smart Forests Atlas (2024), https://atlas.smartforests.net/en/radio/burnbot.

9 For example, see Mia M. Bennett et al., "The Politics of Pixels: A Review and Agenda for Critical Remote Sensing", *Progress in Human Geography* 46, no. 3 (2022): 729-752; Lila Lee-Morrison et al., "Introduction: Machinic Visions of the Planetary", *Media+Environment* 5, no. 1 (2023): 1-7; and Michael Richardson & Anna Munster, "Pluralising the Planetary: The Radical Incompleteness of Machinic Envisioning", *Media+Environment* 5, no. 1 (2023): 1-24.

10 For example, see Amy Cardinal Christianson et al., "Centering Indigenous Voices: The Role of Fire in the Boreal Forest of North America", *Current Forestry Reports* 8, no. 3 (2022): 257-276; and Robin Wall Kimmerer & Frank Kanawha Lake, "The Role of Indigenous Burning in Land Management", *Journal of Forestry* 99, no. 11 (2001): 36-41.

11 While not directly focused on fire, these parallel registers of disrupting, pluralising, querying, and mobilising sense can be found in research and practice, including Michaela Spencer et al., "Asymmetries and Climate Futures: Working with Waters in an Indigenous Australian Settlement", *Science, Technology, & Human Values* 44, no. 5 (2019): 786–813; Susan Schuppli, *Material Witness: Media, Forensics, Evidence* (MIT Press, 2020); and Matthew Fuller & Eyal Weizman, *Investigative Aesthetics: Conflicts and Commons in the Politics of Truth* (Verso, 2021).

AFTER THE FIRE: CHINA MUERTA

Let's turn to visit one site, China Muerta in the central-South region of Chile, where fires have transformed landscapes, to consider the sensory ecologies that materialise there. Even relatively remote protected reserves, such as China Muerta, are affected by climate change's stresses. A containment zone against climate change, which pervades and irrevocably alters every landscape on Earth, is impossible. China Muerta is a 9,887 hectare forest reserve created in 1968 by the Chilean Ministry of Agriculture.[12] Chilean researchers and Mapuche inhabitants have referred to the site name as a "colonial wound", since it means 'dead China' and carries the residue of violence committed against the Mapuche people.[13] With this colonial violence comes the disruption to traditional fire practices, as well as cosmologies for sensing and connecting to the land through non-extractive inhabitations.

Overview from mountain peak in China Muerta, with a view of *araucaria* trees with varying levels of fire damage. Source: Image by author (2023).

Llaima watches over the reserve—an active volcano that frequently erupts. Many other active volcanoes exist in the area, including the most active in South America, Villarrica, which is more distant but exhibits frequent seismic activity. As with other locations in Chile, China Muerta is subject to multiple environmental hazards, not just in the form of volcanoes, earthquakes, and flooding, but also forest fires. While Chile is typically not described as a fire-dependent environment, it has been relatively fire-resilient, until more recent and intense fires have changed the severity and intensity of

12 "Reserva Nacional China Muerta", Información del Parque, Corporación Nacional Forestal (Conaf), accessed December 2024, https://www.conaf.cl/parques/reserva-nacional-china-muerta.

13 As Noelia Figueroa Burdiles and Francisca Vergara-Pinto write about their research, "The results show how the fire was a scenario that made visible the sociocultural diversity of a territory, involving different subjectivities in the understanding of this socionatural disaster and the territory itself; through the mechanisms of participation, action and containment of the fire, as well as through the questioning about the future of the territory and the name of the 'China Muerta' Reserve, which, in our opinion, reveals a colonial wound that continues until our days". Noelia Figueroa Burdiles & Francisca Vergara-Pinto, "Reserva Nacional China Muerta: Consideraciones en torno a la conservación biocultural de la naturaleza, los incendios forestales y la herida colonial en territorios indígenas", *CUHSO: Cultura-Hombre-Sociedad* 28, no. 1 (2018): 102-127.

these events.[14] A large number of *araucaria* trees populate the China Muerta site. These unique species grow in the temperate rainforests of Chile and have adapted to withstand heat and fire, especially from volcanic eruptions. The thick reptilian bark of the *araucaria* trees constructs an epidermal shield to lava flows and flying embers from this geologically active site.

I am visiting this site as part of a collaboration on forest fires in the La Araucanía region with the art-science group Fundación Mar Adentro and with the guide of Paola Arroyo Vargas, who is a forest and fire ecologist and member of Andres Fuentes's research group at la Universidad de la Frontera in Temuco.[15] The research group has focused on China Muerta since the fire. They have extensive knowledge of how the fire ignited, spread, and re-shaped the landscape. Their work has provided a long-term study of the site, showing how initial regeneration occurred—often through the introduction of exotic species carried by livestock—and how native species have been much slower and less likely to regrow in these post-fire conditions.

In March 2015, a fire started on adjacent private land, sparked by a smouldering bonfire common in the Chilean South, where people

Map of the 2015 wildfire at China Muerta showing severity of fire damage and areas where the Fuentes research group has conducted research. Map by the Fuentes research group, shared by Paola Arroyo Vargas. Source: Image by author (2023).

Araucaria trees with destroyed bark, with a view over an *araucaria* forest decimated by fire. Source: Image by author (2023).

14 Xavier Úbeda & Pablo Sarricolea, "Wildfires in Chile: A Review", *Global and Planetary Change* 146 (2016): 152-161.

15 Fundación Mar Adentro, https://fundacionmaradentro.cl; Andres Fuentes-Ramirez, https://andresfuen.weebly.com.

clear brush, vegetation, and rubbish with *quemas controladas*, or controlled burns. The fire spread to adjoining land, encompassing the China Muerta Reserve and two other protected sites, the Nalca Lolco Reserve and the Conguillio National Park. The fire burned for twenty-three days and scorched 3,765 hectares of forests.[16] This was a "*megaincendio*", or a megafire of high intensity that burned in such a way as to completely consume the landscape, from soil to canopy.

What was left in the post-fire landscape of China Muerta was a charred and blackened landscape, where less fire-tolerant trees such as *Nothofagus* species, including *lenga* and *coigüe*, were completely decimated, along with vegetation ground layers. The usually fire-adapted *araucaria* trees also succumbed to extensive fire damage, with many trees destroyed and others pushed into a semi-living state, partially dead but lingering branches that continued to sprout and send out new growth. Paola tells us that the sap inside the *araucaria* trees can become so hot during a megafire that it can reach boiling point and explode through the top of the tree. We witness many trees with severed canopies, stubs of charred branches stabbing the sky. Paola also suggests the fire could have been much worse if it had not occurred in the Southern Hemisphere's autumn, with winter and cooler temperatures approaching.

This megafire was a sensory alert, triggering action to extinguish the fire. Yet, it was also a provocation to consider the changing sensory ecologies in which forest fires occur. As social sciences researchers Noelia Figueroa Burdiles and Francisca Vergara-Pinto note, the fire surfaced the diversity of ways of experiencing, relating to, and understanding the area within and around the China Muerta Reserve. For Mapuche people, fire exists within a cosmological and ancestral relation. For land managers and other actors, fire is a disruptive event to be controlled.[17] These different relations to fire, and fire technologies, are expressive of different environmental knowledges, modes of sensing and experiencing, and responding and acting to fire as part of ecological processes. Environmental sensing, more broadly, can be a practice that spans expert, Indigenous and citizen science, or that weaves together different worlds of experience. At times, these modes of sensing are likely to be in conflict, especially when land practices and relations are at stake. While environmental sensing could be a way to collectivise sense, it could also pluralise such practices as they make evident different or even incommensurable worlds of experience.

While much attention is given to the cause of fires, with this fire attributed to accidental causes, the reality is that forests and other environments such as grasslands and urban-rural interfaces, are much more fire-prone due to the increasing climate- and land-use related stresses to environments. Dry, hot, and windy conditions, along with the build-up of fuel in dense vegetation, can cause fires to take hold and grow into much more intense conflagrations. Megafires are signals of ecological relations,

16 Andrés Fuentes-Ramirez et al., "Spatio-Temporal Variation in Soil Nutrients and Plant Recovery across a Fire-Severity Gradient in Old-Growth *Araucaria-Nothofagus* Forests of South-Central Chile", *Forests* 13, no. 3 (2022): 1-15.

17 Figueroa Burdiles & Vergara-Pinto, "Reserva Nacional China Muerta".

both in the spark taking hold, and in the way that landscapes transform.[18] Such fires are not a singular event. Instead, they pose ongoing transformations to environmental inhabitations, triggering interconnected alterations within entire ecosystems.

Nowhere is this more evident than in the post-fire landscape at China Muerta. Nine years after the megafire event, the forest reserve is slow to move toward conditions of regeneration. A bleached and exposed congregation of *araucaria* trees files up and down the steep terrain. Scribbles of Chilean bamboo (or *colihue*) fill the forest floor and prevent other vegetation from sprouting. Occasional *araucaria* saplings take hold. Lizards sun on the sun-absorbent charred remains of trees, and occasional mushrooms spring from the seams of barkless *araucaria* trunks.

Neither entirely lifeless nor returning to its prior flourishing forest condition, the China Muerta Reserve hovers within a state of half-life. Fires can bring conditions of renewal, but megafires are more likely to scorch landscapes beyond recognition, pushing them to entirely altered states. This is the case with the Amazon, where extensive and intensive fires, extreme drought, increasing temperatures, and forest fragmentation are pushing the forest into changes of state, so much so that parts of the Amazon are likely to become savannahs or carbon sources rather than carbon sinks. What the work of Andres Fuentes's group has found is that regeneration is slow to take hold, and that it is unlikely to occur without intervention. If forests such as China Muerta are to regenerate, then deliberate planting and reworking of landscapes will need to happen.

The transformations that these events spark are not a mere response and move to safety. Instead, they signal what has been lost, what continues to be lost, and the emerging conditions of detection and response that are now unfolding within these transformed sensory ecologies. Regeneration is unlikely to return to a prior condition. Instead, it is a practice of anticipating and working with land that will increasingly burn, adapting practices to fire ecologies, and creating forms of eco-social organisation that can coexist with (while not amplifying) ongoing fires. How could it be possible to create and open up sensory protocols required for detecting and responding to these transformed environments? How do cosmologies of land, experience, fire, technology, and ecological relations guide the sensory collectives that might need to come into formation to respond to these altered worlds? As multiple researchers have suggested, such openings into other land-fire and forest cosmologies could require "decolonising experiments",[19] as well as other "forest futurisms" that different configure environmental temporalities and relations.[20]

18 For discussions of megafires, as well as the suggestion that current planetary conditions could be characterised as the Pyrocene, see Stephen J. Pyne, *The Pyrocene: How We Created an Age of Fire, and What Happens Next* (University of California Press, 2022); and John Vaillant, *Fire Weather: A True Story from a Hotter World* (Sceptre, 2023).

19 Timothy Neale et al., "Walking Together: A Decolonising Experiment in Bushfire Management on Dja Dja Wurrung Country", *Cultural Geographies* 26, no. 3 (2019): 341-359.

20 Kate Lewis Hood & Jennifer Gabrys, "Keeping Time with Digital Technologies: From Real-Time Environments to Forest Futurisms", *Environment and Planning D: Society and Space* 42, no. 2 (2024): 254–74.

SENSORY PROTOCOLS FOR PLANETARY TRANSFORMATION

A day after our visit to China Muerta, our fieldwork group is back in Temuco, the urban capital of the Araucanía region. From Cierro Ñielol, a ceremonial Mapuche site and urban park, we observe *quemas controladas* in the form of agricultural fires that encircle the city and impart a characteristic smoky smell and haze to the air. In the evenings, these fires can bring a rain of particles to airways, where the sun turns lava red as the evening inversion of the atmosphere takes place. Within this fire landscape, where fires have occurred and will continue to catch light, we find ourselves on the edge of an island river park, shored up by boulders against seasonal floods, and marked by debris that washes in and collects after heavy rains. Informal houses occupy a middle ground while a ruined tower overwatches the site.

Bomberos conducting emergency rehearsal in Temuco, Chile, near the Cautín River. View of Puente Treng Treng Kay Kay, with *quemas controladas* in the background. The name of the bridge is based on a Mapuche legend about two sea- and land-serpents. Source: Image by author (2023).

Uncannily and unplanned, we approach the scene of an emergency rehearsal where *bomberos*, or firefighters, stage the scaling of the bank, funnelling supplies to an imagined disaster scene at the edge of the river, while hoisting simulated bodies in orange rafts up its banks. One *bombero* explained to us the objective of their exercise, which was to test the use of equipment and scenarios. They travel to France every summer to practice drills and then continue their training in Chile. In the slow movements of cords and pulleys being winched into place, and *quemas* billowing white-grey smoke on the near horizon, we find further evidence that this is a region defined by fire. Fire practices are part of land cultivation. Geothermal activity undergirds and surrounds all environments. And increasing drought and heat cause dangerous conflagrations across rural and urban sites, which further require continual preparations for the disasters to come.

What the *bomberos'* exercise demonstrates is that emergency protocols unfold within extended sensory ecologies. They set in motion responses to an anticipated, or actual, emergency. Scenarios are ways of testing and adapting to the potential conditions in which emergencies could play out. When the alarms have already sounded and the fires have blazed through, the practices and infrastructures of environmental engagement require staging other responses to and for these transformed sensory ecologies. Such responses could involve collectivising and pluralising sense,[21] unmaking 'common sense', and working toward different modes of "disobedient sensing",[22] as well as "resonant ecologies" for transversal solidarities.[23] The sensory protocols that could be required to act within these post-fire worlds would then require pacing and testing together—to engage in collective inquiry, to experiment within lived environments, and to pause, iterate, adapt, and work within conditions of planetary transformation for greater eco-social flourishing.

ACKNOWLEDGEMENTS

Thanks are due to the Smart Forests research group, Fundación Mar Adentro, Pablo González Rivas, Paula Tiara Torres, Paola Arroyo Vargas, Andres Fuentes and the Fuentes research group at the Universidad de la Frontera, Temuco, Chile, for contributing to this research. This project has received funding from the European Research Council (ERC) under the European Union's Horizon 2020 research and innovation programme (grant agreement No. 866006).

21 Gabrys, *Citizens of Worlds*.
22 Lorenzo Pezzani & Heller, "AIS Politics: The Contested Use of Vessel Tracking at the EU's Maritime Frontier", *Science, Technology, & Human Values* 44, no. 5 (2019): 881–899.
23 Monika Halkort, "Resonant Ecologies: Reading Solidarity Transversally in the Mediterranean Sea", *International Journal of Communication* 15 (2021): 2724-2742.

WORKS CITED

Bennett, Mia M., Janice K. Chen, Luis F. Alvarez León, & Colin J. Gleason. "The Politics of Pixels: A Review and Agenda for Critical Remote Sensing". *Progress in Human Geography* 46, no. 3 (2022): 729-752.

Christianson, Amy Cardinal, Colin Robert Sutherland, Faisal Moola, Noémie Gonzalez Bautista, David Young, & Heather MacDonald. "Centering Indigenous Voices: The Role of Fire in the Boreal Forest of North America". *Current Forestry Reports* 8, no. 3 (2022): 257-276.

Figueroa Burdiles, Noelia, & Francisca Vergara-Pinto. "Reserva Nacional China Muerta: Consideraciones en torno a la conservación biocultural de la naturaleza, los incendios forestales y la herida colonial en territorios indígenas". *CUHSO: Cultura-Hombre-Sociedad* 28, no. 1 (2018): 102-127.

Fuentes-Ramirez, Andrés, Leonardo Almonacid-Muñoz, Nayadeth Muñoz-Gómez, & Kirk A. Moloney. "Spatio-Temporal Variation in Soil Nutrients and Plant Recovery across a Fire-Severity Gradient in Old-Growth *Araucaria-Nothofagus* Forests of South-Central Chile". *Forests* 13, no. 3 (2022): 1-15.

Fuller, Matthew, & Eyal Weizman. *Investigative Aesthetics: Conflicts and Commons in the Politics of Truth.* Verso, 2021.

Gabrys, Jennifer. *Citizens of Worlds: Open-Air Toolkits for Environmental Struggle.* University of Minnesota Press, 2022.

Gabrys, Jennifer. *Program Earth: Environmental Sensing Technology and the Making of a Computational Planet.* University of Minnesota Press, 2016.

Gabrys, Jennifer, Michelle Westerlaken, Danilo Urzedo, Max Ritts, & Trishant Simlai. "Reworking the Political in Digital Forests: The Cosmopolitics of Socio-technical Worlds". Progress in Environmental Geography 1, nos. 1-4 (2022): 58-83.

Haddad, Waleed, & Jennifer Gabrys. "BurnBot: Mitigating Wildfire Risks through Prescribed Burns". Smart Forests Atlas (2024), https://atlas.smartforests.net/en/radio/burnbot.

Halkort, Monika. "Resonant Ecologies: Reading Solidarity Transversally in the Mediterranean Sea". *International Journal of Communication* 15 (2021): 2724-2742.

Kimmerer, Robin Wall, & Frank Kanawha Lake. "The Role of Indigenous Burning in Land Management". *Journal of Forestry* 99, no. 11 (2001): 36-41.

Lakhina, Shefali Juneja, & Jennifer Gabrys. "Shefali Lakhina: Innovating FireTech with Frontline Communities". Smart Forests Atlas (2024). https://atlas.smartforests.net/en/radio/shefali-lakhina.

Lee-Morrison, Lila, Kathrin Maurer, Rikke Munck Petersen, & Dominique Routhier. "Introduction: Machinic Visions of the Planetary". *Media+Environment* 5, no. 1 (2023): 1-7.

Lewis Hood, Kate, & Jennifer Gabrys. "Keeping Time with Digital Technologies: From Real-Time Environments to Forest Futurisms". *Environment and Planning D: Society and Space* 42, no. 2 (2024): 254–74.

Monteiro, Marko, & Raoni Rajão. 2017. "Scientists as Citizens and Knowers in the Detection of Deforestation in the Amazon". *Social Studies of Science* 47, no. (2017): 466–484.

Mukherjee, Rahul. *Radiant Infrastructures: Media, Environment, and Cultures of Uncertainty.* Duke University Press, 2020.

Neale, Timothy, Rodney Carter, Trent Nelson, & Mick Bourke. "Walking Together: A Decolonising Experiment in Bushfire Management on Dja Dja Wurrung Country". *Cultural Geographies* 26, no. 3 (2019): 341-359.

Petryna, Adriana. "Wildfires at the Edges of Science: Horizoning Work amid Runaway Change". *Cultural Anthropology* 33, no. 4 (2018): 570-595.

Pezzani, Lorenzo, & Charles Heller. "AIS Politics: The Contested Use of Vessel Tracking at the EU's Maritime Frontier". *Science, Technology, & Human Values* 44, no. 5 (2019): 881–899.

Pyne, Stephen J. *The Pyrocene: How We Created an Age of Fire, and What Happens Next.* University of California Press, 2022.

Richardson, Michael, & Anna Munster. 2023. "Pluralising the Planetary: The Radical Incompleteness of Machinic Envisioning". *Media+Environment* 5, no. 1 (2023): 1-24.

Schuppli, Susan. *Material Witness: Media, Forensics, Evidence.* MIT Press, 2020.

Smart Forests. Accessed December 2024. https://smartforests.net.

Smart Forests. "Smart Forests Atlas". Accessed December 2024. https://atlas.smartforests.net.

Spencer, Michaela, Endre Dányi, & Yasunori Hayashi. "Asymmetries and Climate Futures: Working with Waters in an Indigenous Australian Settlement". *Science, Technology, & Human Values* 44, no. 5 (2019): 786–813.

Úbeda, Xavier, & Pablo Sarricolea. "Wildfires in Chile: A Review". *Global and Planetary Change* 146 (2016): 152-161.

Vaillant, John. *Fire Weather: A True Story from a Hotter World.* Sceptre, 2023.

'SOY EL RÍO CAUCA Y MIS AGUAS PODRÍAN AFECTAR TU SALUD'

Ifor Duncan

Walking to the end of a canyon track we arrive at the ferry port and are met by a group of warning signs branded by the hydropower company. One sign reads:

> *"Soy el río Cauca y mis aguas podrían afectar tu salud"*
> [I am the river Cauca and my waters may be harmful to your health]

Here at the beginnings of the long and sinuous reservoir, the furthest point from the dam's wall, a new peninsula of timber and *buchón* (water hyacinths) has accumulated beside the small ferry port of Boca de Niquia. The peninsula is patrolled by vultures that bicker atop a skeleton tree. I was told that, like other rafts of *buchón* in the reservoir, the bodies of people still being thrown into the river upstream accumulate beneath the new green growth on the surface. The peninsula is one part of the company's transformation of the entire canyon through inundation. "*Soy*": the river has become hydropower.

The Hidroituango megadam on the Cauca, Colombia's second longest river, is a 225 metre high embankment dam, which if fully realised would produce around 20 per cent of Colombia's electricity needs. Led by the controversial state-owned utilities company Empresas Públicas de Medellín (EPM), the dam has displaced thousands and submerged the remains of decades of war—including forced disappearances and the sites of the massacres of June 1996 and October 1997 conducted by paramilitary groups and implicating the state—into the river.[1]

A state of emergency occurred when errors in the dam's surveys led to the threat that the dam might collapse in 2018, and the early closure of the dam's gates in February 2019 reduced flow downstream to an ecologically threatening level. The risk of the dam failing and the resulting catastrophic flooding throughout this period meant tens of thousands of people from communities in the canyon had to be evacuated. The project has also produced a myriad of devastating ecological effects: the new growth of *buchón* (water hyacinths); algae blooms across the reservoir surface because of depleted oxygen levels; thousands of fish dying in the receding river down-

1 Massacres perpetrated by the paramilitary United Self-Defense Forces of Colombia (AUC) in June 1996 and October 1997 have been found to implicate state agents. "Ituango Massacres v. Colombia", *Inter-American Court of Human Rights*, July 1 2006, 3, 4, 13, accessed December 2024, http://www.corteidh.or.cr/docs/casos/articulos/seriec_148_ing.pdf.

stream; and the traditional methods of living with the river, such as the local economies of fishing and gold panning, are at risk of disappearance. After the threat of collapse, in 2019 a case was brought against EPM and other parties which involved the declaration of the Cauca as a subject of rights through ruling no. 38 of 17 June 2019 by the Superior Court of Medellín.[2] The ruling has many similarities to the landmark judgment T-622 of 2016 that awarded rights to the Atrato river, in the Chocó region, which has become a precedent for rights of nature in Colombia.[3] Like T-622, the Cauca ruling included the formation of a commission of river guardians.[4]

The activist group Movimiento Ríos Vivos has emerged as a coalition of communities responding to the social and ecological devastation wrought by megadam projects in the country.[5] The group directly opposing Hidroituango have become prominent, challenging the environmental and social impact of the dam while seeking justice for their disappeared loved ones and others who are buried under accumulating sediments deep within the reservoir.[6] Members of Ríos Vivos remain in the canyon despite this violence and continue to be targeted by reemergent illegal armed groups, including regular threats via social media and direct messaging.

Travelling in bullet-proof Toyotas with Ríos Vivos community leaders in April 2024 we, alongside Gerald Bermúdez who acted as my field producer and interpreter, were accompanied by armed guards funded by the state. During this research, we conducted interviews with members of Ríos Vivos, recorded video, and made field recordings with hydrophones towards a documentary artist moving image work on the interlapping politics of Hidroituango.[7] This chapter starts from the sign opposite to engage with the discourse on ecological victimhood and practices that attend to such questions. Considering the relationship between perpetrator and victim in the context of a river, here I consider how hydropower's transformation of the river into a reservoir is an act of violence against both river and community.

2 Tribunal Superior de Medellín, Sentencia de tutela No. 38 of 17 June 2019, accessed December 2024, http://files.harmonywithnatureun.org/uploads/upload837.pdf.

3 Corte Constitucional de Colombia, Sentencia T-622 of 2016, accessed December 2024, https://www.corteconstitucional.gov.co/relatoria/2016/t-622-16.htm.

4 The Atrato was the first river to be awarded legal personhood in the National Court of Colombia in 2016 to redress the devastating impacts of mercury used in illegal gold mining. Subsequently, a number of rivers and wetland ecosystems in Colombia have also been recognised as subjects of rights.

5 Movimiento Ríos Vivos, accessed December 2024, https://riosvivoscolombia.org/.

6 The accumulating sediments also pose a potential threat to the dam.

7 This research would not have been possible without the cooperation of Movimiento Ríos Vivos; the assistance of Gerald Bermúdez; as well as the ongoing support of Hannah Meszaros Martin and Óscar Pedraza of Plano Negativo, Elizabeth Gallón Droste, Nicolas Lozáno, Carolina Neu, Linda Schilling Cuellar, and colleagues at CRA. Our time with Movimiento Ríos Vivos was also shared with a group facilitated by Barcelona based Colectivo Maloka. The fieldwork was part-funded by the Department of Visual Cultures at Goldsmiths and the final writing of this chapter was supported by a postdoctoral fellowship from the European Research Council (ERC) under the European Union's Horizon 2020 research and innovation programme (grant agreement n° 101124393).

EPM warning sign at Boca de Niquia, near to the town of Sabanalarga. Source: Image by author (2024).
Aboard a boat in the centre of the Hidroituango reservoir. Source: Image by author (2024).

ENCLOSING THE RIVER: POSSESSION AND DISPOSSESSION

EPM has branded the canyon through infrastructural investments, new roads, temporary pontoons, informational brochures and shop fronts, as well as the safari-style uniforms of its army of sub-contractors. This visibility is part of the company's possession of the river and surrounding territory. A possession present in the wording of the warning sign, which tells a story of ecological transformation through the processes of extractive capital.

The company's adoption of the first-person position for the river, *"Soy"* [I am], is part of a claim to the river in an attempt to sever ties between the river and the community. In cases like Hidroituango, where armed violence has occurred near to rivers, the water bodies themselves become places of desolation. Fear is produced through the harnessing of both the predictability and unpredictability of a river's watery processes; for instance, when people are disappeared into its flows their bodies might reemerge after floating downstream. The conditioning of hydrographic processes in such a way produces what I have called *fluvial terror.*[8] Part of a wider repertoire of intimidation and violence, this is a form of terror produced in relation to territory: a strategy that employs geographic features in violent acts to produce a disjuncture between communities and their sense of place—often resulting in the displacement of people from rural areas to cities. María Victoria Uribe describes such processes in Colombia as the production of terror with the intention of scaring rural communities from their lands.[9] In many cases this violence has laid the groundwork for the development of major infrastructure projects.[10]

"Mis aguas" [my waters], indicates that these waters are now EPM's, and in becoming theirs they have been made harmful to the health of all who come into contact with them. Central to EPM's possession of the territory was the enclosure of the riverbanks, which were until that point a commons inhabited by riverside communities, including the Nutabe people.[11] The challenge to the dam involved the battle for the Nutabe to be recognised as an Indigenous group. A nomadic people based in the canyon, they were finally recognised in May 2017 by Resolution 0071 of the Directorate of Indigenous Affairs of the Colombian Ministry of the Interior. By this date, however, the town of Orobajo, declared the centre of the community, and Barbacoas, another important Nutabe town, were already submerged within the rising reservoir.[12] Likewise, the local *barequeo* (artisanal gold panning) was made

8 Ifor Duncan, "Hydrology of the Powerless" (PhD thesis, Goldsmiths, University of London, 2021), 124, https://research.gold.ac.uk/id/eprint/29967/1/VIS_thesis_DuncanI_2021.pdf.

9 Maria Victoria Uribe, "Dismembering and Expelling: Semantics of Political Terror in Colombia," *Public Culture* 16, no. 1 (2004): 79-95. See also Ulrich Oslender, "Spaces of Terror and Fear on Colombia's Pacific Coast," in *Violent Geographies: Fear, Terror, and Political Violence*, ed. Derek Gregory & Allan Pred (New York: Routledge, 2006), 111-132.

10 Juan Diego Suárez Gómez calls the facilitation of extractive projects and other infrastructures by paramilitary violence a "para-economy", Juan Diego Suárez Gómez, "The New Imagined Coammunities: The Case Of Hidroituango In Colombia" (PhD thesis, University of Missouri, 2017), 174, https://mospace.umsystem.edu/xmlui/handle/10355/67540.

11 Suárez Gómez, "The New Imagined Communities", 210.

12 "How the Powerful Hidroituango Drowned an Indigenous Territory", *Tierra de Resistentes*, 25 April 2019, accessed December 2024, https://tierraderesistentes.com/en/2019/04/25/el-territorio-indigena-que-ahogo-la-poderosa-hidroituango/.

illegal by the Ministry of Defense decree of 2012 (MDN, Decree 2235), despite efforts to list it as an intangible Cultural Heritage practice. The decree outlawed all mining by those without legal title, thus redefining what economies could be undertaken in the valley where previously no title had existed.[13] In addition to the drawn out recognition of the Nutabe, the mechanisms of defining what could be legally extracted and EPM's enclosure of the riverbanks into private property are pivotal to the process of making the waters of the canyon extractable in the form and scale of a megaproject.[14] Through these mechanisms, with the aim of dispossessing to submerge, the company's occupation of the river transforms it into a reservoir and no longer a river.

RIVER AS VICTIM

In the struggle against the dam, the rights of the living and the dead, as well as future generations, are at the mercy of the multiple parties wrestling for resources: the government, its subsidiary EPM, multinational funders, and paramilitaries. The dam fits into the drive for post-conflict development championed by the governments of Alvaro Uribe, Iván Duque, and Juan Manuel Santos. As Hannah Meszaros Martin and Óscar Pedraza have shown, after more than half a century of war, the process of transitional justice since the 2016 peace accords has excluded the role of extractive industries, thus rendering "environmental violence in the context of war invisible".[15] Cases such as Hidroituango and many others, as Martin and Pedraza argue, show that bringing justice to "mass ecological destruction" necessitates a change in the understanding of what constitutes violence. Such questions are ongoing for the government of Gustavo Petro and its dual promises to end the environmental racism experienced by Black and Indigenous groups while achieving a 'green' energy transition that relies on inherited projects such as the megascale example of Hidroituango. In the political and environmental context of the dam, the Cauca, Colombia, and river justice movements more broadly, how can we reconsider the definition of violence in terms of "mass ecological destruction"?

Elsewhere, I have focused on the weaponisation of rivers as not only the use of infrastructural interventions but also the more complex and dispersed process of conditioning riverine characteristics as discriminatory toward certain communities.[16] This conception of weaponisation is influenced by a relational or *hydrosocial* approach to rivers whereby they are understood as an expanded and dynamic assemblage of water volume, material contents, geomorphology, and the socio-cultural significance of communities with which rivers are co-constitutive.[17] To address the weap-

13 Suárez Gómez, "The New Imagined Communities," 186.

14 Rutgerd Boelens, Arturo Escobar, Karen Bakker, et al., "Riverhood: political ecologies of socionature commoning and translocal struggles for water justice", *The Journal of Peasant Studies* 50, no. 3 (2023): 1125-1156, 1129.

15 Hannah Meszaros Martin & Oscar Pedraza, "Extinction in transition: coca, coal, and the production of enmity in Colombia's post-peace accords environment", *Political Ecology* 28, (2021): 721-740, 723.

16 Ifor Duncan & Stefanos Levidis, "Weaponizing a River", *E-Flux Architecture* (2020), https://www.e-flux.com/architecture/at-the-border/325751/weaponizing-a-river/.

17 Jamie Linton & Jessica Budds, "The Hydrosocial Cycle: Defining and mobilizing a relational-dialectical approach to water", *Geoforum* 57 (2014): 170-180.

onisation of water in this context means to also understand the violence conducted upon it beyond its materiality, and to encompass its expanded socio-ecological dimensions.

On 11 July 2023, a stretch of the river hundreds of miles upstream of Hidroituango in the Cauca region was accredited with the status of victim of armed conflict by the Jurisdicción Especial Para La Paz (JEP), the commission for transitional justice in Colombia. Accreditation AUTO No. 226 was made primarily on the basis of armed violence between 2000 and 2004 (and over a longer time frame between 1993 and 2016), during which time thousands of bodies were disappeared into the river. Central to this ruling is GROUP Case No. 005 of 2018 under the name of "Territorial Situation in the region of Northern Cauca and Southern Valle del Cauca" (from here on Case No. 5), which was requested by Afro-Colombian community councils to address the imbricated use of the river as a cemetery for violence against the communities and contamination from illegal mining.[18] The community groups in the municipality of Buenos Aires, which was particularly impacted, stated that:

> *Es la posición de nuestras comunidades, expresada en el presente informe, que como entidad sujeto de derechos que podrían ser dañados, la naturaleza en sí misma, y en este caso, el río Cauca, puede convertirse en una víctima de las acciones u omisiones que perjudican sus derechos—además de que los seres humanos vean sus derechos dañados también como consecuencia.*
> [It is the position of our communities, expressed in this report, that as an entity subject to rights that could be damaged, nature itself, and in this case, the Cauca River, can become a victim of actions or omissions that harm its rights—in addition to human beings seeing their rights damaged as a consequence].[19]

The declaration of the river as a victim by the JEP was preceded in 2019 by the Superior Court of Medellín's ruling to make the Cauca a subject of rights.[20] This recognition was made to protect the river from the environmental impacts of mining and logging along its banks, but also importantly it was made in direct response to Hidroituango, demanding that EPM provide solutions and compensation for environmental, social, economic, and cultural

18 "El río Cauca fue notificado: ya es víctima acreditado del conflicto armado", *El Colombiano*, 1 April 2024, accessed December 2024, https://www.elcolombiano.com/colombia/el-rio-cauca-fue-notificado-ya-es-victima-acreditado-del-conflicto-armado-OE24137494.

19 *Auto SRVR-226* of 11 July 2023, Jurisdicción Especial Para La Paz (JEP), Salas De Justicia Sala De Reconocimiento De Verdad, De Responsabilidad Y De Determinación De Los Hechos Y Conducatas, October 2024, https://relatoria.jep.gov.co/searchproviapi/Auto_SRVR-226_11-julio-2023.

20 I hold reservations on the role of legal subjecthood in the case of rivers. Criticism of rivers being made legal subjects centre on risks of exposing them to further exploitative features of legal frameworks grounded in property logics, whereby rights become yet a further potential "market mechanism" to already proliferating forms of exploitation and devastation. Boelens, et al. "Riverhood", 1136. The International Law Commission cited in the Cauca victim accreditation stresses the importance of protecting nature as a resource and includes in its potential victims of *environmental damage* companies as well as communities. JEP, *SRVR-226*, 20. The question of river rights and legal subjecthood, however, remains of crucial importance in contexts where it is operative in defending communities, bringing the perpetrators of violence to trial, or in the prevention of the contamination and pollution of river ways even if these legal structures require radical transformation.

damage. As Alejandro Ponce de León articulates: "the court [of Medellín] also declared its decision *inter communis*, extending to 'all individuals and communities tied to the Cauca River, its tributaries, and nearby areas' (Tribunal Superior de Medellín, Sentencia de tutela No. 38, 17 June 2019)".[21] The victimhood accreditation of 2023 does not specifically state *inter communis*.

After spending a day filming at the edges of the reservoir near the town of Sabanalarga, the woman who was our guide described the memory of the river as a "torment" because of the loss of the life that it enabled for her and so many others.[22] This sensibility is also present in the words of the municipality of Buenos Aires in relation to Case No. 5 above. Much of the ruling articulates its extension to ensure the benefits of future generations. The inclusion of the basin within the ruling of rights is important in the context of a megadam to understand the full socio-ecological extent of the possession of river and canyon by the company as a spatio-temporal concern.[23] While it emphasises future generations and the river basin, the Cauca Rights ruling does not mention the impact on *comunidades étnicas* or any spiritual significance of the river, as in the example of T-622, thus ignoring the Nutabe.[24] By contrast, the 2023 JEP victim ruling does acknowledge the need to reconcile the "ties of harmony, spirituality and solidarity development that unite human and non-human ecosystems" after years of armed conflict.

Although the JEP ruling does not directly include the area affected by the dam, the terminology of victimhood with regards to the Cauca is used by people downstream in the canyon around Hidroituango. Members of Ríos Vivos know their connection to the processes that have led to the river being declared a victim upstream all too well, one man describing the river to us as a "source" and a "victim" of violence. In an incredibly moving conversation, one of the lead organisers of Ríos Vivos equated the loss of the river to the disappearance of her loved ones; as the river was the *patron* for the entire community its loss impacted everyone. She was not the only person to make this comparison, but it is important to stress that in many ways these two violences are inseparable.[25]

21 Alejandro Ponce de León, "Testimonies from a Mourning Planet: Art, Representation and Justice Beyond the Human in Latin America", Institute of Languages Culture and Society, Institute of Advanced Study, University of London, 18 September 2024, accessed December 2024, https://ilcs.sas.ac.uk/blog/.testimonies-a-mourning-planet-art-representation-and-justice-beyond-human-latin-america.

22 The members of Ríos Vivos who we interviewed remain anonymous at their own request.

23 The extension of this ruling as *inter communis* is in continuity with the Atrato ruling, which sought to challenge contamination brought by mining practices in the specific interests of the *comunidades étnicas* of the entire basin affected including its tributaries, and the Te Awa Tupua (Whanganui River Claims Settlement) Act 2017 in Aotearoa (New Zealand). Both account for the cultural significance of the rivers with the Atrato ruling stating the need to sustain the survival of spiritual and cultural relationships to the territory, and for the Whanganui "*Ko te Awa te mātāpuna o te ora*: the River is the source of spiritual and physical sustenance", an "indivisible and living whole from the mountains to the sea, incorporating the Whanganui River and all of its physical and metaphysical elements". Te Awa Tupua (Whanganui River Claims Settlement) Act of 20 March 2017, 14, accessed October 2024, http://files.harmonywithnatureun.org/uploads/upload711.pdf.a.

24 Tribunal Superior de Medellín, No. 38 of 17 June 2019.

25 Elsewhere, I have called these processes *necro-hydrology*. Ifor Duncan, "Necro-Hydrology", *E-Flux Architecture* (2023), https://www.e-flux.com/architecture/hydroreflexivity/543089/necro-hydrology/.

A mechanical gold dredger downstream of the dam. Source: Image by author (2024).
A young man listens into the reservoir above the flooded town of Orobajo. Source: Image by author (2024).

Here, I consider a further set of questions: is a river a victim when humans are disappeared into it? Do these acts produce wounds within the river? One argument would be that a river is wounded, or is a victim, when the materials introduced into it have produced an ecological imbalance—such as major pollutants from illegal mining, the impacts of deregulated treatment and management, or the intervention of a megadam.[26] For example, in January 2024, Ríos Vivos posted about the traces of pollution leaving a line along the sides of the reservoir and changing the colouration of the flesh of *bocachico* fish.[27] However, as Case No. 5 shows, systematic violence was perpetrated in such intensity near to Buenos Aires between the years 2000 and 2004—substantially by the paramilitary United Self-Defence Forces of Colombia (AUC)—that it turned the river into a "mass grave", contributing, alongside illicit mining and the processing and distribution of coca, to the degradation of the water body and the species that inhabit it.[28] Here, as elsewhere, the same characteristics of the water that are weaponised often bear the impacts of this violence in turn. In other words, although access to water is repeatedly affirmed as an inalienable human right, here, the river's waters have been co-opted as the method of human rights violation.

Tracing socio-ecological transformations does not stop at the surface of the river as a confined site of investigation, but requires the reassessment of the realm of water within processes of political violence. Sensing and thinking *with*, around, and through river ecosystems can reveal the workings of ecologically obscured spaces of political violence.[29] If water is a relational and all-pervasive material, what does it mean to think about conflict in relation to rivers and other water bodies? By "relational" and "pervasive", I take my cue from Dilip Da Cunha and Anuradha Mathur's conception of the world *in a moment of wateriness*, where water is not marginal or contained within mapped lines, but is centred in the experience across its different diffuse physical states such as through rain and in the air.[30] Astrida Neimanis's writing on "becoming a body of water" is likewise central for addressing the concentrations and dispersals of both the methods and traces of political violence in water. She takes the conception of the world in a moment of water a step further, emphasising cycles of embodiment in the world through water's material flows into and around the porous thresholds of plants, human bodies, and more-than-human bodies.[31]

At some points while driving through the canyon it was not possible to see the reservoir, and yet the entire territory is shaped by the dam infrastructure. I tried to imagine how much further below the river itself once flowed. One Ríos Vivos organiser described the increased humidity in the

26 See the CRA MA Live Project "Tainted Water" from 2023-24, https://www.taintedwater.co.uk/.

27 https://www.instagram.com/p/C2LGP6jOCGQ/?igsh=OWVocGgwMmttMTlh.a

28 JEP, *Auto SRVR-226*, 2023, 21.

29 Especially productive for thinking with water as a quintessentially relational substance, within wider political spheres is eco-feminist literature. Particularly: Cecelia Chen, Janine MacLeod, & Astrida Neimanis, eds., *Thinking With Water* (McGill-Queens University Press, 2013).

30 Anuradha Mathur & Dilip da Cunha, "Anuradha Mathur and Dilip da Cunha - Wetness Everywhere", online video, uploaded by GIDEST, 7 August 2017, accessed December 2024, https://vimeo.com/228719234.

31 Astrida Neimanis, *Bodies of Water: Posthuman Feminist Phenomenology* (Bloomsbury, 2017).

canyon produced by the reservoir, and how the water evaporating off its surface rises as a freezing fog in the higher reaches of the surrounding hills:

> *—Por el espejo de agua, en la mañana usted ve que sube una neblina. Usted donde divise bien la represa, en la mañana usted ve un cordón de nube por toda la presa, entonces esa agua se levanta, esa nube se levanta, cuando llegan a nuestros cultivos esa nube quema, quema las flores, quema los cogollitos que van saliendo.*
> —¿Por el frío?
> *—Sí, entonces nos mata la agricultura.*
> [—In the morning you see a fog that rises over the still water surface... Wherever you get a clear view of the reservoir, in the morning you see a wall of cloud. And so that water rises, that cloud rises. When it reaches our crops, that cloud burns, burns the flowers, burns the buds about to bloom...
> —Because of the cold? Like a frost?
> —Yes. So, it kills our agriculture.]

This new fog kills the crops cultivated by the communities in the towns above, including people who have been displaced previously from the river by the dam. The extended hydrological impact of the reservoir adds a further threshold to the limits of the effects of the dam to include meteorology. Thinking of the violence enacted against and through the river to incorporate fog adds to the conception of the river as a victim. At Hidroituango, the victimisation takes place across an expanded scale that includes: the flooding of towns, the displacement of communities, the devastation of the river ecosystem, and the near disappearance of riverside economies, as well as the burial sites and remains of both the corpses recovered from the river and the cemeteries of the those massacred in the canyon.

In this context, where Afro-Colombian and Indigenous people have been subjected to violence and had their recognition disputed, it is important to consider the concept of victim and victimhood. The terminology of victimhood risks redoubling the assault on the person, a reduction of them and their life to the sole status of a victim when their life world and socio-cultural relations are infinitely more complex than this. A warning is clear in the context of declaring a river and its community victims when, until only recently, Indigenous peoples and more-than-human entities have not been considered subjects of the law within structures inherited from colonial European legal forms that have, for centuries, subjugated non-white people.[32] Likewise, addressing the violence against river ecosystems and communities on the same plane risks lessening the weight of the violence against humans who have been disappeared into the river as a result of paramilitary violence. Unless practiced genuinely, such a ruling can reduce these people to 'nature' once more, instead of raising what is considered nature into the sphere where

32 As Paolo Tavares argues, the 2008 Ecuadorian constitution that foregrounded Pacha Mama was designed to break up the existing social, political, economic and legal regimes that excluded Indigenous people and exploit the environment, "reframing the role of the environment within the economy and opening up spaces of political participation for Ecuador's large indigenous population". Paolo Tavares, "Rights of Nature," *Forensis: The Architecture of Public Truth* (Sternberg: 2014), 566.

the violence enacted upon it can be understood to have extensive social impacts, let alone be something to protect on its own account.

When the relationship between river and community are entangled, political and ecological violence are inseparable. Such a framing aligns with existing literature that draws connections between genocide and ecocide, crimes against nature and crimes against humanity.[33] In some ways, a company such as EPM understands this entanglement. When EPM exerts pressure, and paramilitaries spread terror, they intend to displace the existing community and form a new population based on servicing the dam in turn.[34] Thus, to distinguish between environmental and human violence at the point of the act and in its aftermath would be impossible. As the twenty-nine authors of the 'Riverhood: political ecologies of socionature commoning and translocal struggles for water justice' article state: "Social and ecological river communities not only depend on and co-constitute each other, they also co-experience multiple (in)justices".[35] What the example of Hidroituango shows is that a more encompassing understanding of the river as victim must also expand to its wider socio-ecological system, as what might be called a *hydro-social victim*. In such a scenario, it is abundantly clear that to defend human rights requires defending environments, and to defend the environment necessitates a defence of the human community.

RIVER SOUND

I have often heard the question asked in academic and art contexts: how do we speak for rivers and their multispecies communities? Having interviewed zoologists who study the vocalisation of fish in the Venice lagoon, I have long held the impression that rather than thinking who speaks *for them*, if you know where and how to listen, they already communicate a great deal for themselves. This applies to fish and animal inhabitants, as well as the river and its subaqueous flora. Although perhaps not in the form of a speech act, a river's sounds communicate much about its conditions.

It is important to clarify that having expressed this, river guardians provide a crucial role within the present legal reality in advocating for the river and river communities. In the context of the Atrato, the artist and anthropologist Elizabeth Gallón Droste describes "voicing rivers" as a practice whereby guardians articulate the river's needs derived from listening spaces. They acknowledge themselves as continuities with the river in the intention of opening space for a more-than-human listening and attunement to water's

33 Susanne C. Knittel, "Ecologies of Violence: Cultural Memory (studies) and the Genocide–Ecocide Nexus," *Memory Studies* 16, no. 6 (2023): 1563-1578, 1564.

34 Juan Diego Suárez Gómez thoroughly outlines the company's aim to assert control over both river and population in the interest of maximum energy production at the cost of the existing socio-ecology. Suárez Gómez, "The New Imagined Communities".

35 Boelens, et al. "Riverhood", 1133.

socio-environmental and cultural relationality across time.[36] Ponce de León similarly describes the role of sound during the final part of the ceremony where the Cauca was declared a victim, held on its banks near the town of Buenos Aires, where those in attendance:

were met with a final performance: the amplified voice of the river, projected through speakers connected to microphones placed along the banks. The once-silent atmosphere buzzed with the vibrancies of a lively, moving river weaving all together in a shared cadence—gurgling currents, murmurs, rustling palms, a child's laughter, the echoes of prayers.[37]

Such ceremonies have the aim of restoring the relationship between the community and the river.[38] Ponce de León argues that this ceremony opens a route to attending to rivers "as polyvalent, agentic forces that exceed the limits of any single form of representation". And that such a *polyphonic* approach is crucial to the realisation of the rights of nature.[39] Gallón Droste argues that included within this listening are the other modes of sensory perception, such as the changing colour of the river. Perceiving optical changes, she argues, is a sensing of the rhythms and temporalities of the river and is itself an aspect of the practice of listening.

Each river has its own colour specific to its chemical and sedimentary composition. During interviews with members of Río Vivos, a clear refrain emerged that the river is not recognisable: its colour has changed, its chemical composition and pH levels have changed, its surface bears none of the eddying shapes that curl and wind across the flowing river. One person we spoke to on the Cauca described the loss of the signature muddy golden colour of the river, laden with sediments that both fertilised the land and were panned for its small valuable alluvial gold. The colour of the river is a defining characteristic, it communicates its changing sedimentary contents and mineral health.[40] Some went as far as to suggest that, in fact, this is no longer a river at all. The river, like their loved ones, had been "kidnapped".

We heard a haunting local legend of a Faust-like pact between the community and the river that was, for so long, both the patron of the community and the medium of political violence.

36 Elizabeth Gallón Droste, "Voicing ~ listening to rivers of gold", in *Wasser Botschaften*, ed. Katharina Nowak & Johanna Wild (Museum am Rothenbaum – Kulturen und Künste der Welt –MARKK, 2023), 248-265. Gallón Droste's practice follows a path of revealing the sound of water and its multi-species inhabitants including her sonic-visual navigation with the Atrato River Basin, 2024, in collaboration with Pablo Torres Gómez. Elizabeth Gallón Droste, "The Snoring of the Bocachico", audio-visual piece, 2024, accessed December 2024, https://vimeo.com/1009891816.

37 Ponce de León, "Testimonies from a Mourning Planet".

38 Jurisdicción Especial Para La Paz (JEP). Chamber for the Acknowledgement of Truth, Responsibility and Determination of Facts and Conduct, Auto SRVR - 226 of 11 July 2023. p.3, accessed October 2024, https://relatoria.jep.gov.co/searchproviapi/Auto_SRVR-226_11-julio-2023.

39 Ponce de León, "Testimonies from a Mourning Planet".

40 Writing about the colour of the Atrato river, one of the river guardians pointed out to Gallón Droste the brown colour from gold dredging on the Quito river that mixes with the Atrato at their confluence. Elizabeth Gallón Droste, "What Color is the River? Evocations between the Atrato and Guadalquivir Rivers", in *Meandering: Art, Ecology, and Metaphysics*, ed. Sofia Lemos (Sternberg Press, 2024), 155-159, 159.

Close-up of the algae that streaks across and below the surface of the Hidroituango reservoir.
Source: Image by author (2024).

EPM-branded temporary pontoon—this road once led to a bridge across the canyon. Source: Image by author (2024).
The coverage of *buchón* (water hyacinths) that shrouds large parts of the reservoir. Source: Image by author (2024).

> *Porque el río Cauca todos los días bajaba una cabeza. Podía ser de res, de gato, de perro, de cristiano, de lo que fuera... pero todos los días. Un trato que se hizo una leyenda... "usted me regala una pucha de tierra todos los días, un me regaló una cabeza". Entonces se le dio la cabeza porque si todos los días se echa una pucha de tierra, hubiera tocado el territorio.*
> [A head would float down the river Cauca every day. It could be from a cow, a dog, a person, from anything... every day. A deal that became a folk tale... *you give me a piece of land everyday, someone gave me a head.* So we offer the head because giving a piece of land everyday would have left us with nothing.]

In the stretch of the Cauca that is now a reservoir, however, the exchange of land for life with the river has changed, the tussle of erosion between land and water now takes the form of landslides as the reservoir exerts pressure on the young geology of the canyon. In a context where rivers have been the medium of the enforced disappearance of humans, has the river itself disappeared within the now shapeless surface of the reservoir?

At Hidroituango, I made hydrophone recordings at several locations; many of these are silent other than the sound of distant boat engines and ferries crossing the reservoir. One of the most seemingly inaudible recordings I produced was from a boat above the flooded Nutabe towns of Barbacoas and Orobajo, and the river island/sand bank of La Arenera, occupied in 2014 and 2015 by people who were made refugees by the dam and where protests against displacement took place.[41] They occupied this sedimentary space alongside Ríos Vivos, holding workshops and feeding people before they were violently removed by riot police as the waters of the reservoir began to rise around them.

What meaning was produced when I submerged a hydrophone into the reservoir above such locations? The activist art group Ultra-red's mission statement might provide some direction: "exploring acoustic space as enunciative of social relations, Ultra-red take up the acoustic mapping of contested spaces and histories utilising sound-based research (termed Militant Sound Investigations) that directly engage the organizing and analyses of political struggles."[42] Where I recorded from a boat above Orobajo and Barbacoas, the silence communicates the possession, the enclosure, and the displacement of the river community as the acoustic aftermaths of dispossession at sensible and insensible scales.[43] Like an image taken within turbid water or shrouded in fog, sound, even at an ambient register, offers an entry into spaces which are often entirely unmediated by what Macarena Gómez-Barris calls the extractive view.[44] The challenge and complexity of exploring such cases is never more evident than in the work of artists who embed their

41 Suárez Gómez states that "La Arenera plays a double role: as a concentration camp, and at the same time as a space of resistance." "The New Imagined Communities", 189.

42 Ultra-red, *Mission Statement*, accessed December 2024, http://www.ultrared.org/mission.html.

43 Kathryn Yussof makes the important instruction to remain with the insensible, particularly in the case of the deep ocean, so as not to disregard the sites and spaces within which mass extinction occurs. Kathryn Yussof, "Insensible Worlds: Postrelational Ethics, Indeterminacy and the (K)Nots Of Relating", *Environment and Planning D: Society and Space* 31, (2013): 208-226.

44 Macarena Gómez-Barris, *The Extractive Zone: Social Ecologies and Decolonial Perspectives* (Duke University Press, 2017), 104.

The morning fog seen across the reservoir towards the dam, taken near the town of Toledo.
Source: Image by author (2024).

practices within frontline river activism. This includes Carolina Caycedo, who adopts *submerged* methods to counter the very *submergence* and dispossession produced by hydropower.[45] To develop such a methodology requires adjusting your imaginary to the material and processual specificities of these subaqueous spaces. The stillness of the reservoir is a far cry from the turbulent canyon river that was once heard above the surface. Just as its colour has changed, the river does not sound like it once did; in fact, it barely makes any sound at all.

I am still trying to figure out what attending to the silence of the reservoir might communicate: no longer a flow, no longer the sounds of the community and their own practices. No courtroom would take such ambient recordings operationally, and indeed they are not intended for evidentiary purposes but instead stress a need for collaboration. Perhaps the silence, like Rachel Carson's silent spring, communicates the very loss of community and the aftermath of the deathscapes produced by extractive capital. It is as though in addition to the force of its flows the dam has extracted the river's sound. The silence attends to what is at stake for the members of the Cauca River communities that remain defiant against the forces of hydropower: an attention to the organisation of political struggles in submerged spaces that are either hard to access or bear little perceptible trace. The silence

45 Gómez-Barris, *The Extractive Zone*, 93; Carolina Caycedo, "Yuma: Land of Friends, Descolonizando La Jagua", video, 2014, https://vimeo.com/94685623.

accentuates the need for the community to speak as a witness to the violence perpetrated on and through its waters, or more accurately, to speak of the river as a co-victim.[46]

CONCLUSION

After dinner one evening we spoke with one of the guardians of the Cauca on the front porch of her house, which she had built from the Siemens branded crates that brought the turbines to the river. Overlooking the canyon with the lights of the dam in the distance, she declared: "to defend the Cauca is to defend its tributaries."

> *Porque nosotros defendemos el río Cauca,*
> *pero al defender el río Cauca estamos defendiendo todos sus afluentes,*
> *que son los que nos conforman el río Cauca, toda la cuenca.*
> *Yo soy guardiana del río Cauca.*
> *Una sentencia que salió*
> *que el río Cauca es sujeto de derecho.*
> *Entonces en el movimiento habemos cuatro guardianes,*
> *dos guardianas y dos guardiáns.*
> *Estamos divididos en las tres subregiones.*
> *Nosotros siempre hacemos, pero...*
> *la elección que todas las tres subregiones*
> *y que sean hombres y mujeres.*
> [Because we defend the Cauca River,
> but in doing so we are defending all its tributaries,
> which make up the Cauca River, its entire basin.
> I am a Guardian of the Cauca River.
> According to a judicial ruling
> the Cauca River is a holder of rights.
> There are four Guardians in the movement,
> two women and two men.
> We are divided into three sub-regions.
> We always choose, but...
> We include all three sub-regions
> and choose both men and women.]

This was the same woman who equated the loss of the river to the loss of family, and she had been displaced multiple times by the dam and paramilitary violence. When community members are making the direct equation between the loss of rivers and the loss of close family members, then importance of ensuring the *inter communis* ruling of rights should be extended to victimhood. Furthermore, in the case of a river being declared a victim of violence within the jurisdiction of such an *inter communis* ruling, but only applicable to a specific period of violence geographically denominated on

46 At the end of the description of the project *Ríos de Vida y Muerte* by Rutas del Conflicto, a woman is quoted in relation to Case No.5 making an exclamation suppressed almost to a whisper, "if the Cauca River could speak". Rutas del Conflicto, "El Río Cauca", Ríos de Vida y Muerte, accessed December 2024, https://rutasdelconflicto.com/rios-vida-muerte/rios/r-o-cauca.

the river, where does this wound, this victimhood end? Where were the boundaries of the river's influence and the cosmology of socio-ecological relations it produced? And, where are the thresholds of the influence of the dam now?

Seeking social-justice in such contexts requires parsing the full socio-environmental extent of such violence. Whether in affirming rights or seeking judicial retribution for past violence, an *inter communis* ruling must be practiced to allow for a plurality of beliefs, cosmologies, and practices. One which acknowledges that the same features of the environment carry different meanings for different people, thus resisting replacing one singular meaning for another. Each person we spoke with described a personal and communal relation to the river; so there are many Cauca Rivers interlapping spatio-temporally from the submerged present to the sedimentary layers left by past courses.[47] As Ponce de León writes, when awarded legal personhood in 2019 it extended to "all individuals and communities tied to the Cauca River, its tributaries, and nearby areas": "doing so, the court expanded what a river is to the State, recognizing it not only as a body of water but as an ecology that includes its basin and more-than-human inhabitants. However, as of July 2024, the court's decision remains largely unimplemented."[48] In the context of Hidroituango, where its socio-environmental impact extends to such a phenomenon as fog that kills crops in the highlands, the entire socio-hydrologic continuity of the valley and the canyon is a victim of this violence.[49] This includes the community living in an altitudinal relation to what was once the river, from the bed of the reservoir to the crops planted high above in the surrounding hills.

Bloated, eutrophic, speckled with algae, what was once a sediment heavy river is now a lurid flat green surface; this is no longer a river at all, but a waterbody shaped, inhabited, and possessed by extractive capital. The river has disappeared into the reservoir even if its sediments still accumulate at the foot of the impounding wall.

The morning mist has long risen. Under the harsh midday sun, we ask for silence and lower the hydrophone. Passing the headphones to the people sitting on the boat in the middle of the reservoir, we listen in search of the scraping sound of the circular motion of sediments being panned and for even a murmur of the once turbulent river, now disappeared 100 metres below.

47 Thinking the cultural/geological layering of rivers in the context of dams I often return to Wilson Harris, the Guyanese poet, novelist, theorist, and at one time hydropower surveyor in the employ of the British colonial administration, who conceived of the multiple banks of the Macusi/Potaro river as a "tapestry of waters". He wrote of a flute sculpted from the voices of three drowned Macusi children "that sings of an ancient riverbed one hundred fathoms deep, far below the Potaro River that runs to the waterfall. Two rivers then. The visible Potaro runs to the Waterfall. The invisible stream of the river of the dead runs far below, far under our knees. The flute tells of the passage of the drowned into the river of the dead. The flute tells that the river of the dead and the river of the living are one quantum stream possessed of four banks. We shall see!" Wilson Harris, *The Four Banks of the River of Space* (Faber and Faber, 1990), 43.

48 Ponce de León, "Testimonies from a Mourning Planet".

49 Ifor Duncan, *Hydrology of the Powerless*, 41-44.

WORKS CITED

Boelens, Rutgerd, Arturo Escobar, Karen Bakker, Lena Hommes, Erik Swyngedouw, Barbara Hogenboom, Edward H. Huijbens, Sue Jackson, Jeroen Vos, Leila M. Harris, K.J. Joy, Fabio de Castro, Bibiana Duarte-Abadía, Daniele Tubino de Souza, Heila Lotz-Sisitka, Nuria Hernández-Mora, Joan Martínez-Alier, Denisse Roca-Servat, Tom Perreault, Carles Sanchis-Ibor, Diana Suhardiman, Astrid Ulloa, Arjen Wals, Jaime Hoogesteger, Juan Pablo Hidalgo-Bastidas, Tatiana Roa-Avendaño, Gert Jan Veldwisch, Phil Woodhouse & Karl M. Wantzen. "Riverhood: political ecologies of socionature commoning and translocal struggles for water justice". *The Journal of Peasant Studies* 50, no. 3 (2023): 1125-1156.

Caycedo, Carolina. "Yuma: Land of Friends, Descolonizando La Jagua". Video, 2014. https://vimeo.com/94685623.

Chen, Cecelia, Janine MacLeod, & Astrida Neimanis, (eds.). *Thinking With Water.* McGill-Queens University Press, 2013.

Corte Constitucional de Colombia. Sentencia T-622 of 2016. Accessed December 2024. https://www.corteconstitucional.gov.co/relatoria/2016/t-622-16.htm.

Duncan, Ifor & Stefanos Levidis. "Weaponizing a River". *E-Flux Architecture* (2020). https://www.e-flux.com/architecture/at-the-border/325751/weaponizing-a-river/.

Duncan, Ifor. "Necro-Hydrology". *E-Flux Architecture* (2023). https://www.e-flux.com/architecture/hydroreflexivity/543089/necro-hydrology/.

Duncan, Ifor. "Hydrology of the Powerless". PhD thesis, Goldsmiths, University of London, 2021. https://research.gold.ac.uk/id/eprint/29967/1/VIS_thesis_DuncanI_2021.pdf.

"El río Cauca fue notificado: ya es víctima acreditado del conflicto armado". *El Colombiano*, 1 April 2024. Accessed December 2024. https://www.elcolombiano.com/colombia/el-rio-cauca-fue-notificado-ya-es-victima-acreditado-del-conflicto-armado-OE24137494.

Forensic Architecture. *Forensis: The Architecture of Public Truth.* Sternberg Press, 2014.

Gallón Droste, Elizabeth. "What Color is the River? Evocations between the Atrato and Guadalquivir Rivers". In *Meandering: Art, Ecology, and Metaphysics*, edited by Sofia Lemos. Sternberg Press, 2024.

Gallón Droste, Elizabeth. "Voicing ~ listening to rivers of gold". In *Wasser Botschaften*, edited by Katharina Nowak & Johanna Wild. Museum am Rothenbaum – Kulturen und Künste der Welt –MARKK, 2023.

Gallón Droste, Elizabeth. "The Snoring of the Bocachico". Audio-visual piece, 2024. Accessed October 2024. https://vimeo.com/1009891816.

Mathur, Anuradha, & Dilip da Cunha. "Anuradha Mathur and Dilip da Cunha - Wetness Everywhere". Online video, uploaded by GIDEST, 7 August 2017. Accessed December 2024. https://vimeo.com/228719234.

Gómez-Barris, Macarena. *The Extractive Zone: Social Ecologies and Decolonial Perspectives.* Duke University Press, 2017.

Harris, Wilson. *The Four Banks of the River of Space.* Faber and Faber, 1990.

"How the Powerful Hidroituango Drowned an Indigenous Territory". *Tierra de Resistentes*, 25 April 2019. Accessed October 2024. https://tierraderesistentes.com/en/2019/04/25/el-territorio-indigena-que-ahogo-la-poderosa-hidroituango/.

"Ituango Massacres v. Colombia". *Inter-American Court of Human Rights,* 1 July 2006. Accessed December, 2024. http://www.corteidh.or.cr/docs/casos/articulos/seriec_148_ing.pdf.

Jurisdicción Especial Para La Paz (JEP). Salas De Justicia Sala De Reconocimiento De Verdad, De Responsabilidad Y De Determinación De Los Hechos Y Conductas, *Auto SRVR - 226* of 11 July 2023. Accessed December 2024. https://relatoria.jep.gov.co/searchproviapi/Auto_SRVR-226_11-julio-2023.

Knittel, Susanne C. "Ecologies of violence: Cultural memory (studies) and the genocide–ecocide nexus". *Memory Studies* 16, no. 6 (2023): 1563-1578.

Linton, Jamie, & Jessica Budds. "The Hydrosocial Cycle: Defining and mobilizing a relational-dialectical approach to water". *Geoforum* 57 (2014): 170-180.

Meszaros Martin, Hannah & Oscar Pedraza. "Extinction in transition: coca, coal, and the production of enmity in Colombia's post-peace accords environment". *Political Ecology* 28, (2021): 721-740.

Neimanis, Astrida. *Bodies of Water: Posthuman Feminist Phenomenology.* Bloomsbury, 2017.

Oslender, Ulrich. "Spaces of Terror and Fear on Colombia's Pacific Coast". In *Violent Geographies: Fear, Terror, and Political Violence*, edited by Derek Gregory & Allan Pred. Routledge, 2006.

Ponce de León, Alejandro. "Testimonies from a Mourning Planet: Art, Representation and Justice Beyond the Human in Latin America". *Institute of Languages Culture and Society*, Institute of Advanced Study, University of London, 18 September 2024. Accessed December 2024. https://ilcs.sas.ac.uk/blog/testimonies-a-mourning-planet-art-representation-and-justice-beyond-human-latin-america.

Rutas del Conflicto. "El Río Cauca", Ríos de Vida y Muerte. Accessed December 2024. https://rutasdelconflicto.com/rios-vida-muerte/rios/r-o-cauca.

Suárez Gómez, Juan Diego. "The New Imagined Communities: The Case Of Hidroituango In Colombia". PhD thesis, University of Missouri, 2017. https://mospace.umsystem.edu/xmlui/handle/10355/67540.

Tavares, Paolo. "Rights of Nature". In *Forensis: The Architecture of Public Truth*, edited by Forensic Architecture. Sternberg Press, 2014.

Te Awa Tupua (Whanganui River Claims Settlement) Act of 20 March 2017, 14. Accessed October 2024. http://files.harmonywithnatureun.org/uploads/upload711.pdf.

Tribunal Superior de Medellín, Sentencia de tutela No. 38 of 17 June 2019. Accessed December 2024. http://files.harmonywithnatureun.org/uploads/upload837.pdf.

Ultra-red. *Mission Statement.* Accessed December 2024. http://www.ultrared.org/mission.html.

Uribe, Maria Victoria. "Dismembering and Expelling: Semantics of Political Terror in Colombia". *Public Culture* 16, no. 1 (2004): 79-95.

Yussof, Kathryn. "Insensible Worlds: Postrelational Ethics, Indeterminacy And The (K)Nots Of Relating". *Environment and Planning D: Society and Space* 31, (2013): 208-226.

SOIL POLITICS

João Prates Ruivo

In August 2016, I visited the colonial soil archives in Lisbon currently housed in the recently renamed Pedoteca, a term that designates a pedological library or a library of soils. Having been relocated from the extinct Junta de Investigação Tropical—a colonial agency for scientific research that operated until the overthrow of the fascist dictatorship in Portugal in 1974—the soil samples and reports from colonial pedological missions are today gathered at the Instituto Superior de Agronomia (ISA), the Agronomic University of Lisbon. I first came across the Pedoteca while conducting research on the practice and legacy of Amilcar Cabral, one of the founding leaders of the African Party for the Independence of Guinea and Cape Verde (PAIGC) and a theorist of anti-colonial struggle. Cabral had a background as a practicing agronomist, graduating from the same university that now holds the archives with a thesis dedicated to the study of soil erosion in Alentejo, a rural region in the south of Portugal. Soon after graduating—according to the testimony of his colleague Rui Pinto Ricardo—Cabral joined three pedological missions in Angola, where he took part in collecting samples between 1954 and 1956.[1] Cabral's trajectory, from working as a soil scientist for the Portuguese state in Alentejo and Angola, to leading the anti-colonial struggle in Guinea-Bissau, is exemplary of the entangled relations that are articulated in the materials deposited in the soil archive.

Located in the basement of the university, the Pedoteca displays a collection of soils extracted from formerly colonised territories exhibited together with soils from mainland Portugal. The multiple geographies and conflicting political histories represented by these samples are flattened in the scientific presentation of the archive, consisting of a series of vertical soil profiles surrounded by corridors lined with glass jars filled with soil samples taken at different depths. In the centre of the room, standing back-to-back, are two rows of soil monoliths that were extracted from Angola and Alentejo during the 1950s and 1960s, two territories valued at the time for their potential for agricultural expansion.

In my research into the politics of soils, I've investigated how the properties of soils were studied, classified, and altered to enable the transition from colonial rule towards late-liberal modes of governance. In particular, I've focused on the global soil survey initiated by the Food and Agriculture Organisation (FAO) after the end of the Second World War, which I position as a defining moment in the transformation of land from earthly matter into a techno-scientific assemblage, one that is invested with the capacity to unsettle and reorganise modes of life. Through the

1 R. Pinto Ricardo, *Rui Pinto Ricardo (Depoimento, 2013)*, IICT, 2014, https://actd.iict.pt/view/actd:MORPR.

spatial analysis of fieldwork conducted by soil scientists in Angola and in Portugal between 1961 and 1974, in parallel with the rise of anti-colonial struggles that occurred over this period, I argue that soils were mobilised as key agents and registers of colonial violence and resistance.[2] Additionally, I observe how these modifications continue to function in the present, constituting an essential feature of the ways in which soils operate as political matter.

Albeit frequently metonymised as *the land*, soil is not a homogeneous entity and must be defined by the heterogeneous nature of its properties, which are unevenly distributed across the surface of the Earth in horizontal and vertical dimensions. As a continuous spatial and temporal medium, soil's properties not only "materially-persist" in the present, but they also have the capacity to reorganise contemporary events.[3] In exploring these capacities, I consider soil as both a medium which carries traces of geopolitical transformations, as well as a technology that operates at the service of these processes.

Traditionally the field of architectural practice has understood soil as an inanimate substrate for the implementation of built form and has thus expressed limited interest in soil's properties beyond its mechanical capacity to bear loads. In my experience as a practicing architect, soil and architecture only meet at a building's foundation: a technical-functional encounter mediated by layers of structural support and impermeabilisation. However, from a research architecture perspective, before becoming a material resource for construction or acting as a milieu for the implementation of built projects, soils are in themselves already the outcome of a design project, one that expresses a coordinated strategy oriented towards a future goal.[4] In the sense that their constitution is derived from a series of ongoing interactions including complex techno-scientific processes, which inform and are informed by political decisions that take effect at multiple scales. By focusing on the global soil surveys devised by United Nations agencies FAO and UNESCO, the scope of which was intimately connected with the reconstruction of the environment as a whole after the Second World War, I maintain that the soils covered by this project have been irreversibly transformed through the standardising apparatus of scientific soil taxonomies. Comprised of information and statistics on agricultural practices, population, and their environments, these surveys were the outcome of a twenty-year effort involving the coordination of disparate

2 Mobilisation is a term that I use often to refer to the reconfiguration of the properties of soil as a tactic. I follow scientist and philosopher Isabelle Stengers in noting its military origins: "mobilisation designates the contrary of learning, because the first imperative of armies when they are mobilised is to let nothing slow them down. It is as much a matter of defining the landscape that they cross in abstract terms—there are no longer any inhabitants, cultivated fields or villages, only unbeatable obstacles or possibilities of successful passage—as it is of shutting up those who object or discuss the orders they are given." See Philippe Pignarre & Isabelle Stengers, *Capitalist Sorcery: Breaking the Spell* (Palgrave Macmillan, 2011), 21-22.

3 Peter C. van Wyck, "An Archive of Threat", *Future Anterior* 9, no. 2 (2013): 53–80. The underlying reference here is Walter Benjamin's notion of history as the "now".

4 A project, as architect and theorist Pier Vittorio Aureli pointed out, is "a strategy on whose basis something must be produced or brought out. The project thus addresses a potential future situation, but in doing this it seeks to organize the available means towards a possible end." Pier Vittorio Aureli, *The City as a Project* (Ruby Press, 2013).

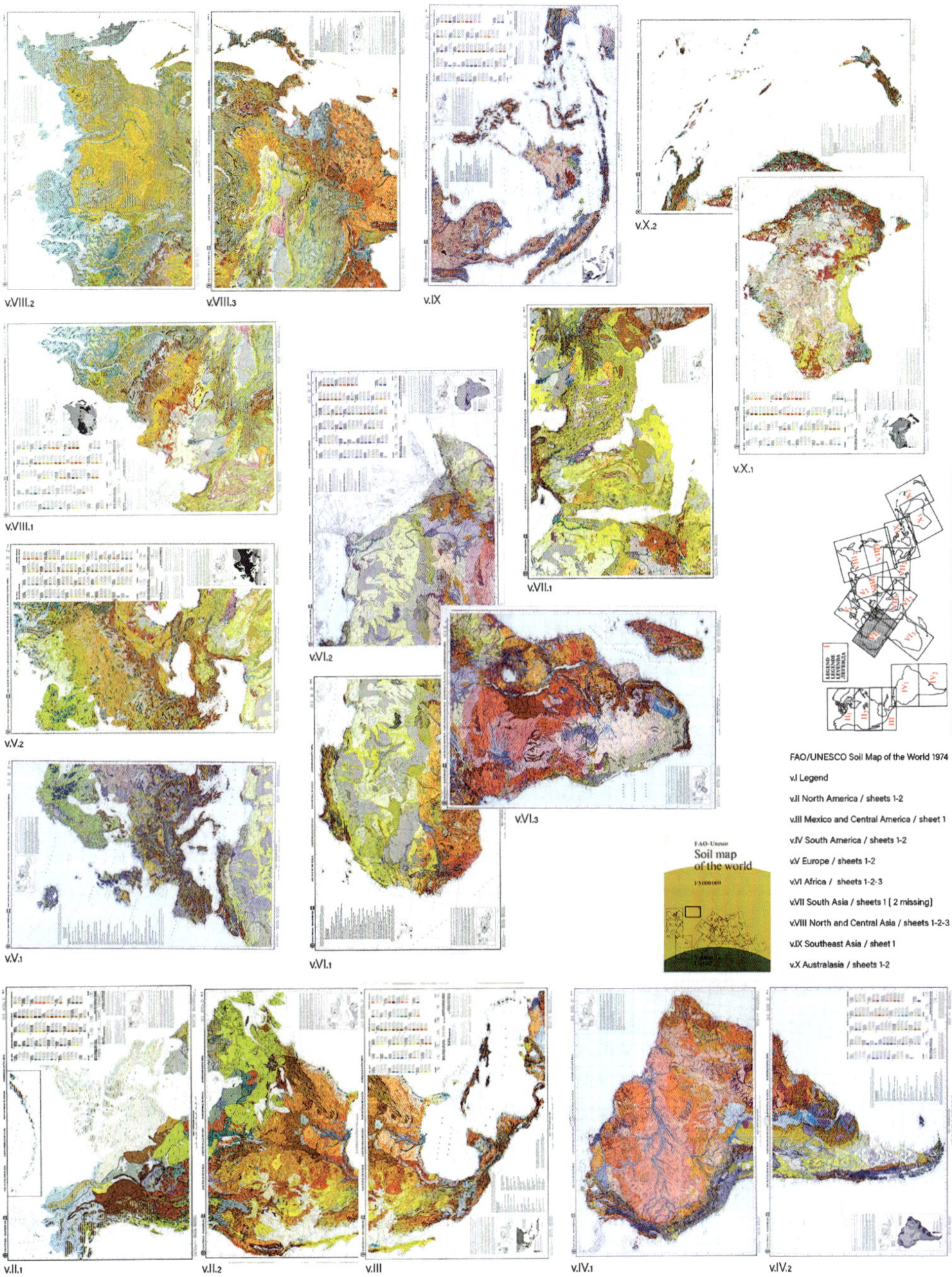

'Soil Map of the World. 1.5.000.000. Vol. I Legend' (Rome (Italy): FAO, 1974).
Source: Image composition by the author.

The ten volumes that comprise the Soil Map of the World are presented here for the first time at a comparative scale, and employ the same taxonomic classification. As a disclaimer of its supposed political neutrality, the map's accompanying legend reads: "the designations employed and the presentation of the material in this publication do not imply the expression of any opinion whatsoever from the Food and Agriculture Organization and or the United Nations Educational, Scientific and Cultural Organization concerning the legal or constitutional status of any country, territory or sea area or concerning the delimitation of frontiers.

national methodologies, and led to a synchronisation of nomenclatures that materialised in the publication of the first Legend of the Soil Map of the World in 1974.[5]

The ten volumes that comprise the Soil Map of the World, are presented here for the first time at a comparative scale, and employ the same taxonomic classification. As a disclaimer of its supposed political neutrality, the map's accompanying legend reads: "The designations employed and the presentation of the material in this publication do not imply the expression of any opinion whatsoever from the Food and Agriculture Organization and or the United Nations Educational, Scientific and Cultural Organization concerning the legal or constitutional status of any country, territory or sea area or concerning the delimitation of frontiers".

While not explicitly referencing FAO's project of the Soil Map of the World, scholars in the humanities have traced the rise of environmentalism as a reaction to the industrial excesses of post-war agriculture in Europe, as well as in its former colonial territories.[6] My research case studies extend their enquiries into the political nature of these ecological and scientific transformations, arguing that neoliberal modes of governance in combination with emergent forms of financial capital have reconfigured soil from a natural medium into a techno-scientific assemblage.[7] Understood within the framework of what I term *soil politics*, soil emerges as an instrument of political projects and a material register of a set of social relations. My analysis concentrates on the spatial and political dimensions of these transformations and inscriptions at different scales, in particular the relation between soil and settlement. Central to my inquiry are the figures of the laboratory, the sample, and the plantation.[8] I consider these to be the primary sites for observing the political dimension of soils, as they reveal the ways in which soils have been tested, exploited, and mobilised at different scales by late-liberal modes of governance. Even when left fallow or uninhabited, the soils that I deal with in my research are inevitably the product of anthropogenic action, since they have been exposed directly or indirectly to the distributed global effects of human presence over time.

Today, these alterations are no longer discernible from their original materials. Together with other anthropogenic environmental transformations—which relied on the evolution of techno-scientific modes of

5 Perrin Selcer, "Fabricating Unity: The FAO-UNESCO Soil Map of the World", *Historical Social Research / Historische Sozialforschung* 40, no. 2 (152) (2015): 174–201.

6 The list is extensive, but my reference here is the work of Maria Puig de la Bellacasa, "Making Time for Soil: Technoscientific Futurity and the Pace of Care", *Social Studies of Science* 45, no. 5 (October 2015): 691–716.

7 I follow Ezequiel Dixon-Roman's reading of assemblage taken from Deleuze and Guattari, which pays attention to the french *agencement*: "it's not a collection of actualities, as would be understood in the English definition of assemblage, but rather a sticky constellation of a multiplicity of forces producing an event, situation, or composite grouping or body. It is a process that functions in relation and connection with other assemblages." Ezekiel J. Dixon-Román, "Algo-Ritmo: More-Than-Human Performative Acts and the Racializing Assemblages of Algorithmic Architectures", *Cultural Studies ↔ Critical Methodologies* 16, no. 5 (2016): 482–90.

8 Here, I follow the tactical use of figures employed by Elizabeth Povinelli, *Geontologies: A Requiem to Late Liberalism* (Duke University Press, 2016). On similar grounds, these four figures are not meant to foreclose the topics of the research, but rather provide a conceptual scale to the different modes of analysis.

monitoring and regulating soil management processes—they have become inscribed into soil and form an integral part of its mineral, chemical, and biological composition.[9] On the other hand, these processes also implied a sustained degradation of the means involved, in particular of the properties of the soil itself. These so-called 'improvements' are one of the elements that constitute what I describe as a form of techno-scientific assemblage. Resulting from centuries of colonial plundering and environmental depredation, they are now embedded in mineral and organic properties of soils through a metabolic cycle that includes the workings of synthetic agents used in monocrop agriculture, such as chemical fertilisers, herbicides, and pesticides. When returned to the soil in the present, improvements are one of the causes of its accelerated destruction. They are not the collateral consequence of environmental degradation, or the secondary effects of climatic alterations, but the very means through which colonial and imperialist projects materialised historically, producing the conditions under

Collection of soil monoliths extracted from Angola in the period between 1946-74, as displayed at the Pedoteca in the Instituto Superior de Agronomia, Lisbon. Source: Image by author (2016).

Located in the basement of the university, the Pedoteca displays a collection of soils extracted from formerly colonised territories exhibited together with soils from mainland Portugal. The multiple geographies and conflicting political histories represented by these samples are flattened in the scientific presentation of the archive, which is comprised of a series of vertical soil profiles surrounded by corridors lined with glass jars filled with soil samples taken at different depths. In the centre of the room, standing back-to-back are two rows of soil monoliths dating from 1950s-60s that were extracted from Angola and Alentejo, two territories valued at the time for their potential for agricultural expansion.

9 In fact, to reflect the impact of humans in soil-forming processes, in 2007 FAO added a new soil category, *technosols*, that includes "soils such as landfills, parks, urban soils, which bear marks of human intervention". Lee Fergusson, "Anthrosols and Technosols: The Anthropogenic Signature of Contaminated Soils and Sediments in Australia", *Water, Air, & Soil Pollution* 228, no. 8 (9 July 2017): 269.

which late-liberal forms of soil management could function in the present.[10] In developing the term *soil politics*, I also seek to describe the specific articulation between these distinct modes of governance, which are bound by the material continuity of soil. Hence soils, in my research, operate as both a political material and as a material archive.

SOIL AS ARCHIVE

The archival capacity of soils is explored through four main propositions that relate to their ontological, biological, structural, and cultural features, which I consider to be distinctive in relation to other types of archives and archival practices. In order to address the ways in which soils function as archives, in opposition to the scientific archiving of soils, I've observed how these ontological properties have enabled soils to "generate their own terms of analytical engagement", a capacity which requires different forms of mediation beyond the positivist scientific paradigm.[11] This archival dimension asserts the autonomy of soil as a concept, setting it apart from other notions, such as the land as *territorial archive*, which in my view fail to recognise the technical specificity of soils that are inextricably linked with their political dimensions.[12]

Soils have a formal structure, insofar as their properties are arranged according to a vectorial order that spans from the geological rock layer until the ground's surface level. This vertical distribution follows a hierarchical logic of distinct horizons, which was first described in pedological terms by soil scientist Hans Jenny, who defined soil as an "anisotropic" entity:

> The spatial distribution of soil characteristics is not randomised but depends on one direction. Along a line extending from the surface of the soil toward the centre of the earth —arbitrarily denoted as Z-axis— the sequence of soil properties differs profoundly from that along lines parallel to the surface. (...) In the language of the pedologist, the anisotropism of soils is usually expressed with the words: "The soil has a profile". [13]

In the practice of pedological sampling, what scientists refer to as a profile refers to a series of parallel *soil horizons*, which can be read both in the positive surface of the continuous portion of the soil extracted, and in the negative space from where it was extracted from. This layered archi-

10 An argument developed by Dipesh Chakrabarty, "The Climate of History: Four Theses", *Critical Inquiry* 35, no. 2 (2009): 197–222. Nevertheless, as Povinelli reminds, the collapsed frames of reference described by Chakrabarty were not shared by everyone.

11 Martin Holbraad, "Things as Concepts", in *Savage Objects*, ed. Godofredo Pereira (Imprensa Nacional-Casa da Moeda, 2012). See also Martin Holbraad & Morten Axel Pedersen, *The Ontological Turn: An Anthropological Exposition* (Cambridge University Press, 2017).

12 The land as a territorial archive is a concept by Peter C. Van Wyck, *The Highway of the Atom* (McGill-Queen's University Press, 2010). "There is the land—the territorial archive, as I have come to think of it—upon which time is etched at various locations, although the legibility of this inscription is difficult and contested" (p.16). A precise account of the historical and political distinctions between land and territory can be found in Stuart Elden, *The Birth of Territory* (The University of Chicago Press, 2013). In my research, I understand territory as "a political technology for organizing social and economic relations that has both spatial and non-spatial elements". Sandro Mezzadra & Brett Neilson, "Extraction, Logistics, Finance: Global Crisis and the Politics of Operations", *Radical Philosophy* 178, March/April (2013): 8.

13 Hans Jenny, *Factors of Soil Formation: A System of Quantitative Pedology*, McGraw Hill Publications in the Agricultural Sciences (McGraw-Hill, 1941), 3.

tecture both stores and organises the material residues from past events, while simultaneously recording in real-time the effects of their exposure to present conditions, including atmospheric and geological events, climate variations, and human intervention. Each vertical profile of soil is thus a continuous record of the stratified evolution of the Earth's surface over time. From the perspective of soil studies, this surface is not an abstract frontier, but rather a three-dimensional entity, with a variable depth and history.[14] Since three centimetres of top-soil can take up to a thousand years to be generated, a large segment of the Earth's history is thus contained in these 1.5 metre sections known as soil monoliths.[15] For example, samples from soil profiles such as those obtained from the surveys in Angola and Alentejo, which are currently on display at the Pedoteca in Lisbon, can be studied to measure carbon concentration historically over extended timeframes. And while remaining linked through the epistemic device of the colonial archive, these soil samples retain their situated autonomy embedded in their material properties.

Soils in my project are not merely climate proxies of past events, nor do they simply offer mediated accounts of history. Soils are rather the material remnants of events in themselves, carrying and registering relations between human and more-than-human agents, all of which combine to inscribe themselves in their mineral and organic components. This second proposition follows feminist materialist perspectives which refuse an ontological difference between past, present, and future events, in particular Karen Barad's insight that memory is "a pattern of sedimented enfoldings" that is "written in the fabric of the world".[16] Barad describes the processes of history as a permanent iterative reconfiguration of material inscriptions. In her words: "the world 'holds' the memory of all traces; or rather, the world *is* its memory."[17] In my research, I investigate how these material inscriptions are made legible or become invisible in the physical and chemical properties of soils, forming part of what I define as their archival capacity. Similar to materials deposited in conventional archives, soils' biophysical properties work both with and against recording. Soils thus operate as a living archive, a dynamic ecology that actively transforms and is transformed by the elements and organisms that constitute it.

Defined in scientific terms as "the upper layer of the Earth's crust", including its liquid and gaseous components, soils are an interface and a threshold between its spheres, which scientists describe as functioning as

14 Here I seek to add to and further problematise Nigel Clark's question in asking why "modern western political discourses have come to focus overwhelmingly on the organization of the surface of the earth rather than on its layering or multi-dimensionality". In Nigel Clark, "Politics of Strata", *Theory, Culture & Society* 34, no. 2–3 (1 May 2017): 214.

15 When referring to the Earth's history, I am also including the inscriptions from different "onto-epistemic worlds", or "ahistorical practices", as described by Marisol de la Cadena: "*Ahistorical* as concept stresses the partial connections with history—the way they are together and *also* remain different". In Marisol de la Cadena, *Earth Beings: Ecologies of Practice across Andean Worlds*, The Lewis Henry Morgan Lectures 2011 (Duke University Press, 2015): 150.

16 Karen Barad, "Quantum Entanglements and Hauntological Relations of Inheritance: Dis/Continuities, SpaceTime Enfoldings, and Justice-to-Come", *Derrida Today* 3, no. 2 (November 2010): 261.

17 Barad, "Quantum Entanglements".

A field cultivated in superintensive mode, outside of Cuba, Alentejo, where Cabral conducted his fieldwork on soil erosion in 1956. Source: Map by author (Basemap: EDIA. Ortophoto. False color (IVRG) 2022. Spatial resolution (m): 0.25 m.

In Alentejo, a southern region of Portugal affected by the recent expansion of industrial plantations, the former presence of trees such as cork oaks and their companion species remains inscribed in the soil, and manifests itself in distortions in the linear pattern of super-intensive cultivation.

a "biochemical reactor".[18] And while soils are not considered living entities in themselves, their role in sustaining life on the planet is recognised as one of their key attributes. Through means of organic decomposition and biochemical reactions, soils as archives are not static repositories of material information, but instead constitute a lively "domiciliation" of events.[19] The chemical reactions involved in these processes produce traces, which allow for intergenerational communication between plants. Trees, for instance, are able to imprint their genetic traces on a site to interact with

18 Turlough F. Guerin et al., "Editorial: JSS — J Soils & Sediments", *Journal of Soils and Sediments* 1, no. 1 (2001): 1.

19 A term borrowed from Derrida's canonical theorization of the archive, found in Okwui Enwezor, *Archive Fever: Uses of the Document in Contemporary Art* (Steidl, 2008). In the wake of Stuart Hall, my use of the term here is meant to reverse Derrida's formulation of domiciliation as a form of "house-arrest", and instead to consider the living qualities of archives: "'living' is strongly counter-posed to the common meaning accorded to 'tradition', which is seen to function like the prison-house of the past." In Stuart Hall, "Constituting an Archive", *Third Text* 15, no. 54 (1 March 2001): 89.

future generations, while also establishing their presence against other species, in a pattern described by soil scientists as soil competition. These more-than-human interactions below ground support scientific claims that soils possess a type of "pedological memory", in the sense that they enable partial access to multi-temporal events.[20] Through my fieldwork I recorded the ways in which these multi-species ecologies are currently considered the 'competition' to the reductionist model of monocrop.

In Alentejo, a southern region of Portugal affected by the recent expansion of industrial plantations, the former presence of trees such as cork oaks and their companion species remains inscribed in the soil, and manifests itself in distortions in the linear pattern of super-intensive cultivation.

But decomposition can also be read as the natural capacity of soils to *bear witness* to the technical processes which inform its destruction. This capacity, which I attribute to soil's archival dimension, is inevitably political, as it cannot be disentangled from the techno-scientific processes that have been mobilised in its modification over the last seventy years. Described from scientific and non-scientific perspectives, decomposition as a process challenges the capacity of soil as a medium to record events and store information. When utilised as a metaphor for other processes and metabolic transformations, it operates as a cultural inscription.[21] But when considered as a biological process, decomposition pertains to soil as a living entity; in this case, discourses oscillate between affirmations of vitality and/or decay that propel interrogations on the subject matter of life itself.[22]

Through my case studies, I explore this evolving division between life and non-life through the figure of erosion, which I consider from a conceptual and scientific perspective. Within the field of soil sciences, erosion is studied under pedology, the branch concerned with the study of soil in its natural environment. In pedological terms, erosion is understood as the geological process of soil formation, and as one of the main threats to its sustainability. In other words, it defines both its genesis and its destruction.[23] As the boundary that negotiates the limits of life on the planet, erosion is the process that articulates the transitions between living and non-living creatures, organic and non-organic matter. Erosion thus troubles and complicates straightforward distinctions between life and non-life because of its metabolic processes, which involve geological desegregation, biological reactions, and chemical transformations.[24] Soils are simultaneously dead and alive: in a state of permanent becoming.

20 Jonathan D. Phillips & Daniel A. Marion, "Pedological Memory in Forest Soil Development", *Forest Ecology and Management* 188, (2004): 363–380.

21 In artist Filipa César's filmic practice, decomposition features as a register of conflict, both external in the case of the damage inflicted on the film archives, and internal in the case of the chemical self-destruction of the filmic support itself. Filipa César, Mined Soil (italics), documentary, short (Spectre Production, 2015). Short (Spectre Production, 2015).

22 Managed processes of decomposition can also act as forms of active resistance against industrial agriculture, as Anthropologist Krystina Lyons argued in her research on the situated knowledges of Colombian jungle farming practices. Kristina Lyons, "Decomposition as Life Politics: Soils, Selva, and Small Farmers under the Gun of the U.S.–Colombia War on Drugs", *Cultural Anthropology* 31, no. 1 (23 October 2015): 56–81.

23 Jean Poesen, "Soil Erosion in the Anthropocene: Research Needs", *Earth Surface Processes and Landforms* 43, no. 1 (2018): 64–84.

24 I follow Povinelli in interrogating the limitations of biopolitics' fixation on biological life. Elizabeth Povinelli, *Geontologies: A Requiem to Late Liberalism* (Duke University Press, 2016).

Soils have an endemic nature. Although it is possible to extrapolate and predict the properties of soils from one location to another through mapping and modelling techniques, each soil sample remains unique in its localised constitution, even when displaced. In the colonial soil archives I visited in Lisbon and in the Centre for Soil, Agrifood and Biosciences at Cranfield University in the UK, each soil sample held is labelled and geo-referenced to the sites from where the samples were originally extracted. But even in the absence of this external metadata, researchers are still able to extract a signature profile from a soil sample that can be matched to a precise geographical location. Soils' "ubiquity and transferability" can therefore provide valuable evidence to both determine or eliminate proof of origin, and also link individuals or things to particular sites, a capacity increasingly being explored in criminal and environmental investigations.[25]

Lorna Dawson, a leading expert in the discipline known as Soil Forensics, whom I met during an encounter with soil scientists in London in 2016, explained how soil samples are being used differently in each forum.[26] In the case of environmental forensics, soil is "a matrix carrier for physical evidence", while in the case of criminal forensics, "soil itself is the physical evidence".[27] This uniqueness is currently endangered by what soil scientists define as the genetic erosion of soil systems, referring to the transformations of natural soils caused by industrial anthropogenic actions such as large-scale farming. Such processes have contributed to a decrease in soil diversity, whereby "each soil loses its own natural genetic configuration that allows to distinguish soils as well as it happens for the living systems: plants and animals."[28] But this erosion of differences in soils is also intimately linked with the ways in which scientific modes of knowing soils are mobilised by the agro-industry, as soils are tested in laboratories for their lack or excess of mineral elements considered essential for plant growth. In particular the concentration of nitrogen (N), phosphorus (P), and potassium (K). Hence when soils are collected for the purpose of agricultural 'improvements', their classification is predicated upon a norm; an ideal condition for ensuring maximum yield and also a deviation from that norm, which can nevertheless be 'corrected' with the application of synthetic chemical inputs. These technical corrections and their aftermath have further consequences beyond genetic erosion effects that I explore in the soils of Angola and Alentejo.

In this sense, it is important to distinguish what I described earlier as an archival capacity embedded in soils' natural processes. Before being deposited in the archives, soils are in themselves already an archive, in that they are composed of many different elements that carry trace evidence of their localised conditions, from their metallurgical and chemical make-up

25 See Lorna A. Dawson & Stephen Hillier, "Measurement of Soil Characteristics for Forensic Applications", *Surface and Interface Analysis* 42, no. 5 (2010): 363–77.

26 See Dawson & Hillier, "Measurement of Soil Characteristics".

27 Lorna A. Dawson & Robert W. Mayes, "Chapter 12 — Criminal and Environmental Soil Forensics: Soil as Physical Evidence in Forensic Investigations", in *Introduction to Environmental Forensics (Third Edition)*, ed. Brian L. Murphy & Robert D. Morrison (Academic Press, 2015), 457–86. See also Dawson & Hillier, "Measurement of Soil Characteristics".

28 Giuseppe Lo Papa, Vanessa Palermo, & Carmelo Dazzi, "The "Genetic Erosion" of the Soil Ecosystem", *International Soil and Water Conservation Research* 1, no. 1 (1 June 2013): 11–18.

Milho da Conceição, *Practical works for removing a soil monolith.* Undated. Collection: *Execução de um monólito de solo.* Ref. AMC004011. Source: Universidade de Lisboa/Instituto de Investigação Científica Tropical (Ulisboa/IICT).

According to pedologists I interviewed at ISA, Conceição was the main expert in the process of extracting and assembling a soil monolith. He also recorded visually his laboratory and fieldwork, in a series of photo albums that provide insights into the progress of the pedological campaigns on the ground. This undated image from his collection appears also in a separate archive of pedological materials, and refers to a soil profile labelled 206/67, extracted in 1967 from the province of Huíla, Angola.

to decayed vegetative matter. Soil, in effect, bears many similarities to other archival procedures. To understand soils as archives opens up a series of research questions. What possibilities does a reading of soils as a sensate archive enable? How can we access the archival potential inherent in soils differently from that of the archived soils in scientific and colonial archives? What modes of interactions, what types of sensing and what forms of mediation might be required? And what kinds of practices can be mobilised in this effort to repoliticise soils?

UNARCHIVING SOILS

Soil becomes political when one begins to comprehend its operation as a techno-scientific assemblage and as an archive. To conceive of soils as an archive, one needs to make a distinction between the archival capacity embedded in soils' natural properties and processes and the state's scientific archives of soils that were collected and deposited as natural materials. In the archive of the latter, soils are reduced to a discrete series of material samples that are organised and stored first according to their geographical provenance, and second labelled under their scientific taxons, which describe soils comparatively in relation to their mineral and chemical properties. My case study focuses on the present-day uses of soil samples extracted from Angola under colonial occupation in the period between

Milho da Conceição, *Sample collection for micropedology studies*, P206/67. 1967.
Source: Universidade de Lisboa/Instituto de Investigação Científica Tropical (Ulisboa/IICT).

These images were taken upon the extraction of soil profile labelled as P206/67, extracted from the province of Huíla, Angola. They document both the collection of individual soil samples for laboratory analyses, taken at different depths, and the separate process of extracting a soil profile vertically to form a monolith for exhibition.

1946 and 1974 with a specific emphasis on the period leading to the outbreak of the independence struggles in 1961. This time frame enables me to examine the ways in which the materials archived in Lisbon intersected with the history of the anti-colonial struggle.

According to pedologists I interviewed at the ISA, Conceição was the main expert in the process of extracting and assembling a soil monolith. He also visually recorded his laboratory and fieldwork in a series of photo albums, which provide insights into the progress of the pedological campaigns on the ground. This undated image from his collection appears also in a separate archive of pedological materials, and refers to a soil profile labelled 206/67, extracted in 1967 from the province of Huíla, Angola.

Removed from their original environments, these soil samples become static repositories of the complex set of relations from which they were extracted.[29] This process of reduction and simplification is meant to generate legibility, what anthropologist James C. Scott argued was created by the utilitarian state to maximize value extraction. For Scott, legibility produces a type of "synoptic view", that allows the state to concentrate only on the essential elements in detriment to everything else which is not only reduced from the field of vision, but simultaneously erased in the

29 My use here of the term *original* is meant to describe both the specific geographic location from where the samples were extracted, and the geological origins of soil mineral substrate, or what scientists term parent material. See James G. Bockheim, "Soil Endemism and Its Relation to Soil Formation Theory", *Geoderma* 129, no. 3 (1 December 2005): 109–24.

process of selective abstraction.[30] I reverse this operation by exploring the multiple potentials that arise from examining soil archives through a different lens from that of the state. Taking into consideration the historical, cultural, and political context from which the materials in the archive emerged, I examine the inscriptions of war and resistance from the situated vantage point of the soil sample.[31]

These images were taken upon the extraction of soil profile labelled as P206/67, extracted from the province of Huíla, Angola. They document both the collection of individual soil samples for laboratory analyses, taken at three different depths, and the separate process of extracting a soil profile vertically, to form a monolith for exhibition.

As political theorist Achille Mbembe has maintained, colonial violence operates as a form of graphism.[32] While acknowledging that colonial occupation operates mainly through violence, the metabolic capacity of soils overwrites the effects of such inscriptions beyond the surface level. A fundamental shift in scale and perspective that has enabled me to examine the samples deposited in the colonial archives beyond their value as historical artefacts within the realm of soil science, but as active agents in the present transformation of soils and politics. As mentioned, my methodology is indebted to feminist approaches to ecology in the humanities, which refuse the totalising gaze of science in exchange for situated forms of testimony.[33] However, in my case studies, these two perspectives do not function as competing knowledges, but rather as complementary fields of inquiry. Anthropologist Vanessa Agard-Jones has made use of a similar method when taking the body's perspective to unpack the environmental effects of chemical contamination in Martinique, an approach inspired by the work of Haitian anthropologist Michel-Rolph Trouillot: "he demanded not only that we do research in small places but also that *we look from them*—a shift from looking at a small unit to looking from its place in the world."[34] Thus to look from the soil samples outwards implies a reversal of perspective. In this case, the sample offers two conflicting vantage points:

30 James C. Scott, *Seeing like a State: How Certain Schemes to Improve the Human Condition Have Failed* (Yale University Press, 1998), 11, 263.

31 A genealogy of the ways in which *inscription* has been used to describe the workings of coloniality would have to begin with Gayatri Chakravorty Spivak, "The Rani of Sirmur: An Essay in Reading the Archives", *History and Theory* 24, no. 3 (1985): 270.

32 Achille Mbembe, "Aesthetics of Superfluity", *Public Culture* 16, no. 3 (2004): 373–405. Graphism also defined the system of racial segregation, as Mbembe notes: "territorial segmentation was a key form of the state's inscription of power into the landscape. But the main site of this inscription was the black body itself" (p.390). Furthermore, for Mbembe, the inscription of the apartheid state's power on the body and on the territory was a matter of "writing on the ground of a new set of social and spatial relations". A. Mbembe, "Necropolitics", *Public Culture* 15, no. 1 (1 January 2003): 25.

33 A foundational reference for this *recalibration* can be found in Donna Haraway, "Situated Knowledges: The Science Question in Feminism and the Privilege of Partial Perspective", *Feminist Studies* 14, no. 3 (1988): 589. "I am arguing for the view from a body, always a complex, contradictory, structuring, and structured body, versus the view from above, from nowhere, from simplicity."

34 Vanessa Agard-Jones, "Bodies in the System", *Small Axe: A Caribbean Journal of Criticism* 17, no. 3 (42) (1 November 2013): 183. My emphasis. Albeit focused primarily on the body, Agard-Jones' approach is invested in exploring it in relation to the other systems and scales: "a Trouillotian and feminist *materialist recalibration* of the body is just the approach for the kind of scale-jumping that helps us think Caribbean bodies in systems, moving us from the innards of embodiment to the space of global capital." Agard-Jones, "Bodies in the System", 187. My emphasis.

the site of extraction, and the site of the archive. Against the vertical unidirectionality of the positivist scientific gaze, these samples constitute a unique vantage point from which to analyse the various operations enabled by soil as political material.

In doing so, I remain attentive to how attributing historical value to the materials in the archive has been used to facilitate and perpetuate colonial expropriation through the incorporation of scientific materials as cultural artefacts. As artist and theorist Ariella Azoulay explains succinctly, the notion of "historical value" became "a major excuse for the accumulation of other's worlds, which is materialised in the archive as institution, cannot be understood independently of the archival regime and subsequent practices."[35] Soil archives are, in most cases, the material and epistemic repositories of colonial projects, and thus not only bear the traces of colonial politics, but are also in themselves constitutive of the discursive and systemic logics of colonialism and its permanent project of settlement and order. Historians have described how nineteenth century colonial powers saw the imperial enterprise as a monumental bureaucratic challenge, which required the deployment of a new epistemic structure.[36]

While early scientific missions amassed vast quantities of data extracted from colonised territories and subjects, there were concerns that the information gathered could either be lost or interfered with in travel. Archives were thus conceived as systems to control the accumulation of information, which was subsequently processed, classified and stored in the metropolis, but also as a means to deal with a mounting "awareness of the problem of interference in transmitting knowledge (...) just as the possibility of *positive knowledge* began to be perceived as *eroding*."[37] The logics that informed archival practices were also the product of scientific developments in Britain around the eighteenth century, in particular the concept of entropy.[38] While the term was introduced to define the measure of information loss, it became indexical of the fear of imperial powers to lose control over their colonised subjects.[39]

As Azoulay also notes, long before the archive was accepted as the site of a "universal world history", it was "a regime based on the allocation of differential roles and places to masses of people who were supposed to

35 Ariella Azoulay, *Potential History: Unlearning Imperialism* (Verso, 2019), 145.

36 On the British: "they surveyed and they mapped. They took censuses, produced statistics. They made vast lists of birds. They then shoved all the data they had collected into a shifting series of classifications." Thomas Richards, *The Imperial Archive: Knowledge and the Fantasy of Empire* (Verso, 1993), 47. While departing from Richard's historical analysis of archival formations, I reject his notion of "fantasy", in order to acknowledge the concrete relation between imperial archival practices and colonial violence.

37 Richards, *The Imperial Archive*, 73. My emphasis.

38 Richards, *The Imperial Archive*, 75. Following Michael Foucault, these scientific developments also came to impact Political Economy: "in the 1860s Marx certainly had regarded the capitalist economy as founded on the capital of low entropy with which the planet is endowed; the *Grundrisse* is essentially an anatomy of the process by which the earth's resources are transformed into commodities. Although Marx does not go so far as to place absolute and inexorable ecological limits on capitalist expansion, he is perfectly aware that free energy cannot be used more than once." Richards, *The Imperial Archive*, 94.

39 As Richards points, "By the turn of the century many of the empire's communications glitches had been defined as examples of entropy, or the tendency of matter to move from an organized to a disorganized state." Richards, *The Imperial Archive*, 75.

be kept in their 'right place'."[40] If we are to accept entropy as the new axis around which knowledge production was structured, a number of questions arise in relation to its extractive nature: first, since it was the product of extensive surveying and mapping of colonised subjects, the archive must be understood as a system that is not only concerned with collecting and organising the knowledge of others, but also invested in generating the rules for restructuring environments and modes of life. This in turn raises a second question, which points to the contradictory nature of the archive: how was this fear of erosion of information during transmission compatible with the utter disregard which is commonly assumed as the colonial attitude towards the sources from where this knowledge was extracted? Furthermore, what is the relation between this perceived erosion of the accumulated knowledge of others, and the construction of the notion of *positive knowledge*?

In the wake of these questions, the emergence of a colonial archival complex cannot be understood as a static representation of the colonised, but rather a productive agent of colonial relations. As Gayatri Chakravorty Spivak insisted when proposing to "read" colonial archives against "hegemonic nineteenth-century European historiography", these archives are not a "repository of 'facts'", but in fact they construct the object of colonial representation that is afterwards effectively realised.[41] In this respect, Azoulay's proposal to distinguish between "the *institution* of the archive, the *regime* of the archive, and *archival practices*" is thus useful to understand the role of different components of the archival machinery.[42] While recognising that archives are in most cases the product of colonial operations of extraction, and that the archive is "first and foremost a regime that facilitates uprooting, deportation, coercion, and enslavement, as well as the looting of wealth, resources, and labour", this distinction provides an entry point for intervention, as it sheds light onto the ways in which some of the components can be put to work otherwise. This operation should not be limited to "forever write alternative histories to settler worldviews", but should instead be open to a continued practice of "unlearning imperialism".[43]

CASE STUDY: ANTI-COLONIAL STRUGGLES & SOIL SURVEYS IN ANGOLA

Following these insights, I approached the colonial soil archives in Lisbon to inquire into the possibility of reading the inscriptions of the anti-colonial war in the soil samples, specifically the traces of counter-insurgency operations of uprooting and forced settlement of populations in Angola. Since many of them were collected from areas which had been subjected to military action, these samples are potentially the material records of unrecognised war crimes committed during the anti-colonial struggles, specifically the use of napalm ammunition in the first stages of the conflict. The scientists in charge of the Pedoteca, Professors Madalena Cunha and Fernando Girão, whom I have met and interviewed on a number

40 Azoulay, *Potential History*, 45.
41 Spivak, "The Rani of Sirmur".
42 Azoulay, *Potential History*, 149.
43 Azoulay, *Potential History*, 171.

of occasions, initially rejected my hypothesis, claiming instead that the anthropic factor is deemed irrelevant when analysing the processes of soil formation in pedological terms.

The main issue for pedologists is the geological scale of transformations, which they consider incommensurable with the short period of colonial occupation.[44] Instead, they explained to me how the soil archives perform a pedagogical role within the Agronomic University, both as historical and scientific materials. But while claiming an ideological independence of scientific activity from politics, the reality of the archive's role in the present contradicts their position. When asked who approaches the Pedoteca nowadays from outside of the University, and for what purposes, their answer was revealing of other interests. I was told that often private entities looking to invest in the former colonial territories covered by the soil surveys seek the archives to inquire into the soils' productive potential. In this instance, the surveys fulfil their original objective, which is to render the territory legible for the purpose of agricultural projects. The primary difference being that the colonial cultivation model that was developed after the end of the Second World War—consisting of white settler family units and corporate plantations—has been replaced in the present by industrial-scale agribusiness.

Evidence of the complicity between soil science and the state can also be found in several recorded testimonies from scientists who took part in the colonial missions that have been made available to the public during the last years. In these interviews, scientists give detailed accounts of the intricate relation on the ground between the survey teams and the populations during the period of the anti-colonial conflict: a "consented presence" some argue, which was nevertheless defended by military force. Cabral's colleague Pinto Ricardo, one of the main pedologists who worked in the missions collecting soil samples, claimed to have been working "for the future of Angola", since the independence of the territory was at that point to be expected.[45] Their differing trajectories are revealing of their active role in constructing alternative futures. While Ricardo remained at the service of the Portuguese State, Cabral left his job as a soil scientist to fight against colonial occupation.

Hence, these testimonies from scientists, while offering valuable first-person accounts of the direct experience of the surveys on the ground, also reinforce the historical narrative from the perspective of the coloniser. Against their so-called "consented presence", the role of soil scientists in facilitating these operations should also be put into question. A counter-testimony is urgently needed, in order to interrogate and possibly debunk the myth of scientific neutrality. And this is precisely what I have in mind when engaging with the soil archives: to investigate what other possible functions or uses are derived from the collection of samples in the present beyond the

44 In a later interview, conducted on the 8 January 2019, he conceded that the late colonial project of white agricultural settlement in Angola, in particular the failed experiment of Cela, had a negative impact on the degradation of the soils.

45 In Ricardo, *Depoimento de Rui Pinto Ricardo - Actd.* For a critical perspective on the interviews of the pedologists, see Cláudia Castelo, "'Não tem a classificação americana, não existe!': História oral, ciência do solo tropical e imperialismo(s)", *História Unisinos* 18, no. 1 (24 June 2014): 136-145.

sole purpose of their historical and academic value as scientific knowledge, in order to trouble the prevailing narratives of political non-involvement on the part of soil science.

INSCRIPTIONS OF WAR

The materials at the Pedoteca are synoptically arranged in a series of rooms and long corridors which are evocative of curator Okwui Enwezor's description of a stereotypical archival space, "a dim, musty place full of drawers, filing cabinets, and shelves laden with old documents, an inert repository of historical artefacts".[46] In the case of the exposed soil profiles stored in Lisbon's colonial archive, dust from two different origins is incorporated in the soil's chemical constitution: that which accumulates at the surface of the profiles and the layered dust particles from where the samples were extracted. Since dust is in itself a form of "displaced urban soil" combined with suspended atmospheric aerosol particles, it continues some of the geochemical processes that occur in the natural soils.[47] Furthermore, through laboratory analysis, these materials can be read anew in relation to the sites of extraction, thus providing a reference point against which to measure the continuous effects of environmental transformation. In this sense, the dynamic properties of the samples in the archives seem to fulfil Enwezor's call for an "active" archive. But above all, the samples stored in Lisbon remain a significant source of information which continues to be mobilised nowadays by different agents, thus extending the colonial reach of the archives into present day politics.

This map includes all the survey points that have been georeferenced by the ISA. I classified the surveys by year, and included here the fieldnotes that are contained in 1,603 of the samples, from a total of 4,500 samples collected between 1946 and 1970.

The soil samples are supplemented by field reports, hand-written forms containing geographic and ethnographic data outside of the direct scope of the missions, which were essentially organised around recording information to produce detailed pedological cartographies. Before being subjected to the classificatory synchronisation of universal soil taxono-

46 Enwezor, *Archive Fever*. These words are taken from the catalogue of an influential exhibition, whose title pays tribute to Jacques Derrida's homonymous essay. Against this immovable architecture, Enwezor proposed instead that the archive should be understood and engaged with as "an active, regulatory discursive system". The formulation is indebted to Michel Foucault, who defined the archive as the system of enunciation which regulates the form of statement-events, while at the same time exposing the logics that govern their formation: "nor is the archive that which collects the dust of statements that have become inert once more, and which may make possible the miracle of their resurrection; it is that which defines the mode of occurrence of the statement-thing; it is the system of its functioning." Michel Foucault, *Archaeology of Knowledge*, trans. Alan Sheridan (Routledge, 2002), 146. As has been noted by multiple scholars that have departed from this statement, Foucault fell short in investigating further the political structures that supported this system, at least beyond their western manifestations. See Simone Browne, *Dark Matters: On the Surveillance of Blackness* (Duke University Press, 2015).

47 L. Ferreira-Baptista & E. De Miguel, "Geochemistry and Risk Assessment of Street Dust in Luanda, Angola: A Tropical Urban Environment", *Atmospheric Environment* 39, no. 25 (August 2005): 4501–12. On the politics of dust as a form of material witness, see Susan Schuppli, "Impure Matter: A Forensics of WTC Dust", in *Savage Objects*, ed. Godofredo Pereira (Imprensa Nacional-Casa da Moeda, 2012).

mies, which govern the territorial representations in the soil maps, each soil sample was numbered, dated, and tagged according to its geographical provenance.[48] An important layer of qualitative information can be found within these captions and field reports that includes a series of annotations regarding the toponymy of rural settlements, driving directions, geographical remarks and pictures of the locations where the samples are taken. This set of analogue metadata is in excess of the quantitative output of the maps, offering a palimpsest of otherwise unregistered information, which further challenges the claims of autonomy and neutrality made by the scientists.[49]

From the abstracted territory of the maps that were produced as the outcome of the soil surveys towards the concrete reality of the samples, these archival materials possess qualities akin to a kind of soil metadata, which can be continually reinterpreted and thus also exploited.[50] Beyond the analogical metadata that already exists in the archives, such as fieldnotes and labelling, I am also interested in approaching these soil archives as a kind of technical media. In this case, the metadata in the samples becomes a tool to read other patterns beyond those studied under the domain of pedology.[51] With the specific case study of the soil samples located in the archives, the operations produced by the soil sample renders visible not only the procedural workings of modern techno-science and its ambitions to capture a totalising view of soil that could be activated by the colonial imaginary, but also the political conditions that have reactivated the archive in the present.

When reading the inscriptions of war and resistance from the vantage point of the sites from where the samples located in colonial archives were extracted from, what emerges is a clear correlation between scientific soil surveys and anti-colonial struggles in Angola. Despite the fact that the soil scientists whom I interviewed claim independence between their work and politics, my analysis of the classification of the data obtained from the soil samples stored in the archive in Lisbon is revealing of a striking pattern. As the soil survey campaigns intensified in the decade leading to the beginning of the war, the activity of soil scientists in 1960 coincides precisely with the area from where the first actions of organised armed resistance erupted in 1961, in the northern provinces of Zaire and Uige. This finding adds a layer of potential complexity to existing historical accounts that attribute the beginning of the conflict to the over-exploitation of land

48 In my research I track in particular the taxonomy developed by the FAO/UNESCO Soil Map of the World in 1961-1974. Eric C. Brevik et al., “Soil Mapping, Classification, and Pedologic Modeling: History and Future Directions”, *Geoderma* 264 (2016): 256–74.

49 Johanna Sassoon has written on the role of captions as a palimpsest of information, and which often gets excluded when archived photographic materials get digitised. See Joanna Sassoon, “Photographic Materiality in the Age of Digital Reproduction”, *Photographs Objects Histories: On the Materiality of Images*, 2004: 186–202.

50 I am employing the stratified concept of *metadata* advanced by Matteo Pasquinelli, who described it as “the vertical accumulation of information about information”. See Matteo Pasquinelli, “Metadata Society”, in *Posthuman Glossary*, ed. Rosi Braidotti & Maria Hlavajova (Bloomsbury Academic, 2018), 253.

51 The term *pedology* was introduced in 1862 by pioneer German soil scientist Friedrich Albert Fallou, and was used by Dokuchaiev in Russia the following decade. The widespread use by soil scientists globally only occurred after the First International Congress of Soil Science, held in 1927 in the United States. See Roy W. Simonson, “Origin and Acceptance of the Term Pedology”, *Soil Science Society of America Journal* 63, no. 1 (January 1999): 4–10.

resources. My research thus contributes to this analysis in situating soil science literally at the scene of these events.

Based on a spatiotemporal analysis of the data extracted from the soil surveys in relation to the timeline of the anti-colonial conflict, fieldwork undertaken by soil scientists in the north of Angola coincides with the outbreak of the independence struggles in 1961.

In mapping the entanglements between soil surveys and anti-colonial struggle, I seek here not only to observe the complicity of soil scientists with colonial occupation, but simultaneously to acknowledge the lasting impacts of colonial science. In recent years, new projects have emerged in the territories that were previously surveyed for the purpose of intensifying land-use. These new extractivist initiatives, located mainly in Alentejo, Portugal and in South Kwanza, Angola, claim to make use of the data from the surveys as a reliable source of information for their future operations.[52] Thus the soil samples archived in Lisbon function not only as inert sources of historical scientific knowledge, but as active agents of colonial extraction in the present. Yet, from a different vantage point, this historical knowledge can also be mobilised and put to work otherwise, in forms of active resistance against the depredations of financial capital. As the area of monocrop plantations expands, so does the resistance prompted by its environmental impacts.

During recent years in Alentejo, a growing number of citizen movements, informed by an assemblage of scientific and non-scientific knowledges and practices, have been organising to counter this unregulated growth. In extending my conversations and engagements with scientific practices, I aim at giving continuity to the work of activists and invested soil scientists, such as Cabral, who advocated for the protections of the soils, as well as of the rights of those who live and depend upon them as a means for subsistence. In fact, in their everyday practices, activists from disparate backgrounds interpret and work with the same techno-scientific and juridical knowledge in order to challenge the hegemony of agribusiness, as do investors and scientists. But while some risks are directly visible in present changes in the landscape, others remain concealed by the distributed nature of their processes. The negotiation between these multiple scales remains one of the main challenges for environmental activists, who are confronted in their struggles with the increasing pressures of financial capital. A new appreciation of the distinct properties of soils is needed, not only from the vantage point of science, but also from the perspective of those directly involved with maintaining other forms of relations with soils that are dependent upon it for multiple uses beyond ag-

52 In both cases, upon the remnants of large-scale hydroelectric projects from the 1950s. In Alentejo with the completion of the Alqueva dam in 2001, and in South Kwanza with the reactivation of the former colonial settlement of Cela, now renamed Projecto Aldeia Nova (PAN). Forming part of a wider pacification plan, the project was conceived and implemented in 2003 by a company and technical staff from Israel, the LR group, which sought to transpose to Angola the cooperative model of agricultural production of the *moshav*. But despite advertising their services as a philanthropic organization, the company LR has been accused of supplying arms for the civil war in Angola. See Gur Megiddo, "The Israeli Fighter Pilots Who Got Rich Off Angola's Civil War and Their Link to a Massive Cyberattack", *Haaretz*, 1 January 2019, https://www.haaretz.com/israel-news/.premium-the-israeli-businessmen-who-got-rich-off-angola-s-war-and-their-ties-to-cyberattack-1.6792027.

ricultural productivity. In other words, it is not so much about challenging the stability afforded by the foundations of applied sciences, but rather about interrogating how the impacts of scientific knowledge about soil are experienced from the vantage point of the sites from where the samples were once extracted.

Standing on the land shaped by the Soil Map of the World in the present, my work in collaboration with that of other activists tries to shift and destabilise the ground, and thus soil, from under the feet of financial investors. In unearthing the invisible strata of financial capital from the soil samples in colonial archives, I seek to return to these seemingly silent and immovable soils, their rift, their uncertainty, and their politics.

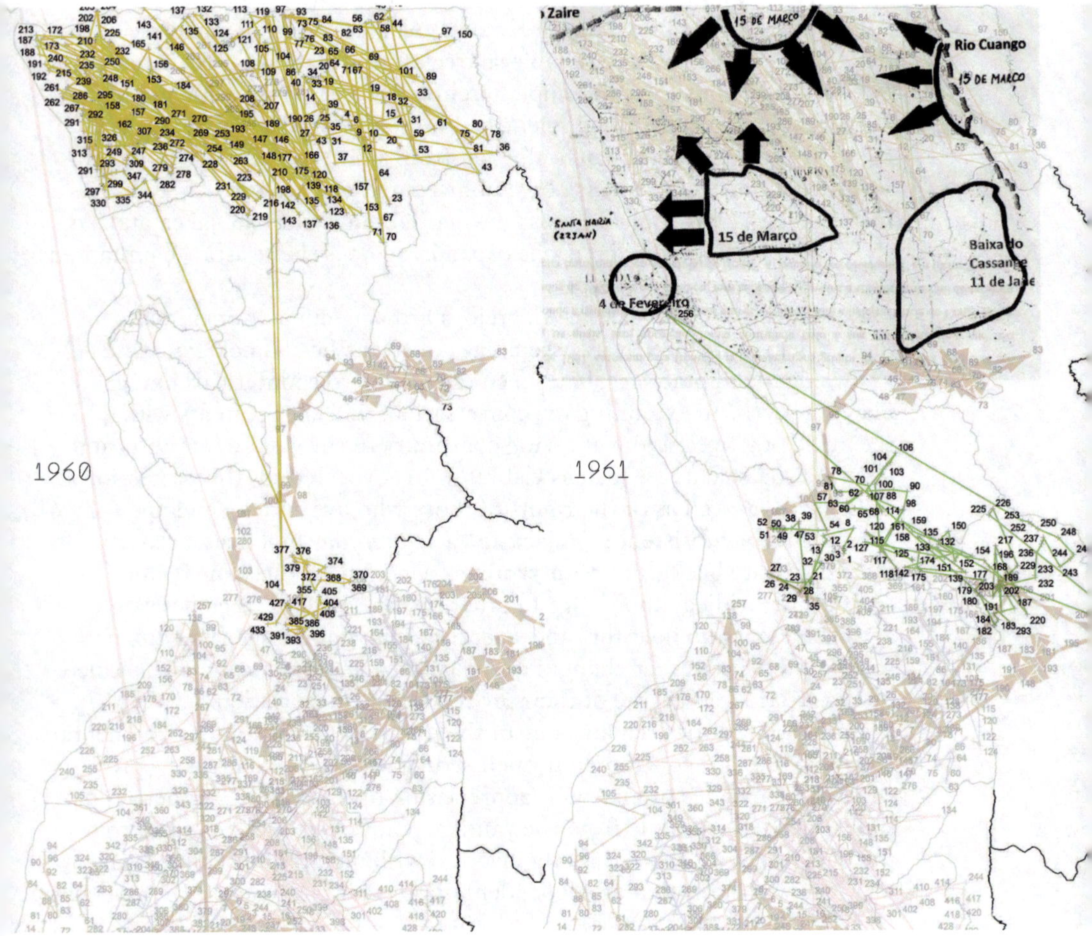

Soil Surveys in Angola, between the years 1960-61. Source: Map by the author.
Base raw data courtesy of Ulisboa/IICT.

Colour classification of the samples extracted by year of collection. Based on a spatiotemporal analysis of the data extracted from the soil surveys in relation to the timeline of the anti-colonial conflict, fieldwork undertaken by soil scientists in the north of Angola coincides with the outbreak of the independence struggles in 1961.

WORKS CITED

Agard-Jones, Vanessa. "Bodies in the System". *Small Axe:* 17, no. 3 (42) (1 November 2013): 182-92.

Aureli, Pier Vittorio. *The City as a Project.* Ruby Press, 2013.

Azoulay, Ariella. *Potential History: Unlearning Imperialism.* Verso, 2019.

Barad, Karen. "Quantum Entanglements and Hauntological Relations of Inheritance: Dis/Continuities, SpaceTime Enfoldings, and Justice-to-Come". *Derrida Today* 3, no. 2 (November 2010): 240–68.

Bockheim, James G. "Soil Endemism and Its Relation to Soil Formation Theory". *Geoderma* 129, no. 3 (1 December 2005): 109–24.

Brevik, Eric C., Costanza Calzolari, Bradley A. Miller, Paulo Pereira, Cezary Kabala, Andreas Baumgarten, & Antonio Jordán. "Soil Mapping, Classification, and Pedologic Modeling: History and Future Directions". *Geoderma* 264 (2016): 256–74.

Cadena, Marisol de la. *Earth Beings: Ecologies of Practice across Andean Worlds.* Duke University Press, 2015.

Castelo, Cláudia. "'Não tem a classificação americana, não existe!': História oral, ciência do solo tropical e imperialismo(s)". *História Unisinos* 18, no. 1 (24 June 2014): 136-145.

Chakrabarty, Dipesh. "The Climate of History: Four Theses". *Critical Inquiry* 35, no. 2 (2009): 197–222.

Clark, Nigel. "Politics of Strata". *Theory, Culture & Society* 34, no. 2–3 (1 May 2017): 211–31.

Dawson, Lorna A., & Stephen Hillier. "Measurement of Soil Characteristics for Forensic Applications". *Surface and Interface Analysis* 42, no. 5 (2010): 363–77.

Dawson, Lorna A., & Robert W. Mayes. "Chapter 12 - Criminal and Environmental Soil Forensics: Soil as Physical Evidence in Forensic Investigations". In *Introduction to Environmental Forensics*, edited by Brian L. Murphy and Robert D. Morrison. Academic Press, 2015.

Dixon-Román, Ezekiel J. "Algo-Ritmo: More-Than-Human Performative Acts and the Racializing Assemblages of Algorithmic Architectures". *Cultural Studies ↔ Critical Methodologies* 16, no. 5 (2016): 482–90.

Elden, Stuart. *The Birth of Territory.* The University of Chicago Press, 2013.

Enwezor, Okwui. *Archive Fever: Uses of the Document in Contemporary Art.* Steidl, 2008.

Fergusson, Lee. "Anthrosols and Technosols: The Anthropogenic Signature of Contaminated Soils and Sediments in Australia". *Water, Air, & Soil Pollution* 228, no. 8 (9 July 2017): 269.

Ferreira-Baptista, L., & E. De Miguel. "Geochemistry and Risk Assessment of Street Dust in Luanda, Angola: A Tropical Urban Environment". *Atmospheric Environment* 39, no. 25 (August 2005): 4501–12.

Foucault, Michel. *Archaeology of Knowledge.* Translated by Alan Sheridan. Routledge, 2002.

Guerin, Turlough F., Thomas Knacker, Werner Kördel, Jörg Matschullat, & Willie Peijnenburg. "Editorial: JSS — J Soils & Sediments". *Journal of Soils and Sediments* 1, no. 1 (2001): 1–1.

Hall, Stuart. "Constituting an Archive". *Third Text* 15, no. 54 (1 March 2001): 89–92.

Haraway, Donna. "Situated Knowledges: The Science Question in Feminism and the Privilege of Partial Perspective". *Feminist Studies* 14, no. 3 (1988): 575.

Holbraad, Martin. "Things as Concepts". In *Savage Objects*, edited by Godofredo Pereira. Imprensa Nacional-Casa da Moeda, 2012.

Holbraad, Martin, & Morten Axel Pedersen. *The Ontological Turn: An Anthropological Exposition.* Cambridge University Press, 2017.

Jenny, Hans. *Factors of Soil Formation: A System of Quantitative Pedology.* McGraw-Hill, 1941.

Lyons, Kristina. "Decomposition as Life Politics: Soils, Selva, and Small Farmers under the Gun of the U.S.–Colombia War on Drugs". *Cultural Anthropology* 31, no. 1 (23 October 2015): 56–81.

Mbembe, A. "Necropolitics". *Public Culture* 15, no. 1 (1 January 2003): 11–40.

Mbembe, Achille. "Aesthetics of Superfluity". *Public Culture* 16, no. 3 (2004): 373–405.

Mezzadra, Sandro, & Brett Neilson. "Extraction, Logistics, Finance: Global Crisis and the Politics of Operations". *Radical Philosophy* 178, no. March/April (2013): 8.

Mined Soil. Documentary, Short. Spectre Production, 2015.

Papa, Giuseppe Lo, Vanessa Palermo, & Carmelo Dazzi. "The 'Genetic Erosion' of the Soil Ecosystem". *International Soil and Water Conservation Research* 1, no. 1 (1 June 2013): 11–18.

Pasquinelli, Matteo. "Metadata Society". In *Posthuman Glossary*, edited by Rosi Braidotti & Maria Hlavajova. Bloomsbury Academic, 2018.

Phillips, Jonathan D., & Daniel A. Marion. 'Pedological Memory in Forest Soil Development'. *Forest Ecology and Management 188 (2004) 363–380*, 2004.

Pignarre, Philippe, & Isabelle Stengers. *Capitalist Sorcery: Breaking the Spell.* Palgrave Macmillan, 2011.

Poesen, Jean. "Soil Erosion in the Anthropocene: Research Needs". *Earth Surface Processes and Landforms* 43, no. 1 (2018): 64–84.

Povinelli, Elizabeth. *Geontologies: A Requiem to Late Liberalism*, Duke University Press, 2016.

Puig de la Bellacasa, Maria. "Making Time for Soil: Technoscientific Futurity and the Pace of Care". *Social Studies of Science* 45, no. 5 (October 2015): 691–716.

Ricardo, R. Pinto. *Rui Pinto Ricardo (Depoimento, 2013).* IICT, 2014. https://actd.iict.pt/view/actd:MORPR.

Richards, Thomas. *The Imperial Archive: Knowledge and the Fantasy of Empire.* Verso, 1993.

Sassoon, Joanna. "Photographic Materiality in the Age of Digital Reproduction". In *Photographs Objects Histories: On the Materiality of Images*, edited by Elizabeth Edwards & Janice Hart. Routledge, 2004.

Schuppli, Susan. "Impure Matter: A Forensics of WTC Dust". In *Savage Objects*, edited by Godofredo Pereira. Imprensa Nacional-Casa da Moeda, 2012.

Scott, James C. *Seeing like a State: How Certain Schemes to Improve the Human Condition Have Failed.* Yale University Press, 1998.

Selcer, Perrin. "Fabricating Unity: The FAO-UNESCO Soil Map of the World". *Historical Social Research/Historische Sozialforschung* 40, no. 2 (152) (2015): 174–201.

Simonson, Roy W. "Origin and Acceptance of the Term Pedology". *Soil Science Society of America Journal* 63, no. 1 (January 1999): 4–10.

"Soil Map of the World. 1.5.000.000. Vol. I Legend". Rome (Italy): FAO, 1974.

Spivak, Gayatri Chakravorty. "The Rani of Sirmur: An Essay in Reading the Archives". *History and Theory* 24, no. 3 (1985): 247–72.

Van Wyck, Peter C. *The Highway of the Atom.* McGill-Queen's University Press, 2010.

Wyck, Peter C. van. "An Archive of Threat". *Future Anterior* 9, no. 2 (2013): 53–80.

SOUNDSCAPES OF THE PETROCHEMICAL CORRIDOR

Margarida Mendes

As I am rowing down the Mississippi, my body becomes one with the pulling strength of the river. I am slowly projected by the kinetic lure of its course, drifting along the side lanes of the river channel where barges and tankers manoeuvre. The sun reflects its rays on the mirrored water, where muddy vortexes keep forming. I am surrounded by low engine sounds and the distant hum of incessant pumping. There is little silence on this stretch of the river as we approach the Gulf. Human voices are replaced by the sounds of occasional birds, as the machinic-steering boats and factory supply infrastructures become a constant presence. My senses are wide awake, merging with the enveloping soundscape as the pull of the river sets the pace to my paddling. My canoe team proceeds in silence as the rhythm of these encircling entities becomes the commanding force that draws our vessels forward. The raging flux of the waters becomes one with the muscular strength of our paddling, as we become synchronous with the river. As I attune to the incessant rush of its flowing waters, a meditative state falls upon me: I realise that I am no longer autonomous from the flowing rhythmic architectures of the river that surrounds me.

We were a group of fifteen people travelling down the petrochemical corridor.[1] We travelled by three canoes, composed of a core team that came rowing down from Minnesota on a hundred-day journey. The canoes were used by intermittent teams, alongside artists, environmental science scholars, and students. The teams rotated when the group made occasional stops for topical field stations and presentations on land. During these, they had the chance to contact activist communities and local specialists, as well as carry out site visits to industrial facilities, riverine infrastructures, and memorial sites along the way. The River Semester participants were encouraged to develop research around the river site, choosing the methodological frameworks and tools that best suited their projects. Many of us collected data and water and sediment samples along the way. We also documented the different stretches of the river, either by visual or audio recordings.

Aware that, at the time, there were no existing acoustic ecology studies of this stretch of the river, I joined the River Semester on the last

1 In the context of the River Semester and the Mississippi. An Anthropocene River project, organised by Haus der Kulturen der Welt (HKW), Berlin, and the Max Planck Institute for the History of Science, Berlin, together with, together with Augsburg and Tulane Universities.

leg of its journey, travelling down from Baton Rouge to New Orleans.[2] I pursued a project titled "Sounding the Mississippi", in which I collected sound recordings of the riverine soundscape, while engaging in ecological debates and meeting local activists and community members. I had proposed to document the lower Mississippi River petrochemical corridor acoustic space by using an audio recorder and carrying listening sessions as a way of reflecting on this ecosystem. I recorded the environment with a hydrophone and zoom recorder stereo microphone both above and below the water line as we canoed down the river towards the Gulf, or whenever we stopped on the riverbanks. By registering the exceedingly industrialised soundscape of these riverine embankments and surrounding industrial facilities, I tried to study the continuity between bodies and the environment.

I sensed my way through the riverine soundscapes, as I reflected on the rhythms that the industry may imprint on matter and existing life forms. While seeking sonic marks of industrialisation, I revisited my thoughts about the impermanence of matter and the mutability of the hydro cycle.[3] These reflections led me to conceptualise the river in my research as a living geological stratum and its surrounding river system as a complex metabolic site where numerous transactions occur. How can listening contribute to a deeper riverine understanding?

In the following sections, I introduce my journey through a description of the Mississippi soundscapes surveyed, narrating encounters I had with artists, activists, and community members around New Orleans during several visits in 2019. While cross-referencing direct reports from the field, I also expose the adaptation of the methodological processes I developed over time to address this case study, specifically in response to the conditions of imposed remoteness and inaccessibility to the field forced upon me by the COVID-19 pandemic. If, at times, the distance became ever too real, not allowing for further sonic registry and connection with the ecosystem under study, the constant revision of my notes and follow-up conversations with the Anthropocene Curriculum fellows allowed for debates about transdisciplinary activist and artistic practices to flourish.[4] This incited further research questions and allowed for new experimental pedagogical methodologies to emerge.[5] In this sequence, I was motivated to carry out a subsequent series of interviews and conversations conducted with an array of practitioners based in New Orleans and Minnesota between 2020 and 2021.

Sonic tools provide compelling methodologies to register the complexity of the petrochemical corridor as an ecosystem. Sonic modes of sensing can offer insight into ecosystem relations before they are fully legible in the landscape as visual evidence. Sound operates in a diffuse way that alters the behaviour and interaction of entities. But, as a process of conduc-

2 Information obtained in an interview with Natalia Sidorovskaia, senior researcher at University of Louisiana at Lafayette who conducts work in the Gulf monitoring oil drilling impacts in the cetacean community. Natalia Sidorovskaia, interview by Margarida Mendes, October 2020, online.

3 I was seeking these sonic marks by tuning into the repetitive patterns generated by boat engines and industrial facilities, while listening also to the hums of the broader soundscape.

4 "Mississippi. An Anthropocene River" project included an iteration of the Anthropocene Campus in New Orleans, comprising a series of workshops, keynotes, and field trips.

5 *The Shape of a Practice* was a program hosted at HKW in November 2020.

tion and reverberation, sound resists fixation, although it does inscribe its effects into matter. As such, sonic tools may expose forms of intersubjective connection while helping to provide evidence of existing power dynamics, exposing sonic marks and decibel thresholds that lead to changes in behavioural and migratory patterns of different species.

Aware that most of the sonic research conducted on the river is situated on the Gulf, leaving behind the Delta communities or other animals and humans on land, I decided to enter this habitat as an attentive listener. I experienced the river through various sound media and reported it through extensive journaling and field notes. Afterwards, I conducted interviews and research that reiterate the cumulative impacts that the presence of industry's sonic emissions can cause on bodies and reflected on the incremented harms that chemical toxicity brings to this context. Through these processes , I introduce how different living species have different perceptions of the sonic, adapting differently to the challenges of industrialised ecosystems and rising background noise, as reported by scientists I interviewed. I also include reflections on the role of orality, storytelling, and witnessing, and how these may help bridge personal experiences across changing soundscapes.

Through a series of sounding exercises, recordings, and conversations with environmentalists, I set out to explore the limits of the sensing body and investigate the chemical and vibrational continuity between bodies and the environment. In doing so, I speculate how different sensing ontologies, perceptions of the bodily, and mechanisms of registration can lead to different forms of environmental attunement. Pursuing my research directly in the field, I ask what sensing systems, modes of existence, and parts of the spectrum are accounted for and which ones lie suppressed by current biopolitical regimes that pay more attention to the human *sensorium*. By 'reading' the riverine ecosystem as a living stratum and the anatomical body as a whole auditory, endocrinological, and sensing system, I explore the subjective experience of acoustics. This has led me to question what kinds of restorative sonic practices may lead to ecosystem awareness and regeneration, and how these listening and sounding practices might work against the dispossessing partitions that generally govern ecosystem management.[6]

Drawing my attention to practices of sensing, both in human and other-than-human entities, I dive deeper into how we can rebuild a sense of care for the planet, one that refuses the partition between bodies and the environment and the hierarchisation of life forms. By pursuing this fieldwork, I wish to rework what it is to hear, to sense, and to register the world, by incorporating techniques of imaginative listening as a restorative and situated practice. I have tried to expand my comprehension of the human body, and that of other living organisms, by reimagining ourselves as antennas immersed in a sea of pulsating waves—whole sensuous bodies that vibrate beyond discrete epidermal borders and live as interconnected beings in intersubjective spaces. Only through this attunement to different sensorial systems can we re-

6 A good example is the "Underwater Sound and Coral Reef Restoration" project. See: https://dosits.org/underwater-sound-and-coral-reef-restoration/.

define our relation to the natural world and find common spaces for listening where different sonic sensibilities can come into conversation. This might lead us to read an ecosystem through plural and novel perspectives, more conscious about diverse forms of inhabitation that decentre the human, while potentially bringing consciousness to species interrelations and allowing for more reciprocal forms of engagement and mutual care.

RIVER JOURNEY – PROLOGUE
bad weather, river stream ran too fast, stayed ashore
visited Baton Rouge museum, a former plantation
walked next to huge petrochemical where neighbourhoods
have been displaced - busted by police

The stretch of the Mississippi River between Baton Rouge and New Orleans is known as the petrochemical corridor. It was formerly referred to as Plantation Country, due to the 400 plantations that existed on the land from Plaquemine's Island downriver.[7] Two hundred oil refineries have now replaced these. These days, the petrochemical corridor is known as Cancer Alley or Death Alley, due to the extremely high cancer rates among local communities. "The level of toxicity increases with the darkness of the skin", said local activist Wendi Moore O'Neal, who has been working with singing and story circles as community healing tools.[8] In the petrochemical corridor, forms of labour and land dispossession have been taking place over centuries as the plantations were eventually replaced by petrochemical industries and carceral institutions.[9] The flux of water has become a strategic asset for the military, and the land privatised by international corporations has expropriated local communities while erasing memorials and exercising control over the health of ecosystems. The massive alteration of Louisiana's changing landscapes is a direct consequence of the intensification of agriculture and the refining of petrochemicals downstream. While upriver, logging and mining have immersed local communities in a sense of *solastalgia*—a state of psychological distress that communities experience when alienated from their homelands due to intensive industrialisation, extractive intervention, and landscape transformation.[10] If one was able to navigate

7 This is how local inhabitants previously named the land.

8 Connecting to the riverine landscapes, Moore O'Neal claims that the river is the root of her spiritual practice, under the hypervigilant state of grief that submerges the local population. Songs are a powerful form of Indigenous medicine that has travelled intergenerationally over the years, affirming modes of collectivity, interspecies codependency, and environmental interconnection connected to a particular site. They are vehicles of spiritual elevation that have circulated for long in the Southern landscapes as a mode of narrating the precarious life of shrimpers, land workers, and other Delta inhabitants, long connected with histories of geotrauma. See: https://jaliyahconsulting.com/.

9 Katherine McKittrick, "Plantation Futures", *Small Axe* 17, no. 3 (2013): 1–15.

10 Solastalgia was a term first coined by philosopher Glenn Albrecht in his 2005 article. Glenn Albrecht, "Solastalgia: a new concept in human health and identity", *PAN: philosophy activism nature* 3 (2005): 44-59.

the shifting timescales of the chemical infrastructural incursions along this river, one could sense the symptoms of mass extinction slowly infusing the surrounding landscape.[11]

In the Lower Mississippi, along with its haunting plantation history and the imprint of settler colonialism erasing the presence of Indigenous peoples, massive infrastructural projects have been developed over the years, significantly altering its landscape. The Mississippi River dates back to the Cretaceous period and became the primary drainage system of the Central United States about 15 million years ago.[12] The river has changed its course innumerable times as the Delta gyrated across Louisiana, the water having flown down courses up to 150 kilometres apart over the last few millennia. Currently, the river's kinetic pull is pushing it into the Atchafalaya River, only to be detained by the continuous intervention of the Army Corps of Engineers. "Seen from the air, the Mississippi Delta looks like a gigantic cancerous lung, excoriated with ten thousand miles of oil and gas canals, widened and widening over decades into a cast disassemblage of open water", says marine biologist Jeremy Jackson.[13] With the settlement of industrial and agricultural facilities, the need to control the river's course incited the construction of 16,000 kilometres of canals, water diversions, and levees. These significantly changed the conservation status of the local marsh, while providing the industry with new shipping lanes. This project of harsh containment has permanently altered the ecosystem and the lives of those who inhabit it, as we can read in the statements delivered by the inhabitants I interviewed along my journey.

The Mississippi passes through thirty-one American states and has many tributaries. Its importance in the region is highly connected to its dependency on the river as a source of hydro maintenance for refineries—particularly in the petrochemical corridor, which contains 25 per cent of the nation's production capacity in the combined petroleum and chemical industries.[14] Not to mention its role as a transportation canal for international shipping: crude oil, natural gas, coal, steel, soybeans, maize, chemical fertilisers, animal feed, wheat, and sugar are a few of the major products traded along its course. The Mississippi Delta holds 8 per cent of the total US gas reserves, processes 3.3 million barrels of crude oil per day, and is the third largest coal exporting port in the United States.

Most of the community members and activists I encountered have shared a sense of nostalgic restlessness and environmental grief that shapes their riverine relationship, while being exposed to high levels of industrialisation and environmental harms. The massive containment projects of river conservation have led to internal disputes and personal distress, since not all the communities have been consulted equally.

11 Statement by artist Claire Pentecost during her presentation at the Anthropocene Campus, Tulane University 2019.
12 Jeremy B.C. Jackson & Steve Chapple, *Breakpoint: Reckoning with America's Environmental Crises* (Yale University Press, 2018), 49.
13 Jackson & Chapple, *Breakpoint*, 45.
14 Jackson & Chapple, *Breakpoint*, 53.

RIVER JOURNEY — DAY 1
camped in Plaquemine Island in front of DOW Plant
canoed 22 miles
restless and intense pumping sounds at night
from the refinery
- the sleepless factory —
listening to the refinery flame subbass

Houma Nation descendant and artist Monique Verdin paddled with me in the canoe. She is known for her long-standing community activism in the lower Mississippi. Her photography and documentary filmmaking practices expose the impacts of toxicity and the controversial entanglements of petrochemical investments in the region. On our journey, Verdin mentioned that she had never seen the petrochemical corridor from the river's perspective, even though she had worked in the area for decades. She was born to a family of shrimpers out in Bayou St. Bernard. She had a close relationship with her grandmother, from whom she inherited her weaving skills and connection to land cultivation rhythms and medicinal plants. In the Bayou, water flows up and down to the rhythm of not only climatic but also industrial pulls, just as the income of the community is decreasingly tied to the seasonality of the land and the nourishments of the Delta's water, and is instead generated by the wages of the petrochemical industry. A process of dispossession and redistribution of labour that will be difficult to reverse.

These factory complexes have worked their way around the alchemical fantasies of molecular shapeshifting to provide many derivatives from oil refining. Some of them have emerged because of the intensive demands of local agriculture, which are highly dependent upon fertilisers and pesticides. As such, the water has become filled with nitrogen and phosphate which destroy marshland roots, thus allowing storms to rush through them more easily. Moreover, the increased salinity of the marshes due to incoming Gulf waters has allowed coastal erosion to seep in, weakening the land and contributing to further alteration of the water chemistry. The combined effects of these changes have profoundly affected the water's oxygen levels, creating so-called dead zones in the lower Mississippi and the Gulf. As a consequence, it also impacts its biodiversity, thus profoundly affecting the Bayou communities who have always subsisted through securing food sovereignty, as Verdin told me.[15]

Verdin was deeply affected by the aftermath of Hurricane Katrina due to a lack of psychological, economic, and political support from the state, which had been incapable of providing an emergency response.[16] She was brought up to the sonic plurality of musical genres that envelop New Orleans, from jazz to Cajun blues and swamp pop; but it is the industrial soundscape that sets the backdrop to her locality. Refinery hums echo through the skies,

15 A dead zone emerges because of excessive organic matter and debris accumulation in the river bottom, which makes it impossible for large amounts of carbon to be processed and converted to oxygen. Jackson & Chapple, *Breakpoint,* 65.

16 Today the aftermath of slavery is entrenched in numerous forms of exclusionary politics in the hygienised post-Katrina New Orleans, where many institutions have been shut down, schools have been fully privatised and Black population reduced to 59 per cent.

alongside engines pumping, the sounds of river dredging, and boat traffic. The reverberations of the petrochemical infrastructure expanded through the riverbanks, amplified by the river's mirrored surface, travelling through the depths of its waters at greater speed. This background noise, a constant 24/7 hum, is further punctured by the interceptions of traffic and loud engine sounds. Yet, during my conversations with Verdin she mentioned that the continuous noise had never worried people, as cancer and coastal erosion are the most important battles for riverine communities at this time.

I found it alarming that the rise in background noise and changes in the soundscape of the river were not considered symptoms of the ongoing modes of dispossession experienced in the region. I wondered, then, how different forms of attunement to the rhythmic registers of geotrauma were necessary in order to find connections between the sonic environment and the rhythmic expressions that this very environment has on the bodies that inhabit it.[17] What patterns can be noticed, made obvious, or lie implicit in ecosystems under such intense industrial transformation? Could one develop forms of attunement and restorative listening on soundscapes under constant distress?

RIVER JOURNEY — DAY 2
canoed 15 miles
Syntech + DOW plants, Syngenta
camp Bayou Gullah island mile 173
recorded radio underwater
nonstop pumping sounds
many boats crossing
difficult to face the stream and paddle
against the current
make it a method: listen longer
1962 BP Oil spill, river on fire
the naturalisation of industry

During our journey through the petrochemical corridor, Verdin and our group had continuous conversations about the Mississippi's changing ecosystems, in which the presence of industry is largely naturalised. We camped along the riverbanks, on small beaches, on deserted islands, or outside levee systems where sediments accumulate. These fluctuating intertidal spaces were not seen as private property but as mutable territories, where sand and mud regurgitated by the river form embankments and deposits to be later sold by property developers as valuable resources downstream. The cyclicality of climate change and coastal erosion in the area contributes to massive, unexpected flooding, increasing land loss while at the same time opening 'new business opportunities'. There is a fine line separating government strategy for hydrological planning and catastrophe profit. The same

17 Robin MacKay, on The Cybernetic Culture Research Unit (CCRU) theory of geotrauma: "Geotrauma, or Plutonics, flattens the theory of psychic trauma onto geophysics, with psychic experience becoming an encrypted geological report, the repercussion of a primal Hadean trauma in the material unconscious of Planet Earth." Robin MacKay, "A Brief History of Geotrauma: The invention of Negarestani", Leper Creativity: Cyclonopedia Symposium, 2011, available online at http://readthis.wtf/writing/a-brief-history-of-geotrauma/.

sediments that are being drawn away by the river when it floods peoples' homes, rushing through their foundations, are being sold back to them. As we travelled on our wooden canoes packed with tents and DIY assemblages of technology, we also had a small taste of what it is to become molecular, a small particle in the river system, dominated by long barges, towboats, and tankers circulating night and day to transfer refined goods and other resources from surrounding industrial facilities.

RIVER JOURNEY — DAY 3
water ritual at 9 am
many chemical plants
radioactive waste at sight
hard winds
23,5 miles paddle
recorded a barge loading supplies
and boat enginescamped on a sand bank

The underwater field recordings captured mostly engine sounds and the passing registers of river vessels. The sound of propellers and machinery underwater, and the cyclical patterns produced as they undertook boat diversion manoeuvres, were clearly discernible. The underwater presence of fish or other local crustaceans was rendered imperceptible by the omnipresence of the vessels. The whirring of the engines was only interrupted by the occasional presence of dredging or other pumping devices in the water. Other infrastructural hums surrounded the river, such as that of the refinery complexes and factories' resource supply machinery, connecting warehouses to the river peers. At other times, we were visited by the intense buzz of light aircrafts, spraying pesticides over the crops in their spiralling flight, leaving vibrational traces amplified by the river. Above water, we could also hear the vague presence of birds and other insects, such as cicadas or nocturnal crickets, among the scarce presence of boat horns. These punctured the soundscape, just as the occasional phantom of a refinery's flare resonating from a distance. Sounds propagate from the river, way beyond the horizon, as its waters are maintained and circulate across the infrastructures that sustain it.

In the vicinity of the Delta, an increased number of chemical plants fill the air with dust clouds. "The Rivergator", an online mile-to-mile guide of the river, warns us that there is radioactive material stored in the open air.[18] The river's water flows continuously, and anything that might be produced in these plants will eventually be incorporated into the Mississippi's ecosystem, due both to the river water being used to cool factory tank facilities, and pipe leakages or minor spills that occur when oil and other chemicals are being shipped.

18 "Rivergator is a mile-by-mile paddler's guide written for canoeists, kayakers, stand-up-paddle-boarders, and anyone else plying the waters of the Lower Mississippi River in human-powered craft." "The Rivergator", Rivergator, accessed 4 December 2024, https://www.rivergator.org/.

RIVER JOURNEY — DAY 4
two long recordings of boats while canoeing
boats crossing, two barges, one tanker, one small
(rusty sounds of shifting tracks)
train tracks by sandbank
long recording of water
camp Charlie mile 149
Arriving at Charlie River Angel for the night — listen to the story of the Poché family, who works in the sugar industry and is decimated by cancer. Still, they feel optimistic about the water quality here. Lost my fingerprints, phone ID doesn't work, the waters must be really chemical. Monique says we should be wearing chemical hazard protection suits however the headwater students still walk barefoot in it.
The slow violence of toxicity is indeed invisible (two weeks later and my fingerprints have not fully recovered yet). Dream of the frog song as a way to interpret the environment.

During the upriver journey, educator and activist Brian Holmes described the river not as a linear continuum, stretching from source to sea, but, instead, as a fluctuating aquatic/terrestrial transition zone: a moving littoral that offers up an image of a dynamic process that does not disrupt, but rather, defines the river.[19] In a similar way, architect Dilip da Cunha also revises our concept of a river, asking how we frame it territorially and infrastructurally, and questioning the extent of its course. "What would it mean for designers to take responsibility for the existence of the river?"[20] says Da Cunha, as he questions the naturalisation of infrastructure and the role of design and spatial practices in reinscribing forms of partition in natural systems. He calls for a new kind of river literacy and urges us to rethink the role and mutations of the coastline, the riverbank, and the water's edge at a time when sea-level rise and resource management necessitate the construction of levees and land retirement schemes. He states that "there's no such thing as dryness, there is only wetness in various degrees".[21] This provocation challenges us to reflect on how we can anchor our imagination of the water cycle at other phases of this elemental journey, and on what the reimagination of the river as a human-made infrastructure might enable. But what if this moving littoral and all its processes were to be reconceptualised as travelling within and outside bodies and communities? How would this redefine the continuity between bodies and the environment, and our notion of corporeality and territory? What other kinds of environmental literacy would be needed to reinterpret these ecosystems?

19 Brian Holmes, "Check my Pulse: The Anthropocene River in Reverse", Anthropocene Curriculum: Anthropocene River Journey, 28 August 2020, https://www.anthropocene-curriculum.org/contribution/check-my-pulse.

20 Land retirement is a practice where landowners are paid to take agricultural lands out of production due to poor drainage and soils containing high levels of salt and selenium. Dilip Da Cunha, "The Invention of Rivers", lecture at Harvard GSD, 20 February 2019, https://www.youtube.com/watch?v=39qJ3DKnPkg.

21 Da Cunha, "The Invention of Rivers".

The impermanence of the river and the intensity of the hydro cycle subject the city of New Orleans and its surroundings to the need for a "pacemaker", says architect Aron Chang.[22] He explains that seventy-eight drainage pumping stations work 24/7 to prevent soil from subsiding. Some of these stations are quite loud, and are distributed all across the city and its outskirts. The Army Corps' Mississippi River & Tributaries Project (ACMR&TP) of emergency floodways was designed to grant territorial diversions that temporarily relieve the pressure of rapidly rising river stages.[23] Together with massive levee systems, floodgates, locks, diversions, and spillways, these infrastructures have controlled the movement and presence of water in the area since its first settlements. They inscribe a rhythm to water flow as well as to atmospheric noise, allowing for the circulation of ships and people as they control the riverine flux. The seasonal pulse of water is now replaced by its industrial version.

Addressing the politics of containment and flow, Holmes criticises this permanent techno-fixing and the impacts of the Army Corps' Mississippi River & Tributaries Project. The project's planning, design, and implementation strategies map onto existing zoning practices, which necessarily include some and exclude others. They make territorial decisions without community input or informed public debate to ground and justify such activities. Holmes also criticises the ACMR&TP for creating conflicts in communities while promoting the continued ideology of human mastery over nature. He argues that the river diversion and containment project is in sync with the extractive rhythm of intensive agriculture and oil industry that has defined the ecology of the floodplains to the point of favouring corn, soybeans, cotton, and rice over any other life form. The result, complete with copious amounts of diesel fuel and synthetic nitrogen, is one of the major components of global climate change: a completely industrialised agricultural system, based on fossil fuel inputs oriented toward foreign markets, and exported to the rest of the world as a development model.[24] The seasonal pulse of riverine flooding, which plays a vital role in planetary metabolism, is today determined by the fossil fuel industry and agriculture lobbies, who, through the purchase of "flowage rights" since the 1930s, determine what can get flooded and what may be conceived as more, or less, valuable.[25]

22 Aron Chang, interview by Margarida Mendes, November 2019, audio.

23 Authorized after the 1928 Flood Control Act, the Mississippi River and Tributaries project "was deemed necessary to put into place a comprehensive, unified system of public works within the lower Mississippi Valley that would provide unprecedented flood risk management". See: www.mvd.usace.army.mil.

24 A leading figure addressing the politics of aquatic infrastructures is preeminent activist Vandana Shiva, whose voice has been a powerful force in the struggles for justice experienced by agrarian communities. Her vision of the hydrocommons and the list of "Principles of Water Democracy" are aligned with her critique of the monocultural regime as a legacy of the colonial regime.

25 The flowage rights contracts and the Army Corps' Mississippi River & Tributaries Project stem from the inheritance of a rationale of environmental partition resulting from speciesist hierarchisations, zoning practices, and discriminatory ecopolitics. This selective procedure allows flowage rights contractors to assign a value system to nature, much before the financial concept of natural capital emerged. "Natural Capital can be defined as the world's stocks of natural assets, which include geology, soil, air, water and all living things. From this Natural Capital, humans derive a wide range of services, often called ecosystem services, which make human life possible." https://www.cbd.int/business/projects/natcap.shtml.

How does the rhythmic legacy of these industrial infrastructures infuse different entities with life force? River diversion projects and flowage rights contracts have privileged the extractive rhythm of intensive agriculture, the oil industry, and the survival of certain communities, intervening as a sovereign body that can "make live and let die".[26] To Holmes, "the seasonal pulse of riverine flooding plays a vital role in planetary metabolism", indebted to a plurality of rhythms, both industrial and natural.[27] However, the state-supported contracting schemes for floodplain management always seem to favour the fruits of industry over any other lifeform. In several moments, the levee system was even breached by bombing in order to redirect flooding, such as in the case of the 1927 torrential floods where the levee system was dynamited to salvage nearby sugar plantations and no compensation was granted to local inhabitants. This event left an impressive sonic mark on some of the riverine inhabitants, who, when they hear a loud sound, often fear that a levee has been breached. This story was told to me by a local inhabitant, who shared this vulnerable feeling prior to the militarisation of the hydrological system—one that, despite being built to protect populations, favoured some instead of others, and natural resources over people. During the many conversations that we had during the journey, we understood that this was often a question of environmental racism, as some populations seem to be deliberately left more unprotected and have less access to decision-making processes than others. The river serves all in different manners, and hides under its course stratified layers of bodies that have succumbed to grant its course.

With Holmes' insights in mind, I returned to the questions I had upon my arrival. What are the effects of the reverberations and infrastructural rhythms that industrialisation imposes on the river? How can the cyclicality of these patterns be shown to reinscribe zoning practices and different evolutionary pathways? Sensing the sonic patterns of industrialisation, I revisited my thoughts about the capacity of matter to mutate, analysing the river system as a complex metabolic system where multiple processes occur simultaneously across bodies and physical dimensions. A site where the hydro cycle has an acoustic expression, as everything that lives and goes through the riverine flux leaves a pattern.

RIVER JOURNEY — DAY 5
camped on mile 131, on an island with willows
and beavers
many refineries, nuclear power plant in sight
recorded a 1.5 hour long take under and over the water
recorded the nearby stream and the puddle at lunchtime
(I am still looking for animals underwater
I don't hear any, just a few fish jump in sight)

26 Michel Foucault, *Society must be defended — lectures at the Collège de France 1975-76*, (Picador, 2003), 239.

27 Holmes, "Check my Pulse".

As we camped amid the swampy landscapes and the wetland's changing climate, the perimeter between the interior and exterior of our bodies and tents became very thin, as if we were made out of a fragile membrane continuously exposed to surrounding atmospheric fluctuations. We weathered through the journey, while humidity and noise pierced our bodies. Our epidermal ears extended from the canoe, through the river waters, up along the shores of the riverbank, where sleepless factories pumped incessantly with a roaring drive. The pores and extremities of our nervous systems became interwoven with the cyclical humming of boat engines and the dragged sounds of the queues of barges passing by, only occasionally interrupted by the sound of cicadas and other visiting insects.

If we sense the environment, how does the environment sense us? And how does the variety of life forms in this stretch of the river listen and adapt to the extensive human presence in the region? Certainly, other-than-human entities would have a lot to say about this, as the intersubjective aural space is exceptionally diverse. Different species occupy different parts of the frequency spectrum, depending on their hearing mechanisms, some of which evolved very differently. Alligators, snakes, arachnids, locusts, as well many other insects populate Louisiana. Insects, in particular, have had seventeen independent evolutions of their hearing systems and have very different hearing organs.[28] Locusts hear through a sensing organ on their belly, which changes the thickness of its membrane's constitution according to different diffractions of sound waves. Moths have neurons in their ears, which alter the mechanical structure of the sound collection. Crickets, in turn, attune to specific sounds by moving their tympanums and tuning into particular frequencies. Spiders have developed lyriform hearing organs along their leg joints, with cracks that deform and are extremely sensitive to vibration, using these to catch prey. In all of these species, the hearing process is an open-loop process that connects the sensorial body with the brain and the environment.

Even willow trees and other vegetation surrounding the river would also listen back at us, as their leafy hairs register minute changes and vibrations in the atmosphere, responding chemically to threats.[29] The intersubjective listening moment, an aurally diverse space *par excellence*, is also an environmental space, where life forms and their surroundings respond mutually in a reciprocal process. Sensing is, therefore, an important step towards environing oneself and, crucially, a trigger for evolution. Different species develop behavioural and physical responses to different sonic and vibrational challenges.

Soundscape ecologist Bernie Krause's acoustic niche hypothesis speaks of animal adaptation to anthropogenic noise.[30] He predicts that in a mature ecosystem, species avoid competition by singing at unique bandwidths or pitches and at different times. Therefore, no two species should sing simultaneously at the same frequency. The hypothesis, moreover, sug-

28 For more on insect audition please refer to the work of Natasha Mhatre.

29 For more on plant audition refer to the work of Heidi Apple with Rex Cocroft.

30 Bernie Krause, "The Niche Hypothesis: A virtual symphony of animal sounds, the origins of musical expression and the health of habitats" in *Soundscape Newsletter (World Forum for Acoustic Ecology)*, 1993.

gests that more mature ecosystems will exhibit pronounced partitioning of the sound spectrum. In contrast, young or disturbed ecosystems will exhibit greater acoustic disorganisation, with multiple species interfering in the same bandwidths. The degree of acoustic partitioning in a given soundscape is directly related to the habitat quality and biodiversity of that ecosystem.

This bioacoustic theory focuses on simultaneous spectrum occupation by different species that lay territorial claims to several audio thresholds. Acoustic biologist Mark Bee, who works upriver in the Mississippi, studies similar phenomena and investigates what we can learn from the environment and ourselves by studying frog songs.[31] Bee's lab analyses frog responses to mating calls in spaces of high background noise density. His study has concluded that female frogs are less likely to find a mating partner and reproduce in noisy environments; noise constrains the spatial scale and extent of a female's ability to assess and compare different mates in a chorus. Frogs, like humans, explore similar auditory solutions, exploiting spatial separation as well as pitch differences to reach their listeners. Hence, reading a frog's response to an acoustic landscape could provide evidence about an environment and about the challenges that species face in adapting and reproducing. Much remains unknown about many other species' hearing mechanisms, despite the fact that anthropocentric noise is a pressing reality and that it occupies significant space in the frequency spectrum. Much remains unclear as to what marks the sonic imprints of present industrial interventions leave on sensorial systems in the long run.

RIVER JOURNEY — DAY 6
visit to the Bonny Carrey water spill
camping by the airport in Kenner
massage circle
mile 113, the sound of boats arriving to the city
the jets are very intense
we barely slept

Closer to the city, on one of our most sleepless nights, we camped under the sub-bass of the Louis Armstrong airport lane, whose intense aircraft traffic pounded through our bodily fascia, catalysing the strangest dreams. Awoken successively by the punctured noise of arriving planes, boat engines and horns, the group had very little rest. We were set for an early wake-up call and sunrise paddle to avoid a storm in the evening, which would have blocked our way into New Orleans. As we got stuck in the morning fog, we had time to reflect on the insomniac evening and the eerie place we had stopped. We asked ourselves how these intense bass noises reverberate through the riverine ecosystem and affect local species, without really understanding the connection between sonic emissions and environmental changes. Was the riverine spectrum also weaving through the spectral atmospheres of our dreams, building imaginary refractions in our sensorial

31 Mark Bee, "Frogs, Acoustics, and The Future of Hearing: Mark Bee at TEDxUMN", TEDx Talk, 19 October 2012, 18 min., 22 sec., https://www.youtube.com/watch?v=mvCkrrfpPhc.

systems as we rested? Where does the exercise of listening start and end, and what political, affective, and physical imaginations does it produce?

The previous night, I had gathered the group around the fire to listen to my recordings, hoping for some discussion. I played an hour-long hydrophone recording that I collected when paddling, comprising boat navigation sounds audible underwater. I was curious to hear their reactions, which were quite diverse. Some focused on describing the characteristics and quality of sound as resembling either mechanical or organic sources, soft versus machinic. Others referred to the inescapable condition of animals underwater, who become powerless when submersed in an auditory pool. One of the listeners sitting by the fire said that the monotonous constancy and duration of the engine sounds resemble the soundtrack of science fiction films. Another person enquired if we could also hear fish jump to escape predators amid the persistent pumping sounds. Lastly, someone said that the constancy of noise was making her PTSD alerts rise, destabilising her sensory system and raising her anxiety. This exercise of collective listening began to capture how different people register different sonic sensibilities, reiterating the aural diversity of humans and all living entities who hear, sense, and respond somatically in varied ways to the same auditory stimulus.[32] It also opened up a space for storytelling bridged by intersubjective perceptions and personal confidences, which merged our riverine experience together with past encounters with the noise caused by hydric infrastructures and industries along the river. How does the situatedness of experience travel through time?

RIVER JOURNEY — DAY 7
mile 113-94 NOLA!
We woke up at 5 am to arrive before the storm
there is a lot of fog, we only left at 9 am
I didn't record today because we wanted
to paddle faster
We passed several bridges
in the area near the warehouses of the port of NOLA
many cranes, some freighters
soft paddle with increased speed
we sang by the river before leaving and made an offer
we were welcomed by torrential rain on arrival

32 John Drever, "'Primacy of the Ear' – But Whose Ear? The case for auraldiversity in sonic arts practice and discourse", *Organised Sound* 24, no. 1 (2019): 85-95.

WORKS CITED

Albrecht, Glenn. "Solastalgia: a new concept in human health and identity". *PAN: philosophy activism nature* 3 (2005): 44-59.

Bee, Mark. "Frogs, Acoustics, and The Future of Hearing: Mark Bee at TEDxUMN". TEDx Talk, 19 October 2012. Video, 00:18:22. https://www.youtube.com/watch?v=mvCkrrfpPhc.

Da Cunha, Dilip. "The Invention of Rivers", lecture at Harvard GSD, 20 February 2019. https://www.youtube.com/watch?v=39qJ3DKnPkg.

Drever, John. "'Primacy of the Ear' – But Whose Ear? The case for auraldiversity in sonic arts practice and discourse". *Organised Sound* 24, no. 1 (2019): 85-95.

Foucault, Michel. *Society must be defended — lectures at the Collège de France 1975-76.* Picador, 2003.

Holmes, Brian. "Check my Pulse: The Anthropocene River in Reverse". *Anthropocene Curriculum: Anthropocene River Journey*, 28 August 2020. https://www.anthropocene-curriculum.org/contribution/check-my-pulse.

Jackson, Jeremy B.C. & Steve Chapple. *Breakpoint: Reckoning with America's Environmental Crises.* Yale University Press, 2018.

Krause, Bernie. "The Niche Hypothesis: A virtual symphony of animal sounds, the origins of musical expression and the health of habitats". In *Soundscape Newsletter (World Forum for Acoustic Ecology)*, 1993.

McKittrick, Katherine. "Plantation Futures". *Small Axe* 17, no. 3 (November 2013): 1–15.

Rivergator. "The Rivergator". Accessed 4 December 2024. https://www.rivergator.org/.

SEED MARGINS

Cooking Sections
and Enrico Milazzo

There is a lot of talk about agrobiodiversity [...] *we are not allowed to use seeds from other farmers, it goes against the interests of the industry. Cultural institutions should choose whether they want to talk about these topics or work with us. Institutions and municipalities do not work with us because we work against the industry.*

Germana Fratello (Campi Aperti)

In spring 2024, as fields dried up prematurely, many mid-scale Sicilian farmers decided not to plant food. EU subsidies for leaving land uncultivated, combined with water cuts, made it clear that even heavy agrochemicals on exhausted soils and standardised seeds would not meet financial and climate demands amidst yet another wave of extreme weather. However, other marginal fields remained green, where rare seed varieties—free from industrial patents and commercial ownership—could resist heat and water stress.

Cultivated over generations on the margins of other large-scale farms and agrarian plots, peasant seeds (*semi contadini*) are well-weathered to defy market and legal boundaries determining agrochemical dependencies, adaptation, and propagation. For most of agricultural history, they have been freely (re)produced and exchanged by farmers, a built-in barrier to capital accumulation.[1] As harsh terrain and climate change drive unlikely selections, these lesser-known plants do not adhere to yield, uniformity, or aesthetic standards. They communicate with their wild neighbours, working in symbiosis regardless of yield, which makes them not necessarily reproduce to be 'productive'. Despite being unregistered and increasingly outlawed, peasant seeds play key ecological roles but often reach the market named and disguised under registered varieties.

Building on a multi-year process of field tests and exchanges among small-scale growers, lawyers, activists, and agronomists, our collaborative project *Monoculture Meltdown* exposes how market dependencies have made seeds *uncommon* in southern Italy—not only due to low supply and demand but also because the agroindustry has stripped the commons of the power to resist drought. Patents on 'climate-resilient' crops, largely owned by seed corporations, reinforce a neo-liberal narrative of increasing food production through biotechnologies.[2] These industrialised seeds are deemed 'productive'

1 Jack R. Kloppenburg, *First the Seed* (University of Wisconsin Press, 2005), 8.
2 Anne Saab, "International Law and Feeding the World in Times of Climate Change", *Transnational Legal Theory* 9, no. 3–4 (2018): 288–301.

regardless of the fact that they require high inputs to survive—water, pesticides, fertilisers, cheap labour. Yet, their efficiency falters when externalities are factored in, as seed saver Angelo Giordano notes, likening it to "spending ten to get twelve, versus investing one to get nine".[3]

Italy, known for its unique agrobiodiversity, has intensified monocropping across various plains—from tomatoes and wheat in the Tavoliere delle Puglie and Sicilia, to hazelnuts in Lazio, corn in Pianura Padana, and prosecco vineyards in Veneto. This practice has contributed to making the land and its food production increasingly prone to collapse.[4] Saltwater intrusion into depleted underground aquifers is suffocating crops, and the *Xylella fastidiosa* epidemic has killed more than twenty million olive trees. These are but just two examples of the extended impacts of monocropping. By reconnecting culture and agriculture with the non-conformist seed heritage of Sicilia and Puglia, *Monoculture Meltdown* advances new legal paradigms to cultivate the rights *of* and *to* peasant seeds. It seeks ways for unregistered crops to freely cross-pollinate, ultimately freeing soil care practices from the pressures of heat, water, and market stress.

UNCOMMON SEEDS

In southern Italy, where agriculture is both a cornerstone practice and an extractive industry, drought is literally written into the names of villages. Many are recognisable because of their namesake to local vegetables selected over centuries to withstand climate hardship. *Siccagno* (drought) varieties on the verge of extinction range from the *pomodoro di Aradeo* and *pomodoro pizzutello di Paceco* to the *cece rosso delle Murge* and the *zucca pignatara di Porto Empedocle*. The extensive list, connecting specific tomatoes, chickpeas, or pumpkins to their places of origin, turns the names of villages—and generations of inhabitants—into bearers of drought resistance. For decades, the agroindustry dismissed many of these drought-resistant varieties—branding them as poor seeds for poor people in poor soils. And yet, residents from vil-

Propagation fields under drought conditions without irrigation. Sicily, spring 2023. Source: Image by Enrico Milazzo.

3 Angelo Giordano, public talk at "I Diritti dei Semi", working session at the Rural Parliament hosted by CLIMAVORE x Jameel at RCA at Notte Verde, Castiglione d'Otranto, Italy, 30 August 2024.

4 Marco Armiero, Roberta Biasillo & Wilko Graf von Hardenberg, *Mussolini's Nature. An Environmental History of Italian Fascism* (MIT Press, 2022), introduction.

Drought-resistant *gaghiubbo* melon propagated in Puglia, spring 2023. Source: Image courtesy of Serit Seeds.

Evolutionary population of fava beans. Source: Image by Enrico Milazzo.

Drought-resistant black chickpea (cece rugoso neo della Murgia) propagated in Puglia, spring 2023. Source: Image courtesy of Serit Seeds.

lages in Sicilia and Puglia, the regions with highest aridity, manage to grow them and source food on the margins, preserving a climate heritage that the market ignored. But how can one recognise and revalorise a product when not able to use its name or genetic distinctiveness?

Since 2023, *Monoculture Meltdown* has collaborated with Angelo Giordano and other seed savers like Antonio Capriglia and Eva Polare, alongside a network of twenty farmers and cooperatives, to trace localised, drought-resistant varieties now under threat of extinction. Uncommon vegetables and legumes have been identified and sourced from inconspicuous places. These included a wide range of rare aubergines, beans, capers, chick-peas, lentils, melons, pumpkins, and tomatoes—each with its own name, relatives and characteristics, often differing only slightly in shape, colour, texture, or taste. The hamlet of Miranti in Petralia Soprana, where its eight inhabitants are all named Miranti, provided *corsia*—a semi-wild brassica prolific even in harsh conditions. A car garage in Agira was the source of a retired farmer's red broccoli—a variety that probably mutated its colour by exposure to colder mountain climate. The distinct red chickpea of Cianciana and the red chickpea of Porto Empedocle were sourced from two Sicilian villages only 50 km apart, which seed savers can trace as descendants of the smooth black chickpea of the Di Gesu family in Villalba. The reason some of these highly localised varieties have been forgotten, despite the desire to reproduce them, is not just the scarcity of supply or demand, but the legal obstacles to selling these products through community-supported agriculture (CSA) or community-*supporting* agriculture models.[5] In response, the project also develops cultural tactics to overcome these legal and economic obstacles, particularly around the rights to use peasant seeds, thus reimagining CSA as *culturally*-supported agriculture.[6]

Resisting while growing or being preserved for months to extend their shelf life, these 'drought vegetables' respond to specific microclimates and contribute to agrobiodiversity.[7] They are a collective effort, capable of nourishing multiple species through exchange and adaptation. After harvest, specimens that endured heat waves, pests, or disease are selected. These are understood as engaging in *coevolutionary mutualism*—multiple species learning from each other on how to thrive together in harsh conditions.[8] While evolutionary biology frames learning as genetic plasticity in response to environing conditions, intergenerational transfer of information also happens by other means.[9] Theorist Nicole Seymour, in her critique of heteronormative pro-capitalist futurity, explores how future-thinking can nonetheless function as queer ecological values, particularly when it comes to combating corporate greed and social/environmental injustice.[10] Similarly, preserving food heritage and agrobiodiversity relies on the promiscuity of wild and domesticated plants and seeds—an approach that is incompatible with agribusiness's pursuit to sell standardised seeds selected from the same 'perfect parents' and genetically coded to perform uniformly.[11]

In this sense, promiscuous pollination enables plants to interact and evolve with one another via sexual or appetite arousal, forming horizontal

5 In a CSA, a contractual agreement is established between a farm and a group of consumers, who commit to purchasing the farm's entire annual produce at the start of the season. This arrangement reduces the farmer's commercial risks by providing a guaranteed market, allowing them to plan production regardless of unexpected weather and yield fluctuations.

6 Luigi Coppola, speech at CLIMAVORE Assembly, Rome, 27 October 2023.

7 Daniel Fernández Pascual & Alon Schwabe, "What is Above is What is Below", *E-flux Architecture*, 24 May 2019.

8 Henry F. Howe & Judith Smallwood, "Ecology of Seed Dispersal", *Annual Review of Ecology and Systematics* 13, no. 1 (1982): 201-228. John N. Thompson, *The Coevolutionary Process* (University of Chicago Press, 1994), 167.

9 Tim Ingold, "Evolution without Inheritance: Steps to an Ecology of Learning", *Current Anthropology* 63, no. 25 (2022).

10 Nicole Seymour, Strange Natures: Futurity, Empathy, and the Queer Ecological Imagination (University of Illinois Press, 2013), 183.

11 Ferdinando Branca, Sergio Argento & Alessandro Tribulato, "Assessing Genetic Reserves in Sicily (Italy): The *Brassica* Wild Relatives Case Study", in *Agrobiodiversity Conservation: Securing the Diversity of Crop Wild Relatives and Landraces*, ed. Nigel Maxted et al. (CAB, 2012), 52–58.

kinships. They shift Darwinian evolution to *involution*—momentary improvisations of multispecies practitioners caught together in affectively charged ecologies that do not always promote the 'survival of the best'.[12] *Monoculture Meltdown* promotes the idea of promiscuous genealogies—forms of exchange that allow plants to freely express their differences. Intimate relations and curiosity between growers, climate, and peasant seeds have created rich and fluid ecosystems, spreading qualities regarded as 'nonsensical' from a human/industrial perspective. Together, they surpassed intensive cultivation methods, which were otherwise ill-suited to the rugged landscape.

The friction of the terrain-made non-standardised seeds and non-conformist ways of living under intensive tax-collection regimes flourishes. Such specimens are not just more-than-human in non-state space, but more-than-market species, defying corporate profit.[13] A prime example of low-yield adaptation to avoid parasites or disease is the black fava bean from Lampedusa, which resists the local climate better than industrialised northern Italian varieties, by shrinking its stem enough to prevent a local beetle from nesting inside. Local varieties of drought-adapted Mediterranean plants, such as Lampedusa's black fava, are not only more resilient to their specific terrain, but also boost the growth of beneficial microorganism communities that enhance plant stress tolerance. Besides, this eventually translates into highly nutritional or medicinal compounds for the human diet.[14]

Agroecology is not just a method of cultivation; it is a social practice that requires an understanding of affect and relations, while often needing to navigate a complex balance between volunteer work and self-exploitation. Thus, transitioning to agroecological or syntropic growing is not an easy task, as it relies not just on seeds as isolated objects but also on labour. Workers skilled in non-conventional farming must unlearn and relearn years of land practices, effectively decolonising the field and the mind at the same time. Among the participating farms, many want to be recognised not only as food producers or heritage keepers but, more importantly, as environmental custodians. To become a common good, seeds need a community behind them that evolves with unseasonable (unexpected, unreliable, extreme) weather: no peasant or indigenous seed exists without a community that conserves, uses, nurtures and further develops it within its growing cycles, culture and ecosystem. Within the holistic human rights approach/framework, the right to seeds has been recognised as central to the collective, closely intertwined with the right to food and nutrition, the right to health, the right to work, and the right to culture and self-determination.[15] In constant transformation, vegetables grown through *aridoculture* (the

12 Carla Hustak & Natasha Myers, "Involutionary Momentum: Affective Ecologies and the Sciences of Plant/Insect Encounters", *Differences* 23, no. 3 (2012): 75.

13 Kristin Asdal & Tone Huse, *Nature-Made Economy: Cod, Capital, and the Great Economization of the Ocean* (MIT Press, 2023), 14.

14 Silvia La Scala, Flores Naselli, Paola Quatrini, Giuseppe Gallo & Fabio Caradonna, "Drought-Adapted Mediterranean Diet Plants: A Source of Bioactive Molecules Able to Give Nutrigenomic Effects per sè or to Obtain Functional Foods", *International Journal of Molecular Sciences* 25, no. 4 (2024): 2235.

15 Philip Seufert, Mariapaola Boselli & Stefano Mori, "Recovering the Cycle of Wisdom: Beacons of Light Toward the Right to Seeds", Working Group on Agricultural Biodiversity of the International Planning Committee for Food Sovereignty (IPC), FIAN International and Centro Internazionale Crocevia. April 2021.

Unregistered peasant seeds, freely exchanged and reproduced for generations, are increasingly outlawed and displaced by industrialised hybrids and patents. The celebration of tomato sauce-making is not just a culinary tradition but an act of resistance—ensuring that drought-resistant varieties, cultivated on the margins, continue to circulate beyond corporate seed enclosures. In the image is the harvest of tomato seeds after the first round of planting, as part of the collective celebration *Senza Passata Non C'è Futuro*, Puglia, August 2024. Source: Image by Eleonora Carrozza (courtesy of CLIMAVORE x Jameel at RCA).

practice and culture of dry farming) continue to evolve, demanding care and attention rather than remaining stagnant. Yet peasant seeds face another challenge beyond climate: intellectual property rights (IPR).

DOMINANT CLAIMS

In 1980, a landmark US lawsuit dictated that forms of nonhuman life could be owned. In *Diamond v. Chakrabarty*, a new bacterium, *Pseudomonas putida*, capable of breaking down crude oil to clean up corporate spills, became the sole property of General Electric genetic engineer Ananda Mohan Chakrabarty.[16] While *his* bacterium was aimed at addressing petrochemical pollution (without tackling its root causes), this lawsuit had a profound impact on the financialisation of global agriculture. Previous regulatory frameworks allowed plant breeders to own specific asexually reproduced plant varieties and their seeds, as with Henry A. Wallace's registration of Pioneer Hi-Bred corn 50 years earlier, which led to the Plant Patent Act of 1930. This IPR legal framework expanded in the US with the Plant Variety Protection Act of 1970, which included sexually reproduced plants and paved the way for seed patenting. Chakrabarty's legal victory opened a market of commodifiable plants, turning seeds from the commons into new exploitable subjects—the next currency.

In Europe, agreements on plant patenting led to the creation of the 1961 Union for the Protection of New Varieties of Plants (UPOV) Convention in Paris. Its final form, adopted in 1991, provided monopoly rights to breeders and nothing in return to small-scale farmers, while imposing new agrochemical dependencies.[17] This landscape worsened with the Agreement on Trade-Related Aspects of Intellectual Property Rights (TRIPS), adopted by the World Trade Organization in 1994.[18] Today, just four companies (Bayer, Corteva, Syngenta, BASF) control half of the US $47 billion seed market and, not coincidentally, 75 per cent of the global agrochemicals market.[19] In a post-Brexit landscape, UPOV91 restrictions on seed saving and swapping are back at the forefront of new trade agreements.[20] This increases risks particularly among farmers in the Global South, many of whom rely heavily on these methods to procure seeds.[21]

16 Karine E. Peschard, *Seed Activism: Patent Politics and Litigation in the Global South* (MIT Press, 2022), introduction.

17 "Ten Reasons Not to Join UPOV Global Trade and Biodiversity in Conflict", *GAIA/GRAIN*, 2 May 1998.

18 Keith Oaki, *Seed Wars: Cases and Materials on Intellectual Property and Plant Genetic Resources* (Carolina Academic Press, 2007), introduction.

19 "Who Profits under UPOV?" *GRAIN*, 28 November 2022. See also: Kim van der Borght & Saurav Ghimire, "Seeds and Intellectual Property Rights: Bad Faith and Undue Influence Undermine Food Security and Human Rights", in *Law and Sustainability. Economic and Financial Law & Policy – Shifting Insights & Values*, ed. Koen Byttebier & Kim van der Borght (Springer, 2022).

20 "UPOV 91 and trade agreements: Compromising Farmers' Right to Save and Sell Seeds", *Both Ends*, 11 July 2018.

21 Catherine Early, "Stop Seed Saving Restrictions in UK Trade Deals", *The Ecologist* July 5, 2024. See also: Saurav Ghimire, Nurul Barizah, Intan Soeparna & Kim Van der Borght, "Plant Variety Protection Law and Farmers' Rights to Save, Exchange and Breed Seeds: The Case of Indonesia", *Journal of Intellectual Property Law & Practice* 16, no. 9 (2021): 1013–1025.

Hundreds of biopiracy lawsuits between corporations and indigenous or peasant vegetable varieties have since followed, setting legal precedents. The protagonists of these IPR disputes bring innocent foodstuffs to the courtroom, from tomatoes against Monsanto and broccoli against Syngenta, to the neem tree that resisted being patented as a pesticide or quinoa that sought to remain unpatented and Peruvian.[22] Putting vegetables 'on trial', these cases often see corporations defending the appropriation of Indigenous or peasant knowledge by falsely claiming unique genetic engineering techniques (allowed by the law), despite using conventional breeding methods (which are not). Resistance to IPR is not just about protecting a seed's name but ensuring the free distribution and propagation of seeds so that anyone can freely access them.

Unlike commercial varieties, peasant seeds are more attuned to sensing drought.[23] They forecast atmospheric changes, deciding when to block or trigger germination. If the weather is too hot, they can simply remain dormant. A protein in their cellular membrane acts as a sensor—the site where water potential, light, and temperature are evaluated—which triggers a chemical change to determine the seed's response to its environment. In this process, seeds not only receive data from what's above and ahead, but also sense one another underground. They are literally 'turned on' by their neighbours, aroused by the possibility of germinating as a collective—especially in drought or desert conditions.[24] Like forests, rocks, glaciers, or berries, seeds are sentient entities that communicate the present and anticipate the future.[25] They translate human crop failure into survival success for the plant's progeny.

Banu Subramaniam and Madelaine Bartlett have pointed out that many narratives around plant reproductive biology stem from colonial racial and sexual politics, with evolutionary biology often grounded in racialised heterosexual romance.[26] Nonreproductive sexual activities, frequently viewed as ecological decline, are challenged by non-normative relationships in plant ecosystems, subverting dominant paradigms of control and standardisation; hence the move towards queering the understanding of seeds' role in diversity, resistance to monocultures, and the subversion of industrial agriculture norms.[27] It is thus crucial to imagine new possibilities for plant sex, sexualities, and relationalities beyond the binaries of conventional reproduction, resisting displacement, marginalisation and industrial hierarchies that prioritise market value and human life over other forms of life.

22 For more details, cases: European Patent Office, T 0425/96 (Tomato plants/MONSANTO) 20-09-1999; EP1597965t; ECLI:EP:BA:2005:T041601.20050308.

23 Annalisa De Boni, Antonia D'Amico, Claudio Acciani & Rocco Roma, "Crop Diversification and Resilience of Drought-Resistant Species in Semi-Arid Areas: An Economic and Environmental Analysis", *Sustainability* 14, no. 15 (2022): 9552.

24 Katja Tielbörger & Rüdiger Prasse, "Do Seeds Sense Each Other? Testing for Density-Dependent Germination in Desert Perennial Plants", Oikos 118, no. 5 (2009): 792–800.

25 Janelle Marie Baker, "Do Berries Listen? Berries as Indicators, Ancestors, and Agents in Canada's Oil Sands Region", *ETHNOS* 86, no. 2 (2021): 273–294.

26 Banu Subramaniam & Madelaine Bartlett, "Re-imagining Reproduction: The Queer Possibilities of Plants", *Integrative and Comparative Biology* 63, no. 4 (2023): 946–959.

27 Catriona Mortimer-Sandilands & Bruce Erickson, *Queer Ecologies: Sex, Nature, Politics, Desire* (Indiana University Press, 2010), introduction.

Peasant seeds, with their diverse shapes, mismatched colours, bulky or skinny types, demonstrate adaptability, fluidity, and flexibility in sexual expression. Queer forms of reproduction include asexual citrus rootstock grafted with sweeter-fruiting tops, self-reproducing peanuts, and vegetative propagation in giant garlic or *bianca* prickly pear.[28] These foods blur the boundaries of normative parenthood, increasing malleability, and embracing differences among individuals and their body types, while enhancing collective resistance in isolation or marginal terrain, in the absence of 'conventional' mates under environmental stressors.[29] In the case of grains, evolutionary populations rely on the expression of genetic diversity to resist disease by increasing individual differences, which may lower yield but improve quality and foster collective survival.[30]

Amongst the farmers in this project, some favour allowing seeds to evolve naturally, letting them blur distinct characteristics as they adapt to new soils, eventually adopting a new name tied to that place over time. This approach, considered 'radical' among purist conservationists, envisions a future where plants no longer carry fixed names, but embody a dynamic internal biodiversity as the ultimate expression of local adaptation. Others support evolutionary populations but also emphasise the cultural importance of preserving specific varieties with singular names and characteristics, as bearers of local histories, biographies, and genealogies. Market developments like seedless cucumbers or watermelons, designed to accommodate 'lazy' consumer preferences and limit self-propagation, create dependencies on buying seeds from select providers, eventually contributing to financial collapse among farmers fighting to preserve the specificity of vegetable adaptation. Multispecies kinship, as Kim Tallbear and Angela Willey argue, can move beyond traditional, binary thinking about relationships in the natural world, focusing instead on how queer and Indigenous perspectives offer more fluid and inclusive views of ecological interdependence.[31]

CHALLENGING UNREGISTERED PROVENANCE

The Mediterranean, for French historian Ferdinand Braudel, was defined by the geographic range between the northernmost olive trees and the southernmost date palms.[32] Today, these boundaries no longer define its shores, as human migration, influenced by centuries of European colonialism, reacts

28 Vegetative propagation relies on growing from fragments fallen from the 'parent plant' for quicker adaptation.

29 Daniel H. Nussey, Alastair J. Wilson & Jon E. Brommer, "The Evolutionary Ecology of Individual Phenotypic Plasticity in Wild Populations", *Journal Evolutionary Biology* 20, no. 3 (2007): 831–44.

30 Salvatore Ceccarelli, Stefania Grando, Maedeh Salimi & Khadija Razavi, "Evolutionary Populations for Sustainable Food Security and Food Sovereignty", in *Seeds for Diversity and Inclusion,* ed. Yoshiaki Nishikawa & Michel Pimbert (Palgrave Macmillan, 2022), 121–136.

31 Kim Tallbear & Angela Willey, "Critical Relationality: Queer, Indigenous, and Multispecies Belonging Beyond Settler Sex & Nature", *Imaginations* 10, no. 1 (2019): 5–15.

32 Fernand Braudel, *The Mediterranean and the Mediterranean World in the Age of Philip II* (University of California Press, 1995), 232.

to extractivism and climate emergencies.[33] The perception of arid lands as wastelands, only made fertile through intensive agriculture and exploited labour, stems largely from colonial assumptions and has long driven populations into famine.[34] But as rising temperatures, monocultures, and water dependencies push crops to migrate into new climatic zones, drought's political and financial operations become ever clearer.

The exploitation of migrant labourers in Sicilia's booming greenhouse economy, where plastic enclosures cultivate patented fruits and vegetables year-round despite water scarcity, has dramatically intensified. The region now relies on importing workers, forcing climate demarcations into exploited bodies and territories. While Tunisian men once made up the majority of greenhouse workers, traffickers have shifted to employing Romanian citizens since the country joined the EU in 2007.[35] In places like Ragusa, thousands of Romanian women face not only labour exploitation but also sexual abuse, often facilitated by their own husbands.[36] Organisations like Libera, Proxima, and Fuori Mercato (off-market) are raising awareness, providing shelter flats for exploited workers, and setting up slavery-free greenhouses and social orchards for people to regain their lives. Direct action organised by workers themselves has also gained momentum. In May 2021, The Invisibles, a group of migrant fruit pickers led by activist Aboubakar Soumahoro, exposed the inhumane treatment under *caporalato*.[37] Meanwhile, workers' organisations like La Fabbrica Occupata (the squatted factory) in the Tavoliere delle Puglie, Italy's top-producing tomato region despite being one of the most drought-affected, are resisting the violence of large-scale agricultural markets. When agro-industrial plantations are compromised or destroyed by depleted aquifers, saltwater intrusion, unexpected heat waves or hail storms, it is the workers who suffer increased exploitation and even lower wages to compensate for pre-agreed harvests. Cheap food is not cheap if the human and environmental toll is accounted for.

Peasant seeds, however, resist industrial definitions of aridity, thriving in *poly*culture systems without relying on chemicals or labour exploitation. But farmers still face challenges in commercialising or exchanging peasant seeds without certification.[38] Italy's 2021 decree acknowledged peasant and organic seeds, however the cost and bureaucracy of registering these

33 Diane K. Davis, *Resurrecting the Granary of Rome: Environmental History and French Colonial Expansion in North Africa* (Ohio University Press, 2007), introduction.

34 Diana K. Davis, *The Arid Lands* (MIT Press, 2016), introduction. See also: Mike Davis, *Late Victorian Holocausts: El Niño Famines and the Making of the Third World* (Verso, 2002), Notes on Definitions.

35 Recent waves in forced migration are contributing to a shift towards recruitment of workers from Senegal, Gambia, Nigeria, Bangladesh and India in what has been referred to as the "refugeesation" of agricultural exploitation. See Nick Dines and Enrica Rigo, "Postcolonial Citizenships and the 'Refugeeization' of the Workforce: Migrant Agricultural Labor in the Italian Mezzogiorno", in eds. Sandra Ponzanesi & Gianmaria Colpani, *Postcolonial transitions in Europe: Contexts, Practices and Politics* (Rowman and Littlefield, 2016), 151–172.

36 Lorenzo Tondo & Annie Kelly, "Raped, Beaten, Exploited: The 21st-Century Slavery Propping Up Sicilian Farming", *The Guardian,* 12 March 2017; and Lorenzo Tondo & Annie Kelly, "'Terrible Conditions': Police Uncover Abuse and Exploitation on Farms in Sicily", *The Guardian*, 31 October 2017.

37 *The Invisibles*, directed by Diana Ferrero & Carola Mamberto (Doha Debates, 2020), 00:09:00.

38 In 1971, Italy introduced legal restrictions on seed commercialisation following European Community guidelines (Legge 25 novembre 1971, n.1096, Disciplina dell'Attività Sementiera).

seeds is prohibitive and often requires written records older than fifty years to prove the seed's provenance.[39] At the EU level, additional regulations on Heterogeneous Organic Material (HOM), New Genomic Techniques (NGTs), and Plant Variety Rights (PVR) create further obstacles.[40] Rather than supporting the right to food, agroecology or peasant agriculture, these measures have paved the way for CRISPR technologies that allow partial genetic modification without classifying these seeds as fully GMO.[41] Chloe Mathurin from Via Campesina Europe highlights how NGTs are often used to justify patent claims, even for plants obtained through conventional or peasant breeding methods. This increases costs, legal uncertainties, and dependencies, especially for farmers and traditional breeders, as "access to biological diversity is restricted, threatening the development of locally adapted crops".[42]

Agroecological farmers are thus pushed into grey zones of legality, forced to find creative workarounds. These include crafting packaging and branding to disguise unregistered varieties, exchanging seeds through cultural associations, using frameworks like *agricoltura custode* (custodian agriculture) and *registri di conservazione* (registry of seed cultivation for conservation purposes), or signing collaboration agreements between nurseries and farmers in lieu of seed purchase invoices. While technically legal, these methods fail to recognise the vital role of these heritage practices, pushing both seed savers and their climate-resilient plant resources closer to extinction. Recent legal amendments have introduced the oxymoronic term *varietà prive di valore intrinseco* (varieties without intrinsic value), requiring farmers to declare their labour and produce as having no value to continue operating. However, given the lack of enforcement, many farmers resist these seed enclosures, finding it worth the risk. Seed saving is a right—not an exception or a privilege that can be taken away.[43]

The ability of these seeds to evade human control can allow them to adapt, disguise, and also resist contemporary agroindustry on marginalised terrain. This is also how a unique variety of durum wheat, *timilia*, from the area near Modica, maintained its co-evolutionary connection with the land. Timilia is useless to agroindustry but invaluable to farmers: it is known as a *grano di riparo* (repair grain). When the weather is erratic, southern Italian farmers can rely on *timilia*. It will grow and produce even when planted as late as March. Although the yield is negligible for agroindustry, the flour's quality surpasses that of modern varieties. Despite this, *timilia* has been slowly abandoned, especially due to policies like *contributo accoppiato* (coupled income support), which tie European subsidies to the purchase of registered seeds. In some cases, local farmers outsmarting the system bought the

39 Decreto Legislativo n. 20 2021 (art. 6) and Legge n. 23 2022, Tutela, Sviluppo e Competitività della Produzione (art. 8).

40 Regulation (EU) 2018/848 "On Organic Production and Labelling of Organic Products", and Official Controls Regulation (EU) 2017/625.

41 Erica Borg & Amedeo Policante, *Mutant Ecologies: Mutant Ecologies Manufacturing Life in the Age of Genomic Capital* (Pluto Press, 2022), introduction.

42 "Joint Statement on Patents and New GMO's: Don't Risk the Future of Our Seeds!" *EUROVIA*, 15 November 2023.

43 Karine E. Peschard, *Seed Activism: Patent Politics and Litigation in the Global South* (MIT Press, 2022), 4-5.

registered seeds, planted them, and collected the subsidies. But once the first green shoots appeared in December and after inspectors had reviewed invoices and fields, the farmers quietly re-seeded *timilia* carrying on the unwritten and unwritable history of peasant resistance.

SEED COMMONS: CULTIVATING THE RIGHTS OF AND TO SEEDS

Transforming food systems and promoting free seed circulation requires both addressing the challenges agroecological growers face and recognising that farmers have always understood multispecies relationships. Consequently, climate struggles cannot be separated from cultural shifts, and cultural shifts require new forms of action. While hundreds of food policy reports focus on industrial extractive systems, few incorporate the role of art and culture in shaping new food futures.

In response, in October 2023 we organised the first CLIMAVORE Assembly aimed specifically at revalorising the role of 'culture' in agriculture. The Assembly highlighted the struggles of peasant seeds and interrogated what formats and platforms could create meaningful change in the present. By applying non-normative thinking from queer ecology, the goal was to foster fluid participatory governance capable of dismantling the rigid binary power structures by using "assemblies" as inclusive vessels. In that spirit, this international, intersectional gathering of cultural institutions reimagined their roles as agents of transformation in the climate crisis, reconnecting cultural and artistic programmes with local food infrastructures.[44] The Assembly explored new tactics for ecologically-driven action and policy-making, finding forms of resistance to the norm, while building networks of trust, solidarity, and mutual support.

With over 250 attendees, the CLIMAVORE Assembly brought together growers, seed propagators, and farming cooperatives alongside policymakers, artists, educators, curators, chefs, researchers, cultural producers, activists, and environmentalists. Together, participants explored how to foster civic movements and take action. Occupying two landmark sites in Rome—Museo delle Civiltà (Museum of Civilisations) and Campidoglio (the seat of the City Senate)—the Assembly invited diverse voices to contend and reflect on our collective role in addressing the broken food system and the extinction of peasant knowledge. It emphasised that many cultural institutions (museums with collections connected to colonial origins, land-grant universities, or film propagandists such as Istitute L'Unione Cinematografica Educativa) have historically played a role in cultural erasure; and that when culture is erased, so are peoples and ecol-

44 The Assembly built on two fellowships from the Visible project, which enabled CLIMAVORE to lay the foundation for a long-term project in Italy. The first of which was initiated in collaboration with Locales. It also draws on the experience of the Visible Temporary Parliaments, which, since 2015 have occupied city parliaments with socially engaged art projects, to infuse new perspectives in democratic debates. Research for the CLIMAVORE Assembly to advance foodways in drylands and wetlands has been produced with CLIMAVORE x Jameel at the Royal College of Art, London.

ogies. New alliances require us to rethink what cultural institutions, with their resources, spaces, and public assets could offer farmers in the struggle around drought and seed enclosures.[45]

During the Assembly, food growers called on institutions to support their efforts by using their curatorial and education departments, public programmes, and in-house resources to raise visibility around agrobiodiversity, land access and peasant seeds.[46] They sought to create new narratives around food justice, storying multispecies worlds.[47] Museums, as places of preservation, should extend their role beyond custodians of objects to include networks, ecologies, and common immaterial heritage. As the Palestinian art and agriculture collective Sakiya stated:

permanent culture is a troubled term because permanence in culture takes for granted the ownership of land. To rewild our surroundings, we need to rewild our imagination and the stories and mythologies that we tell.[48]

New alliances for the commons are crucial to challenging the large-scale lobbies of the agribusiness. Building trust within these alliances requires participatory systems based on mutual support, like *garanzia partecipata* (participatory guarantee), which some farms in the project advocate for as a replacement for organic certification. This model relies on personal exchanges between farmers and consumers, transforming economic relationships into social and political bonds. It is a collective, multi-sensory, relational practice overseeing production methods and products. The entire community—market-goers, producers, and co-producers—is encouraged to take responsibility for ensuring the integrity of the producers and their goods, using all of their senses and critical awareness, keeping their eyes, ears, noses, tongues, and brains connected and alert. To achieve this, the Assembly suggested more frequent contact and visits with farmers, customers, and members to foster an attentive understanding of agricultural challenges, which can lead to the formation of a mutual aid fund to help farmers address environmentally-related production issues alongside the community instead of chemicals.

Queering kin is not just about building, preserving, or celebrating chosen family relations between seeds and their human and more-

45 Ravi Agarwal, speech at CLIMAVORE Assembly, Rome, 29 October 2023. See also Marco Notarnicola, co-founding member of XFarm—a community-led growing project on confiscated Mafia property. Speech at CLIMAVORE Assembly, Rome, 29 October 2023.

46 Debates around whether cultural institutions are the best vehicles for change revolved around their mediatic power and societal agency to raise awareness has the power to create impact, even when voices are dissonant. Assembly participants demanded cultural institutions to offer their platforms and support access to land for communities who have lost it; to redistribute and mutualise resources—human, financial or intellectual; to facilitate training and opportunities to come together; to enhance pleasure and create desire, eroticising our sensory experiences; to open up educational departments and collaborate with schools to expand radical pedagogies; to trigger people's imaginations about cooking with healthier ingredients and understanding the ecological relationships behind them; to share their press and communication platforms, amplifying the necessary shift towards supporting agrobiodiversity; and to train and inspire the next generation of farmers and landworkers.

47 Sophie Chao, "(Un)Worlding the Plantationocene: Extraction, Extinction, Emergence", *eTropic* 21, no. 1 (2022).

48 Sakiya, speech at CLIMAVORE Assembly, Rome, 28 October 2023.

CLIMAVORE Assembly at Campidoglio, Rome, October 2023. Peasant seeds are more than genetic material; they are archives of resistance. As corporate control tightens over seed laws, the Assembly's session at the seat of the City Senate debated how legal and cultural infrastructures can uphold the rights of and to seeds. Source: Image by Giulia Valentini (courtesy of CLIMAVORE x Jameel at RCA).

than-market environments. For example, *Monoculture Meltdown* began collaborating with Museo delle Civiltà to challenge seed banks as static top-down repositories and collections that freeze plants or cultural artefacts into unchangeable, untouchable commodities. Instead, the collaboration explores other dynamic conservation processes that allow seeds to engage in queer relationality—adapting and evolving with changing climates. As seed saver Angelo Giordano contests, seed banks have focused on preserving culture in a normative way, disconnecting it from the people and ecologies they co-evolved with, turning diversity into a feared form of genetic *erosion*.

At the core of the collaboration is the use of a public cultural institution as a vessel to create provenance for unregistered seeds. This involved an agreement letter with farmers to grow seeds for cultural purposes, expressing the commitment of propagators to sending seeds to the museum for 'temporary storage', after which the institution will return them to the same or other farmers for the next growing season. Under Italian law, once seeds are documented in a farmer's notebook, they can be self-reproduced. *Monoculture Meltdown* explores the potential of cultural institutions certifying seeds for cultural purposes. In parallel, 'drought nurseries' were created to identify and distribute peasant seeds at risk of extinction. The selection guidelines required seeds to be locally grown, co-evolved with the surrounding climate and communities, self-reproduced, potentially resistant to heat and water stress, and cultivated through agroecological or syntropic methods.[49] In 2024, around 50,000 seeds were planted for propagation, with a goal to collect 250,000 and assign them a temporary cultural provenance.

Under this framework, *Monoculture Meltdown* collaborates with a network of twenty farmers and cooperatives in Sicilia and Puglia, engaged in the observation, cultivation, and propagation of peasant seeds for cultural purposes. The project uses the museum's 'living collection' to foster local alliances between seeds, soils, artists, and farmers, and, ultimately, to bridge the cultural and agricultural divide. Meanwhile, a working group of stakeholders and legal advisors is advancing new model laws that expand the rights *of* and *to* seeds across regional, national, and European frameworks, and use the space of the museum to create *legal fictions* that can already operate in the future present.[50] Thinking through cultural and 'rights of nature' frameworks when applied to *cultivated* nature may reconnect their divide, offering possibilities to counter failing food systems and enhance shared trust, infrastructure, and knowledge networks. The project's participants contribute to the living collections of cultural institutions to create a legitimate origin in the form of a provenance document for drought-resistant seeds, while working with legal scholars to cultivate the rights *of* and *to* seeds.

New opportunities from dry farming and agroecological adaptation can transform foodways and their arid ecologies. However, regulatory challenges persist, from restrictions on commercialisation of self-reproduced seeds to new genomic techniques and non-organic heterogenous plant material regulations. Farmers involved in the project assert that peasant seeds are essential, even for non-agroecological producers, as they often outperform industrialised seeds, even with agrochemicals. Recognising the free adaptation and cultivation of less water-dependent seeds is vital for the agriculture of the future, preserving cultural heritage amid ecological collapse, and ensuring the rights of future generations. As Carla Monteleone from Cooperativa NoE remarked, "there is no human progress without civil disobedience".[51]

49 These guidelines were developed in agreement with the collaborating partners and seed savers involved in the project, following several discussions held throughout spring and summer 2023.

50 Following discussions with rights of nature expert Mari Margil and the PRIN LUMEN group, key project collaborators, this work seeks to leverage the unique space and agency of the museum to present legal alternatives as actionable for cultural audiences today, while simultaneously advocating for legal changes that may take several years to materialize.

51 Carla Monteleone, speech at Arci Porco Rosso, Palermo, 7 May 2024.

Frank Cancian, agriculture after after the Second World War in Lacedonia. Source: Image courtesy of MAVI-Museo Antropologico Visivo Irpino.
Frank Cancian, Women in the procession to the Madonna delle Grazie, Lacedonia, 1957. Source: Image courtesy of MAVI-Museo Antropologico Visivo Irpino.

ACKNOWLEDGEMENTS

The work on dryland microclimates in southern Italy was initiated by Cooking Sections in 2018 as part of *What is Above is What is Below*—a public installation for Manifesta 12, Palermo. The Sicilia & Puglia Station continues its long-term legacy as part of *Monoculture Meltdown*, a project developed within CLIMAVORE x Jameel at RCA. The work in Italy is led by Principal Investigators Daniel Fernández Pascual and Alon Schwabe, project manager Dani Burrows with Research Associate Enrico Milazzo and local coordinators Davide Palmieri and Gabriella Patera, in partnership with Vessel Art Project, Puglia. The research was also informed through the ongoing fellowship at CIFAR's Future Flourishing Program, CIFAR, Toronto, Canada. Collaborating propagators in Sicilia include: Az. Agr. Acquaviva, Capo Granitola, Chiantala & Radice Sicula, Coop. Ciauli, Coop. NoE, Coop. Valdibella & Agricola Mpidusa, Lu Panaru, Tizza, Vallone Wilderness & Gesualdo Faulisi. In Puglia: Amedeco & Roberto Polo, Casa delle Agriculture, Coop. AlterEco, Coop. Karadrà, Coop. Pietre di Scarto, Contrada Serulla, Luna nel Pozzo, SeminAzioni, XFarm, Zilletta di Brancia. Rights of Seeds working group: Mari Margil (Centre for Environmental and Democratic Rights), PRIN LUMEN led by Silvia Bagni (Università di Bologna), Veronica Federico (Università degli Studi di Firenze) and Serena Baldin (Università degli Studi di Trieste).

WORKS CITED

Armiero, Marco, Roberta Biasillo, & Wilko Graf von Hardenberg. *Mussolini's Nature. An Environmental History of Italian Fascism.* MIT Press, 2022.

Asdal, Kristin, & Tune Huse. *Nature-Made Economy: Cod, Capital, and the Great Economization of the Ocean*, MIT Press, 2023.

Baker, Janelle Marie. "Do Berries Listen? Berries as Indicators, Ancestors, and Agents in Canada's Oil Sands Region". *ETHNOS* 86, no. 2 (2021): 273–294.

de Boni, Annalisa, Antonia D'Amico, Claudio Acciani, & Rocco Roma. "Crop Diversification and Resilience of Drought-Resistant Species in Semi-Arid Areas: An Economic and Environmental Analysis". *Sustainability* 14, no. 15 (2022).

Borg, Erica, & Amedeo Policante. *Mutant Ecologies: Mutant Ecologies Manufacturing Life in the Age of Genomic Capital.* Pluto Press, 2022.

van der Borght, Kim, & Saurav Ghimire. "Seeds and Intellectual Property Rights: Bad Faith and Undue Influence Undermine Food Security and Human Rights". In *Law and Sustainability. Economic and Financial Law & Policy – Shifting Insights & Values,* edited by Koen Byttebier and Kim van der Borght. Springer, 2022.

Branca, Ferdinando, Sergio Argento, & Alessandro Tribulato. "Assessing Genetic Reserves in Sicily (Italy): The *Brassica* Wild Relatives Case Study". In *Agrobiodiversity Conservation: Securing the Diversity of Crop Wild Relatives and Landraces*, edited by Nigel Maxted et al. CAB, 2012.

Braudel, Fernand. *The Mediterranean and the Mediterranean World in the Age of Philip II.* University of California Press, 1995.

Ceccarelli, Salvatore, Stefania Grando, Maedeh Salimi, & Khadija Razavi. "Evolutionary Populations for Sustainable Food Security and Food Sovereignty". In *Seeds for Diversity and Inclusion,* edited by Yoshiaki Nishikawa & Michel Pimbert. Palgrave Macmillan, 2022.

Chao, Sophie. "(Un)Worlding the Plantationocene: Extraction, Extinction, Emergence". *eTropic* 21, no. 1 (2022): 165-191.

Davis, Diane K. *Resurrecting the Granary of Rome: Environmental History and French Colonial Expansion in North Africa.* Ohio University Press, 2007.

Davis, Diana K. *The Arid Lands.* MIT Press, 2016.

Davis, Mike. *Late Victorian Holocausts: El Niño Famines and the Making of the Third World.* Verso, 2002.

Early, Catherine. "Stop Seed Saving Restrictions in UK Trade Deals". *The Ecologist,* 5 July 2024.

Fernández Pascual, Daniel, & Alon Schwabe. "What is Above is What is Below". *E-flux Architecture*, 24 May 2019.

Ferrero, Diana, & Carola Mamberto. *The Invisibles.* Doha Debates, 2020. 9 min.

Ghimire, Saurav, Nurul Barizah, Intan Soeparna, & Kim Van der Borght. "Plant Variety Protection Law and Farmers' Rights to Save, Exchange and Breed Seeds: The Case of Indonesia". *Journal of Intellectual Property Law & Practice* 16, no. 9 (2021): 1013–1025.

Howe, Henry F., & Judith Smallwood. "Ecology of Seed Dispersal". *Annual Review of Ecology and Systematics* 13 no. 1 (1982): 201-228.

Hustak, Carla, & Natasha Myers. "Involutionary Momentum: Affective Ecologies and the Sciences of Plant/Insect Encounters". *Differences* 23, no. 3 (2012): 74-118.

Ingold, Tim. "Evolution Without Inheritance: Steps to an Ecology of Learning". *Current Anthropology* 63, no. 25 (2022): 32-55.

Kloppenburg, R. Jack. *First the Seed. The Political Economy Of Plant Biotechnology, 1492-2000.* University of Wisconsin Press, 2005.

La Scala, Silvia, Flores Naselli, Paola Quatrini, Giuseppe Gallo, & Fabio Caradonna. "Drought-Adapted Mediterranean Diet Plants: A Source of Bioactive Molecules Able to Give Nutrigenomic Effects per sè or to Obtain Functional Foods". *International Journal of Molecular Sciences* 25, no. 4 (2024): 22-35.

Mortimer-Sandilands, Catriona, & Bruce Erickson. *Queer Ecologies: Sex, Nature, Politics, Desire.* Indiana University Press, 2010.

Nussey, Daniel H., Alastair J. Wilson, & Jon E. Brommer. "The Evolutionary Ecology of Individual Phenotypic Plasticity in Wild Populations". *Journal Evolutionary Biology* 20, no. 3 (2007): 831–44.

Oaki, Keith. *Seed Wars: Cases and Materials on Intellectual Property and Plant Genetic Resources.* Carolina Academic Press, 2007.

Peschard, E. Karine. *Seed Activism: Patent Politics and Litigation in the Global South.* MIT Press, 2022.

Saab, Anne. "International Law and Feeding the World in Times of Climate Change". *Transnational Legal Theory* 9, no. 3-4 (2018): 288–301.

Seymour, Nicole. *Strange Natures: Futurity, Empathy, and the Queer Ecological Imagination.* University of Illinois Press, 2013.

Seufert, Philip, Mariapaola Boselli, & Stefano Mori. *Recovering the Cycle of Wisdom: Beacons of Light Toward the Right to Seeds.* Working Group on Agricultural Biodiversity of the International Planning Committee for Food Sovereignty (IPC), FIAN International and Centro Internazionale Crocevia. April 2021.

Subramaniam, Banu, & Madelaine Bartlett. "Re-imagining Reproduction: The Queer Possibilities of Plants". *Integrative and Comparative Biology* 63, no. 4 (2023): 946–959.

Tallbear, Kim, & Angela Willey. "Critical Relationality: Queer, Indigenous, and Multispecies Belonging Beyond Settler Sex & Nature". *Imaginations* 10, no. 1 (2019): 5–15.

Thompson, John N. *The Coevolutionary Process.* University of Chicago Press, 1994.

Tielbörger, Katja, & Rüdiger Prasse. "Do Seeds Sense Each Other? Testing for Density-Dependent Germination in Desert Perennial Plants". *Oikos* 118, no. 5 (2009): 792–800.

Tondo, Lorenzo, & Annie Kelly. "Raped, Beaten, Exploited: The 21st-Century Slavery Propping Up Sicilian Farming". *The Guardian,* 12 March 2017.

Tondo, Lorenzo, & Annie Kelly. "'Terrible Conditions': Police Uncover Abuse and Exploitation on Farms in Sicily". *The Guardian*, 31 October 2017.

FIELD

NOTES

TREES, VINES, PALMS, AND OTHER ARCHITECTURAL MONUMENTS

Paulo Tavares

The aircraft is flying over a thick jungle; the image captured by the film camera on board shows a blurry picture painted in various shades of dark. Only the highest palms, which stand out from the canopy mass, can be identified from this birds-eye perspective. The camera pans toward an open field where we see a large human settlement. Its spatial layout is geometrically arranged in the form of a vast arc. The aircraft circles the area, the camera holds on the settlement while the voiceover provides some contextual information: "on the right bank of the das Mortes River begin the domains of the Xavante Indians, the great warrior tribe that became famous for its stubborn resistance against all attempts at catechesis. A few kilometers from the river, protected by the dense *cerrados* [biome], we begin to see the first villages of these forest peoples, which they defend with remarkable determination".[1]

Produced in 1947 by the Indian Protection Service (SPI), the Brazilian agency created to govern Indigenous affairs, *Rio das Mortes* is one of the few documents of the ancient settlements of the Xavante. Fifteen years or so after these images were recorded, all of their settlements had been abandoned or destroyed.

From the 1940s to the late 1960s, the Xavante, an Indigenous nation that has lived in the central Brazilian plateaus since time immemorial, were subjected to a brutal campaign of land dispossession and forced removals to create space for cattle and soy farms. Officially known as "pacification", this campaign was part of a strategy of territorial colonization that the Brazilian state described as "occupying demographic voids". In 1966, at the peak of this campaign, the Xavante communities of the Marãiwatsédé region were deported from their ancestral land. In 1974, the National Indian Foundation (FUNAI), the state agency that replaced the SPI in 1968, issued a certificate attesting that this territory was Indigenous land no more.

Following the publication of the final report, in late 2014, of the Brazilian National Truth Commission—a commission set to investigate human rights abuses committed by the military dictatorship (1964–1985)—my architectural practice, in collaboration with the Bö'u Xavante Association and the Brazilian Public Prosecutor's Office, initiated a project to document the sites of ancient Indigenous settlements in order to provide evidence of their ancestral possession of this territory. This visual essay shows excerpts of this ongoing project. Our methodology is based on the reading of various media, ranging from historic photographs and films to satellite data to the territory itself. The landscape and its representations are interpreted as documentary mediums, archaeological surfaces that bear traces and memories of the ancestral occupation of the land by the Xavante people.

1 Heinz Forthmann, *Rio das Mortes*, documentary (SPI, 1947).

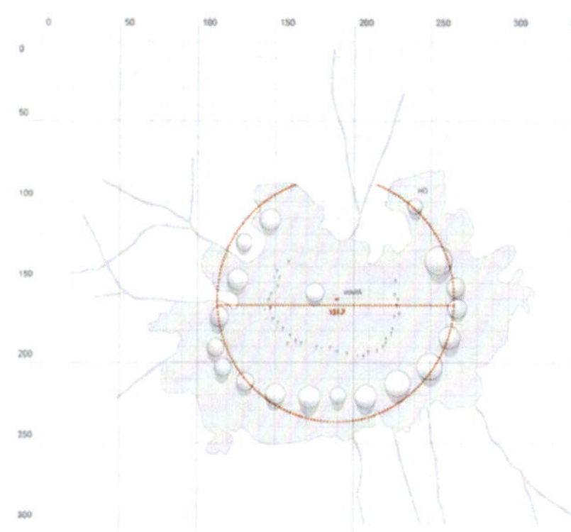

Article on the "pacification" of the Xavante from O Cruzeiro (1946). Identification of the vestiges of the village Sõrepré, the geopolitical centre of the Xavante ancestral territory, probably founded in the early nineteenth century.

IMAGE ARCHAEOLOGY

The 'conquest' of the Xavante country became a mass media phenomenon at the time, with sensational photojournalism stories circulating in popular magazines, depicting the Xavante as peoples and missionaries as redeemers. But these visual records constitute an important source of information about the history of the Xavante territory; through them we can study the spatial arrangement of its ancient settlements.

The research reconstituted the architecture of some of the old villages by working the photographs through a set of digital modeling tools. The villages were traditionally built following a precise circular layout, with the houses distributed in an arc-shaped line forming a great internal plaza. The central patio of the largest village we modeled had a diameter of about 200 meters, though its footprint extended beyond the village's perimeter, defined by the row of houses.

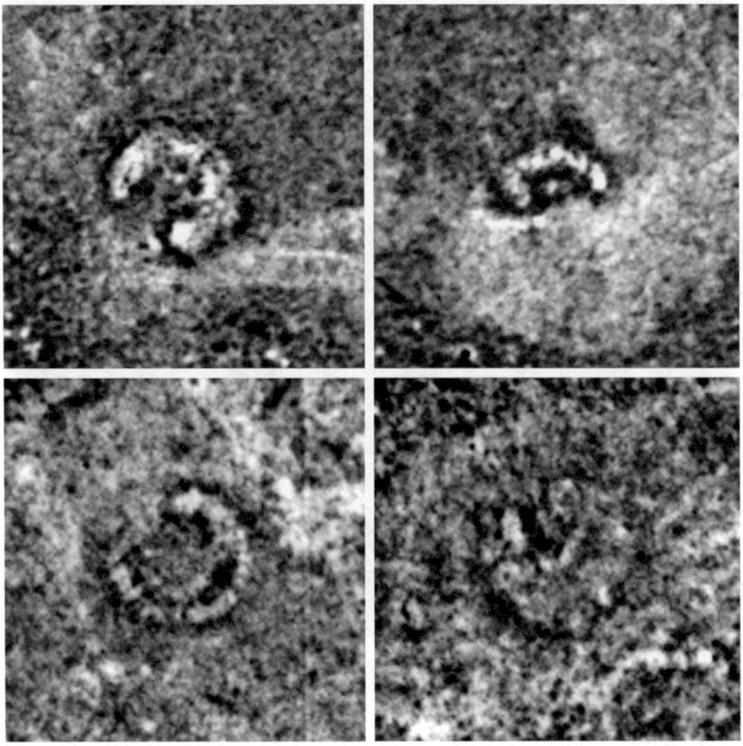

"The ancient village never dies, the vegetation is always reborn in the same place. This photo is the old village Sõrepré. Today this region is divided into four farms. The farmers do not let us enter this area; before we could still do that. So we have to work to regain access to this region." — Jurandir Siridiwê, describing the satellite images of Sõrepré during the project presentation in Etenhiritipá (2017).

The settlements were always situated near streams, with the opening of the arc oriented toward the watercourse. The houses were built as domes structured with wood beams and covered with palm leaves, reproducing the circular logic of the overall urban scheme at the scale of architecture.

Our research also examined a series of satellite images and aerial photographs of cartographic surveys. Despite the dramatic transformations in the landscape caused by the widespread deforestation that followed the forced removals, some of the ancient Xavante settlements seem to have been so old and robust that they left lasting marks in the territory, which are still clearly visible in these images.

Our analysis identified several traces on the ground whose shape, size, location, and disposition indicate the former presence of indigenous settlements. These footprints exhibit an arc-shaped layout that bears striking resemblance to the spatial arrangement of the villages reconstituted from the photographs. Inscribed on the Earth's surface like geoglyphics, these are vestiges of interventions in the landscape that were planned according to a cultural pattern consistent with the architecture of the ancient Xavante settlements documented in the archival records.

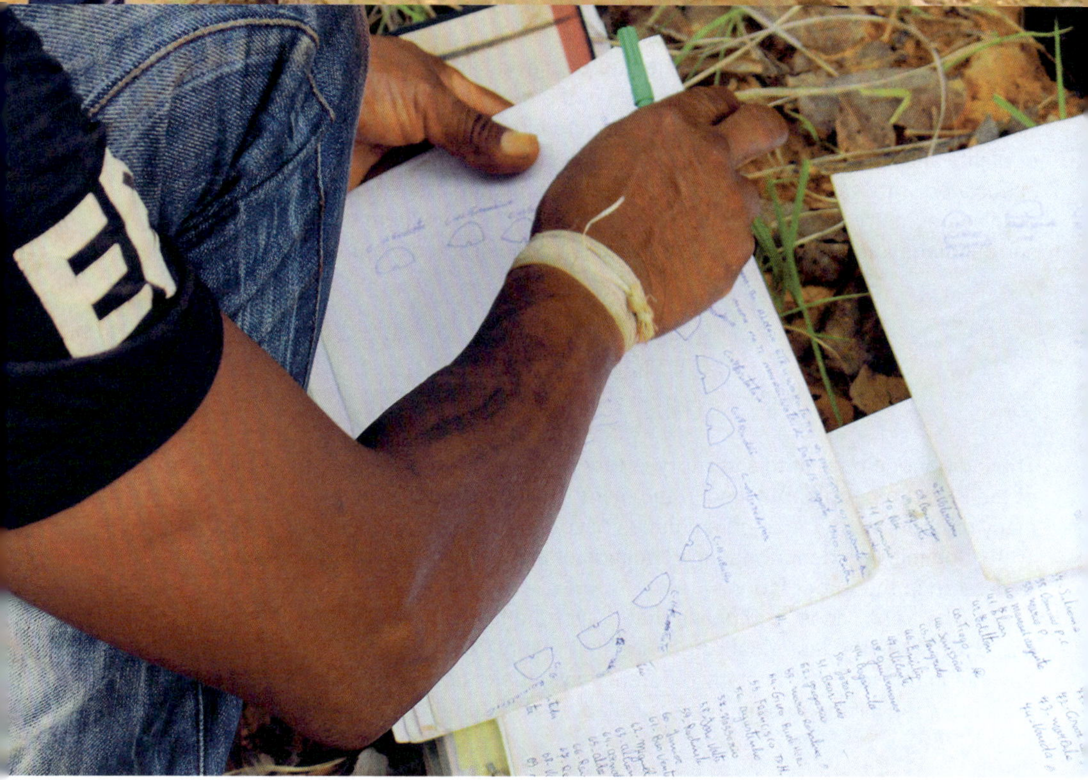

Policarpo Waire Tserenhorã describing the archaeological site of Bö'u, during field documentation (2017).

LANDSCAPE ARCHAEOLOGY

In parallel with the exercises in 'imagery archaeology', the project undertook a series of field expeditions, together with elders of Marãiwatsédé, to document some of the archaeological sites on the ground. Policarpo Waire Tserenhorã, Dario Tserewhorã, and Marcelo Abaré, the elders who guided us, used to be warriors who led their communities in great geographic expeditions through their territory (a cultural practice called *hömono* that was totally eradicated by state policies). They therefore have a very sophisticated knowledge of this land, its environs and history.

Such extraordinary, unique knowledge of the territory, typical of Xavante culture, has been documented by various studies, as illustrated in this passage from anthropologist David Maybury-Lewis's classic 1967 ethnography, *Akwẽ-Shavante Society*: "in their monotonous scrub, where I was unable to tell one bush or thicket from another, and was frequently under the impression that I had traveled through a particular patch of trees only a little before, the [Xavante] can remember the exact place where a kill was made months or even seasons previously and narrate its circumstances in detail".[2] What Maybury-Lewis perceived as an amorphous and homogeneous landscape, the Xavante people identified as specific places saturated with history and memories. In the context of our project, even with the disfigurement of the landscape due to the predatory advancement of pastures and plantations, the elders recognized several archaeological sites, even remembering places where Indigenous massacres occurred. The three localities surveyed—the villages of Tsinõ, Ubdõnho'u, and Bö'u—match precisely the geographical points of the footprints identified in the satellite images.

The ancient Xavante villages can be identified through very peculiar evidentiary signs that are easily recognized by the elders. These include the form and composition of botanic formations, the presence and the disposition of certain trees and palms, and variations in soil type.

All the sites that were documented display a similar remarkable feature wherein a patch of vegetation had grown in the arc-shaped layout of the ancient village. Made of a combination of medium and large trees, palms, and other types of plants and vines, these botanic formations contain certain species that are associated with Xavante ancestral occupation and land management systems. Their precise geometry, as well as their species content, makes them stand out from their surroundings and reveals their anthropogenic, 'constructed' nature.

LIVING RUINS (THE FOREST AS HERITAGE)

The Indigenous past of this territory is recorded not only in the collective memory of the Xavante people, but also in the memory of the Earth itself. In spite of the many different ways these communities have been subjected to what the Brazilian Truth Commission described as a "politics of erasure", their history remains registered in the forest fabric.

The trees, vines, and palms that grew from the fertilized soils of the ancient settlements are the historical landmarks that testify to the ancestral presence of the Xavante in this territory. In many different ways, these botanic formations are the product of the village design, the equivalent to architectural ruins, albeit not dead

2 David Maybury-Lewis, *Akwẽ-Shavante Society* (Oxford University Press, 1974).

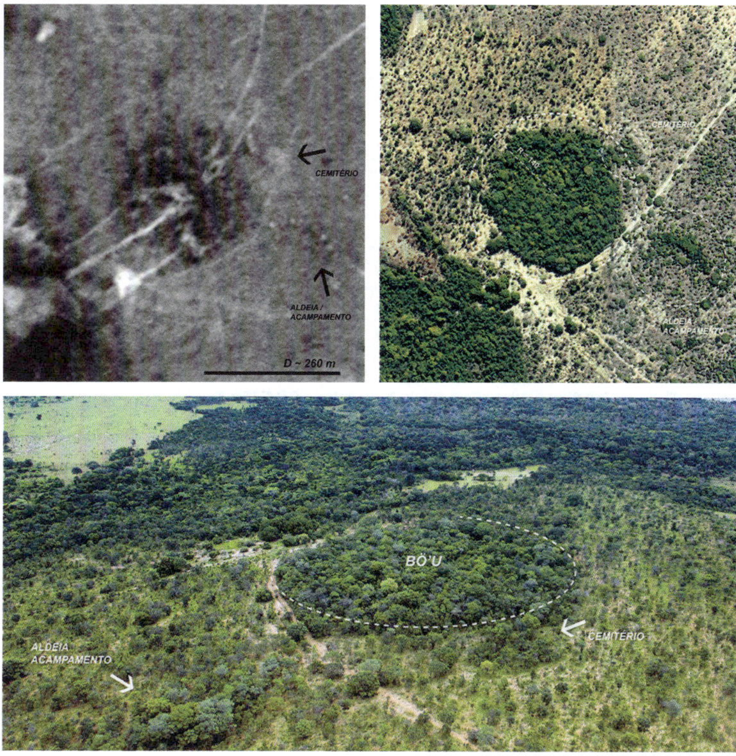

Identification of Bö'u, the old centre of Marãiwatsédé. The site is characterised by a thick jungle formation that has preserved the original circular layout of the ancient village. Bö'u was probably founded in the early to mid-nineteenth century and existed until the forced removals in the 1950s. This region is known as Bö'umoahö, "place of production", in reference to the abundance of natural resources found in the area and to the village's past prosperity.

"This arc of trees used to be a village. The end of the row of houses was there, and the other end over there, far away. The village was enormous, so the vegetation that formed inside the semi-circle is as big as the village was. The center of the village was located around here. That's why this forest is in the middle of the village. Here we used to make warã, our collective meetings." — Policarpo Waire Tserenhorã describing the archaeological site of Bö'u during field documentation (2017).

but living. Can we claim trees, vines, and palms to be historic monuments? Is the forest an 'urban heritage' of Indigenous landscape management systems?

Most of this archaeological heritage is outside the recognized limits of the Xavante reserves, situated within private fenced lands to which the Xavante people do not have access. As such the sites are in danger of being completely destroyed by the advancement of the agribusiness frontier.

In August 2017, following the presentation of our research findings at the Xavante village of Etenhiritipá, we started drawing a petition to be submitted to the Brazilian National Institute of Artistic and Historic Heritage (IPHAN) and to UNESCO calling for the inclusion of these botanic formations on the list of the protected common heritage of humankind. Our petition contends that those botanic formations should be considered archaeological heritage inasmuch as they represent 'architectural artifacts' of the unique culture of the Xavante.

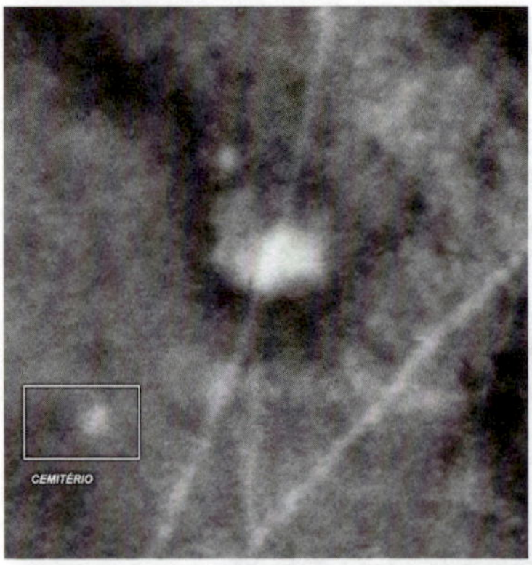

Identification of Tsinõ, a village founded in the early 1960s after the communities of Marãiwatsédé were forced to settle next to the headquarters of the Suiá Missu farm. The farm headquarters are still practically intact. Next to an aeroplane landing strip on the opposite side, it is possible to identify the archaeological site of Tsinõ by a distinct arc-shaped botanic formation. In 1966, the Brazilian Air Force led an operation using this landing strip to transfer the Xavante communities—by that time, about 263 survivors—to a distant region 500 kilometres away.

"We were all displaced from this area, leaving everything behind. And the non-Indigenous took advantage of that and occupied the region, without caring to the fact that we are the original owners of this land. This region is called Suyá. In our language it is called the place of stones. Look to the rocky mountain over there. Next to the mountain there are plenty of yam; this is a very fruitful region." — Policarpo Waire Tserenhorã describing the region where the village of Tsinõ is located (2017).

Beyond the urgency of protecting these sites, in interpreting trees and palms as ruins, the petition seeks to probe the liminal relations between natural and cultural landscapes as they have been defined by colonial categories of thought within and beyond the field of architecture, particularly in the way such categories and cognitive schemes have constrained definitions of heritage, memory, and history. Architectural knowledge often blinds us from understanding the deeply human and historical, properly architectural nature of these forest landscapes, and such is the tacit act by which it becomes complicit in the colonial politics of erasure.

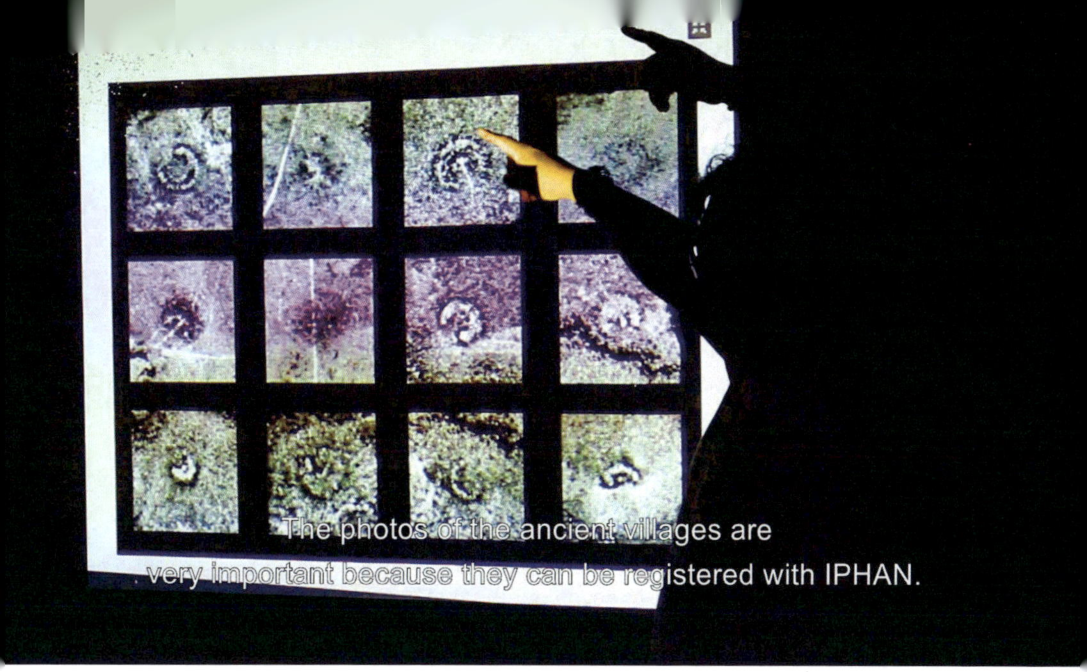

Caimi Waiassé, describing the use of satellite images during the presentation of the mappings in Etenhiritipá. Source: Image by author (2017).

WORKS CITED

Forthmann, Heinz. *Rio das Mortes*. Documentary. SPI, 1947.

Maybury-Lewis, David. *Akwẽ-Shavante Society*. Oxford University Press, 1974.

UNGROUNDING THE GEOTHERMAL ENERGY FIELD

Asıl Uludağ

My research investigates the development of geothermal energy in the provinces of Aydın, Manisa, and Denizli in the Aegean region of Turkey through its long materialisation process starting from the early twentieth century. I examine this process through the legal, scientific, economic, and infrastructural assemblage that drives it, which I call the *geothermal energy complex.*

The provinces are home to sixty-seven geothermal energy plant (GEP) units and counting, which produce electricity from the heat of geothermal fluids, which in this region are as hot as 250°C.[1] These reside in aquifers layered deep in the ground, starting at a depth of 1 kilometre and exceeding 3 kilometres. An electricity-producing deep GEP is composed of boreholes, which bring fluids to the surface, and a power plant including a turbine and a generator, which produces electricity from their heat. While a GEP might only have two boreholes (one for production and one for reinjection), GEPs in this region have up to thirty, spread across a large area, often installed on separate plots. Pipelines running above and below the surface transport fluids from the boreholes to the power plant. There, heat is extracted and used to spin turbines, producing electricity. After heat extraction, the cooled (but not cold) fluids must be returned to the same aquifer through reinjection boreholes to maintain aquifer pressure and prevent surface pollution. This diagrammatic model, however, does not reflect the actual production of geothermal energy, its material economy, and politics in the region.

The GEPs, owned and operated by a total of twenty-one companies, are part of a single mega-project, which renders this region productive for the state and private companies by transforming it from an agricultural zone to an industrial energy field. Enabled by the global green energy transition and the emergence of renewable energy as a profitable sector, the mega-project capitalises on the hydro-geothermal relations that have historically shaped socio-ecological practices, systems, and organisations in the region, reinventing them as an energy resource through legal redescriptions, economic restructuring, scientific sense-making, and infrastructural development.

Built on land plots which were previously olive and fig gardens as well as agricultural fields, the GEPs have changed the socio-ecological fabric of this geography by altering not only its landscape but also its sensed environment. The relationship between the surface and the deep-subsurface is rearranged as geothermal fluids and gasses, saturated with subsurface chemistries, are

1 In many cases, multiple power plant units, although built at different times, are grouped under a single GEP project name by the energy company. This conceals the spatial, temporal, and procedural specificities of each unit, its materialisation, and the overall extent of geothermal energy development. Therefore, in my research, I analyse each unit as a separate formation which is why the number of GEPs I present here does not match the official numbers.

released into the surface environment through vapour release from GEP chimneys, shallow reinjections from boreholes, or by direct discharge into streams and rivers. Repercussions include water and soil contamination, air pollution, acrid smells, groundwater temperature rise, acid rain, and changes in the microclimate (especially humidity levels). All of these combine to negatively impact local populations whose main source of income is agriculture, primarily olive, fig, and grape production. Sensing these environmental changes has mobilised communities around the issue of geothermal energy development in various towns and districts, including Germencik, Kızılcaköy, Yılmazköy, Pamukören, Buharkent/Sarayköy, Sarıgöl, and Alaşehir. Among the many strategies that the resistance groups have utilised to challenge their development, appealing to Environmental Impact Assessment (EIA) approvals granted to planned GEPs has been the most common and effective intervention.[2] Despite winning dozens of cases, this is not a sustainable strategy for the locals. Once a site is marked as a geothermal energy field, there is no way of undoing this designation, as it puts the site on the map for development. Consequently, defensive strategies only function as mechanisms of delay as new EIAs replace old ones, regardless of the cases won by the local resistance groups.

2 MARCH 2020
GERMENCIK, AYDIN

Public Participation Meeting for Efe-8 GEP. Source: Video by Mehmet Güngör, shared on the Germencik Çevre ve Doğa Derneği (GERÇED) Facebook page (2 March 2020).

The Public Participation Meeting (PPM) for the planned Efe-8 GEP took place at a wedding hall in the Ömerbeyli neighbourhood of Germencik. Organised by the Aydın Governorship, the PPM gathered local stakeholders, representatives from the Office of the Governor and the Ministry of Environment, Urbanisation and Climate Change, as well as officials from the energy company and those from the engineering company planning the GEP. During the meeting, the GEP project was to be presented and a report was to be produced, recording the responses from the public. However, before the project presentation could begin, Halil Çetinkaya, a Sarılop fig producer and President of Germencik Çevre ve Doğa Derneği [Germencik Environment and Nature Organisation], stood up to intervene.

2 An Environmental Impact Assessment is a process that aims to mitigate the social and environmental impact of planned projects. In the case of geothermal energy in Turkey, it follows the granting of the production licence. It requires companies to submit a detailed report of the project, potential impacts, and measures to the relevant state bodies. This is the first instance when a planned GEP project is officially announced to the public. The EIA process also includes a Public Participation Meeting (PPM) where company representatives present the project to local communities and record their feedback. To date, not a single EIA application for a planned GEP has been rejected.

> We filed a lawsuit for the said GEP. Seven experts, scientists, came here for this plant.[3] They prepared a report stating that this plant could not be built on Grade-1 agricultural land, and the operation of this plant was halted. I am asking the ministry representatives here, when no GEP exists on Grade-1 agricultural land in any country in the world, how do you, despite the reports of seven experts—scientists—hold this EIA meeting for the second time and stand before the people of Aydın? Do you harbour ill will toward Aydın? Does the Ministry of Environment harbour ill will toward Aydın? [...] We do not want this presentation, and we do not want geothermal either! *Applause*

At the time of the PPM, there were already fifteen GEP units in Germencik, Aydın. Despite local contestation, Efe-8 GEP, composed of two units and thirty boreholes, was built and put into operation in 2020. The same company also owns and operates Galip Hoca, Efe-1, Efe-2, Efe-3, Efe-4, Efe-6, and Efe-7 GEPs, all in the same district. There are seven more GEP units in the district, owned and operated by a different company.

While defensive legal interventions stall the expansion of the geothermal energy complex, it is necessary to explore modes of reappropriation that challenge privatisation, as well as the governance mechanism constructed around a geothermal energy field. What alternate hydro-geothermal relations might be enlisted to challenge the legal, economic, and scientific assertions that marginalise local communities through extraction? Where are the places, and who are the people, that already have alternative attachments to the deep subsurface?

These questions have led me to explore ancient oracular rituals, the sites of historical and contemporary thermal springs and baths, as well as the activities of healing that formed around the hot springs and fumaroles of the region. Hydro-geothermalism, a concept I've developed, refers to practices that have been passed down between people of different cultures who inhabited these lands over millennia through stratified histories of occupation, displacement, and relocation. While some of these practices have been unearthed by archaeologists working in the area, fading memories of more recent ones remain in the minds of the older generation living in the villages. Untold if unasked, their accounts may guide us in understanding how the relationship between the surface and the deep subsurface was once commoned; that is to say, how it was part of communal practices of repair and care. The fieldnotes that follow narrate my search for them in Germencik, Aydın.

11 SEPTEMBER 2023
BOZKÖY, GERMENCIK, AYDIN

I arrived in Germencik early in the morning with plans to meet a few locals and ask them about the old thermal baths. But, as it often happens, they had to reschedule. So I was alone, driving around with little information from unreliable online sources. After searching blind for a while, I found myself on a road called Ilıcalar [Hot springs], which led me into the hills of Bozköy, where I encountered signs to the Elitium Thermal Hotel. It was the only visible clue to any thermal activity, so I decided to pay a visit. I drove past Nezihe Beren GEP and arrived at the hotel a few minutes

3 When an appeal is filed for an EIA approval, the court calls in experts to conduct fieldwork, evaluate the basis of the objection and produce a report which the court uses to make a decision. The expertise of the scientists is determined by the nature of the objection and the conditions of the site. In recent years, however, there have been instances where scientists called in for the GEP cases were experts on distant regions with distinct environments, calling into question the impartiality of the court.

later. At the reception, I met the operations manager. After a brief introduction, he asked me to have a seat in the lobby as he walked away, speaking into his walkie-talkie. He came back with Özgür, an employee of the hotel and a local of Bozköy.

ASLI So, you know what was here before this?

ÖZGÜR Yes, I've been working here the longest. The construction began in 2011. The upper section was built in about five months. But this part was built in 1993. This is the old building.

ANOTHER EMPLOYEE, PASSING BY Probably twenty-five years ago, maybe more [...] My father had a hemorrhoid problem at the time. [...] A friend of his said, "hey, there's some mud down in Bozköy. Let's take you there". It was just dirt, boiling away right there. We held a towel as my dad got in, then we stepped away so that he could rest comfortably. About fifteen to twenty minutes later we went back to find my father sunk into the mud, asleep. He was buried up to here, so we lifted him up. [...] After that, he never had that problem again. That day, still covered in mud, he wrapped himself in a towel, got in the car, and went home, smiling.

MANAGER This place used to belong to the municipality. It still does, but there was no hotel building back then. Think of caravans, tents [...] People would come from the village with their donkeys and sell milk, cheese, pears, grapes.

ÖZGÜR They would even slaughter goats and sheep right down there. The locals would buy the meat and cook it themselves on those gas cylinders.

Our conversation was interrupted as the general manager had become available and invited me to his office. About an hour later, however, I was in Özgür's car, heading up to Bozköy to meet Adem Amca,[4] a village elder. As we drove out of the hotel grounds, Özgür stopped the car at the gates, and a middle-aged man, Ejder, hopped in the back seat. Like many others from Bozköy, he knew the baths well.

EJDER The entrance was here. There were small barracks there. The water would boil naturally. People who came here with a cane would leave without it. I used to herd sheep around here when I was young. People would wrap up their beds and blankets and bring them along when coming here. There were no beds; everyone brought their own. During summer, people would stay two to three months. There was a generator here. We would run it in the summer. At 11 pm, its fuel would run out, and then it would be dark. There was one TV, and once a week, on Saturday, we'd watch a movie [...] People would come here sick and leave healthy.

When we arrived in the village, Özgür parked the car behind a tractor in the square, in front of the coffee house. Adem Amca was there, along with a few others. After a round of "hellos", we had a seat, ordered tea and picked up from where we left off.

ÖZGÜR There were open concrete pools. One side was for women; the other was for men.

ADEM We called the one below Çelik Banyo [Steel Bath]. We used to bathe in that one. It was warm. The one above was too hot. There was a ten to fifteen room hotel at the entrance. It used to belong to the village back then. The municipality ownership came later. They did a build-operate-transfer contract, then the municipality took over.

4 *Amca* means uncle in Turkish, commonly used to refer to older men.

ÖZGÜR It's very old, this place. Look, Adem Amca is seventy-seven years old. It existed before his time.

ADEM Now, on your way here, on the left side, there's Çamur Ilıcası [Mud Thermal]. There's hot water there too. Coming from Germencik, it's the building on your left. You know the vapour, it's there.[5] A two-storey building with fences around it, there. Points in the direction of the hotel. But it's not much.

ÖZGÜR When it's the private sector, Ms. Aslı, no one can enter without permission. But was there security or anything back in our day? People went there with their donkeys. We used to go with my late Alim Nine [Nana]. They'd load grapes, pears, dried fruits, and nuts to sell there. We'd go along.

EJDER We used to sell milk there.

ÖZGÜR You know geothermal [energy plants], when they dug their boreholes, the waters dried. They dig 2000 metres, 3000 metres deep. The hotel's water used to come out on its own. Now, they have to use a submersible pump. It used to spring on its own. The old quality is gone, truly.

ADEM It used to come out naturally. It was good for foot and back pain. We would head straight there after school. Now, you can't dive right in. You need to go in slowly. If you jump in, you'll burn yourself. Once you get used to it, you can stay for an hour if you want.

ÖZGÜR The water would flow 24/7. There was a concrete canal. The water would fill the pools. Then, two hours later, they would be emptied and refilled. [...] The hotel's water is lower now. Since the geothermal [energy plant] is extracting, the water level dropped.

ADEM The hotel supplies its water from the geothermal [energy plant] now, it has to.

ÖZGÜR But they feed it to the outside pools, not the inside ones. You know the ones outside? Did you see them? For the pools inside, they only use the hotel water.

There's another place, Ms. Aslı, when you go up that hill. You know where the road forks? There are two poles right on that bend. There's another water there.

EJDER No, no, it dried up.

ADEM It's gone, lost.

After a brief silence, Adem Amca excused himself and left for his afternoon nap. Özgür and I got in the car and drove back to the hotel.

20 SEPTEMBER 2024
ÇAMKÖY, GERMENCIK, AYDIN

I went back to Germencik a year later to visit the thermal bath Adem Amca mentioned. It's right across the street from Nezihe Beren GEP. I found the owners, Süleyman and Hamdiye Dağılıoğlu, a couple in their eighties, sitting at a table on the porch, looking out at the view dominated by the GEP. The loud and incessant hum and hiss of its continuous electricity production drowned their voices as they welcomed me into their home. I pulled up a chair and joined them at the table.

5 Many elders in the region call the GEPs "vapours" or "where the vapours come out".

Çamur Ilıcası, Hamdiye, and Süleyman Dağılıoğlu's home and thermal bath.
Source: Image by author (20 September 2024).

SÜLEYMAN This is historical water. There used to be a bath here, with mud below. The water used to be here, right under us. They built a canal, and it moved down there.

HAMDIYE There were two small barracks over there, on the other side of the road. You would cover the bath with a straw mat and bathe. Was it this modern back then? No road, no building.

SÜLEYMAN We built the building fifteen years ago.

HAMDIYE We don't get many people now.

SÜLEYMAN People who know, come. Some pay, some don't […] Those who worked in the tobacco fields in Tire, Ödemiş, Milas felt better after bathing here. Otherwise, they got a bad rash, they said. People used to come with their beds and blankets. They said they felt good after staying here for a week to ten days. They'd use the mud, and they'd bathe. The water moved when they built the canal.

HAMDIYE The municipality wanted to use the water here to build a bath in Germencik. It never happened, but they built the canal and our water moved. This was years ago. I was a kid.

SÜLEYMAN You see that over there? *Points at the GEP plot.* It was my brother's. He sold it. They offered a lot of money to us as well, but we didn't sell. We have three daughters-in-law and grandchildren.

SÜLEYMAN They bought so much land around here, and then some more. All the things that happened near this water [...] It existed at the time of my father's grandfather, it's that old. It's a legacy.

HAMDIYE We also have a garden there, among the olives.

SÜLEYMAN The olives were good this year, so were the figs.

ASLI *Points at the GEP.* Don't these affect your figs?

SÜLEYMAN Look down there. All the figs along the pipelines are dry.

Süleyman Amca, holding the hose that leads into the bath. Source: Image by author (20 September 2024).
One of the thermal springs in the garden, by the tree. Source: Image by author (20 September 2024).

HAMDIYE	Look how many of them dried here. There were also some over there that my father had planted. They dried too.
ASLI	Who comes to the bath now, then?
SÜLEYMAN	They come from the east. They fire up their grills, bring their children and stay until sundown. Many come from Aydın as well, of course. But no one stays overnight. They bathe, then they leave.
HAMDIYE	There's no electricity here anyway.

We chatted a while longer; then, they showed me the thermal bath and the hot spring. I asked them where their ancestors were from. They said they were Yörük but didn't know which tribe. "A professor came one day", said Hamdiye, "and told us which Yörük we are, but I don't remember. He said we are the stubborn kind."[6]

Searching for the commons in the deep subsurface of Aydın, Manisa, and Denizli, one finds a complex history of displacement, dispossession, marginalisation, and erasure that conditions the relationships that local communities have with the land. Knowledge and attachments have been lost or weakened. The geothermal energy complex benefits from this fragmentation and exacerbates it by monopolising and altering hydro-geothermal relations between the surface and the deep-subsurface. While its traces are now faint, a hydro-geothermal commons (as opposed to thermal spa tourism) can still be found in memories and in practices taking place in certain parts of the region, such as Germencik. Due to the continued disruption of intergenerational relationality to land as well as marginalisation, what is found in the field is not an internally consistent traditional knowledge base, but an amalgamation of personal experiences, faded recollections, fabrications, rumours, cultural appropriations from past civilisations, and insights gleaned from the fields of medical balneology and hydro-climatology. These entangled geo-social relations are reflected in local modes of sensing and efforts to 'make sense' of the deep subsurface in the region, which the geothermal energy complex simply cuts across. The task at hand is to organise a new geo-thermal commons; perhaps, then, what is lost may resurface from the depths.

INAUDIBLE SURVEYS

George Ridgway

These field notes develop the concept of *thick listening* to probe ecological unravelling and species decline. Listening to three sonic ecological surveys undertaken during 2024 across Southern England, I investigate the roots of barbastelle bat species decline, how sonic and visual worlds are entangled through new technological listening architectures, and how listening to the thick excesses of these representations can foster new collective and non-extractive listening bodies. The insights and reflections that accompany each of the following sections emerge from my position as an ecological bat surveyor within the UK conservation and ecological consultancy sector.

SONIC EXTRACTION

27 JUNE 2024, 22:28,
SURREY, UK.
LOW ACTIVITY/MODERATE.
POSSIBLE EMERGENCE FROM BARB—AT
22:28. PASSES + FORAGING FROM COMMON
PIPS FROM HEDGE BEHIND. PASSES
FROM SEROTINE AND NOCTULE
AND MYOTIS SPECIES?

Four of us are out in the fading light, surveying a suburban home, listening to the static buzz from a bat detector whilst looking up at a tiled roof ridge. We are listening to the ultrasonic range of the acoustic spectrum (20 kHz to 120 kHz), transposed by microphones into registers humans can hear (20 Hz to 20 kHz). Simultaneously, we listen to each other's verbal orientations through our handheld radios. A surveyor calls, a flash occurs in their peripheral vision, and the translated call sounds out as a flurry of electronic beeps. The microphone application identifies the flash as a western barbastelle bat (*Barbastellus barbastellus*) through its inbuilt species auto-identification. As surveyors, we perform a recognition-making practice using echolocations and visual sightings to locate the material crevice from which the bat emerged on the building's roof.[1]

Making sensible biotic subjects and determining ecological baselines through surveying is a basic tenet of conservation practice. Yet, during the last twenty years, a privatised ecology sector has emerged, facilitated by the expansion of planning and construction developments. It employs a neoliberal framework, prioritising the conservation of legally protected species and habitats while permitting the destruction of others deemed less favourable as long as mitigation of loss is 'compensated'. Sound has become a fundamental tool in helping establish baselines (especially within bat surveying), where more-than-human worlds that exist beyond the perceptual capacities of human sensing are made audible, thus demanding ecological protection. Sensing the echolocations of barbastelles enables us to listen

1 The process of emitting sound waves and listening to echoes that reflect off of the material surroundings to aid spatial orientation.

to the depletion of ecological value through colonial extraction. But even the process of listening is subjected to neoliberal governance, as sound is categorised and translated into tradeable currency.

The barbastelle bat that emerged from the roof crevice is classed as 'vulnerable' in the UK under the ICUN protection classification. Barbastelles typically favour old growth (predominantly oak) woodland for day and maternity-colony roosting. Yet, like the majority of UK bat species, they have adapted to inhabit built architectures due to habitat loss. A 2023 scientific paper reported a species decline of 99% in the past 330 to 548 years.[2] A decline that correlates with agricultural expansion as well as the extensive ship-building programmes that extracted hardwoods for British colonial expansion. This maritime architecture required naturally curved and 'outsized' mature oak limbs for bolstering the ship's internal structure.[3] Sourcing these arboreal architectural features became a priority of forest and environmental surveying.[4] Consequently, extensive areas of old growth forest were depleted and fragmented throughout the mid-sixteenth to mid-nineteenth centuries, disrupting barbastelle roost networks in the process. Outsized tree limbs housing cracks and irregularities are considered waste by timber economies, yet the crevices formed by loose bark, splits, and deadwood are inhabited by barbastelles and many other species.[5] For barbastelles, these spaces provide sites for day roosts and, crucially, maternity colonies. Maternity colonies are reproductive spaces where the young first learn to listen and perceive the world through sound, recognising and locating their mothers within the colony

An eighteenth century illustration, with the banner reading "Britain's Glory and Protection". A mature (likely oak) tree, standing before a backdrop of naval ships and other vessels, constructed from its timber. Source: University of California at Los Angeles, William Andrews Clark Memorial Library.

2 Marc Besson et al., "Towards the Fully Automated Monitoring of Ecological Communities", *Ecology Letters* 25, no. 12 December 2022): 2753–75.

3 Patrick Melby, "Insatiable Shipyards: The Impact of the Royal Navy on the World's Forests, 1200-1850", Western Oregon University, 2012.

4 "New Forest Shipbuilding", *The Real New Forest Guide*, accessed 10 October 2024, https://newforestguide.uk/history/new-forest-shipbuilding/.

5 Oak trees have significant contributions to biodiversity, supporting at least 2300 species, with 326 recorded species depending upon the trees for their survival. "Oak Trees and Wildlife", Woodland Trust, accessed 18 December 2024, https://www.woodlandtrust.org.uk/trees-woods-and-wildlife/british-trees/oak-tree-wildlife/.

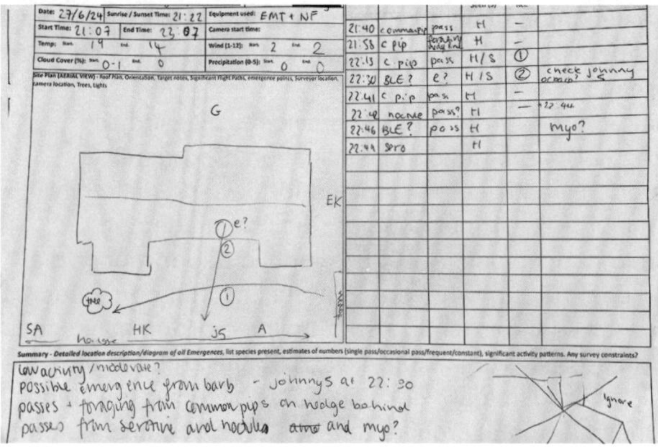

Survey record and notes with time stamps of acoustic and visual records of species present, as well as site plan representing survey activity. All sonic activity is transcribed to text, drawing, or images within field notes, and audio data is reviewed using software such as Kaleidoscope through digitised spectrograms. Source: Image by author, with thanks to Darwin Ecology (2024).

using isolation calls. These calls then develop into echolocations as the bats learn to navigate the negative space of the roost cavity, and later, the surrounding woodland habitat through flight.[6] For barbastelles, these spaces, therefore, foster the development of listening cultures and sonic ways of inhabiting the world.

Attuning to this species through echolocation and through sonically oriented surveying practices ruptures modern colonial conceptions of these sites as mere resources; instead, it values these material structures and negative architectures as sonic habitats. When sonic surveying is only used to produce taxonomic baselines that separate out species, their location, and habitat type, these complex life worlds remain hidden—allowing neoliberal logics to render them as consumable products: silent, replaceable, and tradeable.

LISTENING WITH ALGORITHMS

12 AUGUST 2024, 21:54, 20 DEGREES, CLEAR SKIES. DOGS BARKING TO THE SOUTH, AND THE CONSISTENT HUM OF THE M25 MOTORWAY BEYOND.

I'm walking through thick grass on an old landfill site which has been approved for the construction of film studios, while I stare at a smartphone screen of scrolling frequencies. Through a patterning of colour and saturation, I decipher signal relations and echolocation from 'noise', separating the biological signal of a brown long-eared bat passing overhead from the surrounding acoustic milieu. Deciphering these calls requires multiple registers of transduction and transposition that has increasingly become algorithmic as acoustic flux is converted into durational pressure waves and metricised into statistical data, which in turn is represented as two-dimensional spectrograms. These computational tools make visible the inhabitations of (ultra)acoustic space by more-than-humans. They also afford forensic and poly-perspectival analysis by registering the wider contextual environment, its meteorology, anthrophony,

6 Neil Middleton, Andrew Froud, & Keith French, *Social Calls of the Bats of Britain and Ireland* (Pelagic, 2014).

Ecological surveying, Surrey, UK. Echolocations are transposed to human audible frequencies through ultrasonic microphone applications (Wildlife Acoustics), then transcribed into written survey notes. The records can be used for regulatory licensing to mitigate the impacts of new construction and architectural development by replacing or relocating habitats. Source: Image by author, with thanks to Darwin Ecology (June 2024).

and the materiality of the surrounding architectural space (albeit abstracted) within a single frame.

Planning authorities are increasingly mandating the use of these technologies in developing methodological baselines that prioritise listening for species presence. Other contextual registrations remain either silent or are relegated to 'noise' within this framework. During this technological process, an oculocentric mode of knowledge transference is reinstated to accelerate user interaction and analysis, giving precedence to what is seen on screen over what is heard in the recording. Within these logics, a folded non-Euclidean space of vibratory flux is hierarchised, categorised, and spatially separated into foreground and background, severing the active biological signal from its environmental milieu.

The use of these applications and processes has transformed the interpretation of metric and statistical data, with computation increasingly relying on algorithmic auto-identification systems trained on acoustic indices or deep Convolutional Neural Networks (CNN). A type of deep learning architecture, CNNs learn to search and identify acoustic patterns and audio events that match annotated datasets associated with species-specific vocalisations or ecosystem dynamics.[7] While they directly analyse audio recordings to identify events, they nevertheless rely upon the spectrogram to perform their analysis, embedding its visual and geometric spatial logics into their output models. Not merely measuring sound, they learn to recognise ecological events as numerical relations, constructing a "bridge between the vibrational phenomenon of sound, the computational domain of signal processing, and the cultural level of interpretation".[8]

Echoes, like all sounds, are emergent temporal processes used for orientation, communication, and expression. Whilst the work of surveyors is to locate echolocation calls from an ongoing milieu of vibrations, surveyors repeatedly note that they are unable to discern species difference through the unique timbre, tone, and rhythm of its transduced sound, and rely on the patterning of visualised representations. At stake in these re-cognitions is the question of how sonic knowledges are reproduced in the process. What alternative listening methods and sites of hearing might be required for attending to sonic relations that cannot be translated or represented through these parameters? Remembering that vibration defies anthropocentric categories, listening

7 Thanks to Vincent Lostlanlen for email correspondence on spectrogram and CNN processes, noting spectrograms can serve as a (very) crude mechanistic model of the response of the cochlea (September, 2024).

8 Domenico Napolitano & Renato Grieco, "The Folded Space of Machine Listening", *SoundEffects* 10, no. 1 (2021): 185.

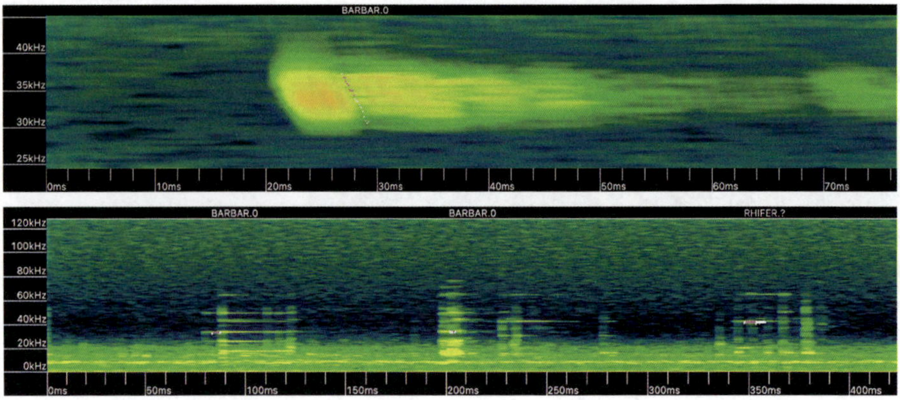

Top, spectrographic representation and auto ID analysis of a barbastelle call and echo with highlighted points in pink matching parameters correlating to barbastelle call patterns; Bottom, misidentified barbastelle call using the same auto ID parameters. Source: Image by author (June 2024).

to the ecological dynamics of a *vibroscape* might offer a pedagogical proposition, one that holds open sonic worlds and relations that exist within the margins and surplus of audibility and perception.[9] If, as theorist Kathryn Yusoff notes, the "knowledge surplus of biotic worlds is not simply a problematic that marks ecology, but its overwhelming condition", how can we find modes of re-cognition beyond 'our' technical abilities to make more-than-human worlds intelligible.[10] This might require developing thick listening practices that are resistant to sonic reduction.

PEDAGOGY OF THE CHORUS

15 JULY 2024, 06:54,
#10
START: 06:45
END: 09:50
TEMP: 22 DEGREES
CLOUD COVER: 0
PRECIPITATION: 0
WIND: 0

In a woodland glade, coppiced and undergoing forest management, two gurgling calls permeate the punctured metal fence erected to keep out deer. The bark of a hidden deer reverberates through the surrounding oak trees. I am not familiar with the gurgle, nor know what specific bird species made it. It folds into the ongoing acoustic flux of the dawn chorus. My smartphone, however, detects the call, listening through the open-source bird sound identification app Merlin. It identifies it as a greater whitethroat—a summer migrant species from the Sahel in Africa.

9 "The entire set of substrate or airborne vibrations that is present in a specific portion of a geographical area." Almo Farina, Alice Eldridge, & Peng Li, "Ecoacoustics and Multispecies Semiosis: Naming, Semantics, Semiotic Characteristics, and Competencies", *Biosemiotics* 14, no. 1 (April 2021): 141–65.

10 Kathryn Yusoff, "Insensible Worlds: Postrelational Ethics, Indeterminacy and the (k)Nots of Relating", *Environment and Planning D: Society and Space* 31, no. 2 (April2013): 209.

The whitethroat's call performs a sonic territory, constantly being iterated through the bird's participation with the thick patterning of the chorus.

If listening to ecological dynamics and biodiversity now inhabits a new space produced by socio-technical networks, it is one that disturbs the binaries and boundaries of organism and machine. Functioning as highly distributed systems of knowledge production, these listening architectures comprise constellations of CNNs, human and non-human listening acts, prosthetic cochleae, material architectures, and (affective) atmospherics of the situated location. Coordinating these to make sense of inaudible dynamics requires collective and critical practices of listening—ones that contribute to new forms of acoustic commoning. Yet within ecological surveying and the sciences, sonic events are increasingly being figured as an index of biodiversity and have thus become sites of transcription and data extraction. The knowledge produced from such remote and passive sensing is rarely one of vibrational participation. Instead, sonic events are configured as techno-social apparatuses: constituted within numerical code, forged out of minerals that make up microphone arrays, mediated by atmospheric conditions that propagate sound waves, and subjected to sociocultural processes that extract meaning from them. Listening to the ways in which these do or do not recognise the thick registrations of the chorus and the acoustic materiality of sonic worlds poses questions of knowledge acquisition and transference. Sonic worlds are inherently relational, and choruses are pedagogical spaces. They are not only a composition of acoustic flux, but also invitations to contribute collectively to political, social, and epistemological reorientation. Throughout the glade in front of me, the whitethroat reiterates its call again, and again, and again, always pausing, then modulating its call before offering its response.

WORKS CITED

Besson, Marc, Jamie Alison, Kim Bjerge, Thomas E. Gorochowski, Toke T. Høye, Tommaso Jucker, Hjalte M. R. Mann, & Christopher F. Clements. "Towards the Fully Automated Monitoring of Ecological Communities". *Ecology Letters* 25, no. 12 (December 2022): 2753–75.

Napolitano, Domenico, & Renato Grieco. "The Folded Space of Machine Listening". *SoundEffects* 10, no. 1 (2021): 173–89.

Farina, Almo, Alice Eldridge, & Peng Li. "Ecoacoustics and Multispecies Semiosis: Naming, Semantics, Semiotic Characteristics, and Competencies". *Biosemiotics* 14, no. 1 (April 2021): 141–65.

Melby, Patrick. "Insatiable Shipyards: The Impact of the Royal Navy on the World's Forests, 1200-1850". Western Oregon University, 2012.

Middleton, Neil, Andrew Froud, & Keith French. *Social Calls of the Bats of Britain and Ireland.* Pelagic, 2014.

The Real New Forest Guide. "New Forest Shipbuilding". Accessed 10 October 2024. https://newforestguide.uk/history/new-forest-shipbuilding/.

Woodland Trust. "Oak Trees and Wildlife". Accessed 18 December 2024.
https://www.woodlandtrust.org.uk/trees-woods-and-wildlife/british-trees/oak-tree-wildlife/

Yusoff, Kathryn. "Insensible Worlds: Postrelational Ethics, Indeterminacy and the (k)Nots of Relating". *Environment and Planning D: Society and Space* 31, no. 2 (April 2013): 208–26.

SENSING SEAWEED AND PRACTISING PHOTOGRAPHY DIFFERENTLY

Sam Nightingale

Seaweed and photography have an entangled history, from Anna Atkins's blue cyanotypes of seaweed specimens to the iodine used by Louis Daguerre to reveal some of the first photographic images. In their differing ways, seaweeds and photography are sensory media: they sense, capture, and transform light, and they both have the potential to record traces of environmental change. This text outlines a creative research practice I call *para-photo-mancy*, which responds to seaweed as a substrate that senses and stores traces of environmental events in its morphological structure. Here, I place seaweeds' ability to sense and modulate light in relation to photography's chemical history, which is rooted in extracting minerals and using plants to make light-sensitive substrates. I consider *para-photo-mancy* an experimental method to reconfigure and reimagine representational modes of photography that provides both an alternative visual approach to environmental photography and the iconography of planetary crises, typified by the large-scale 'Anthropocene' photography of Edward Burtynsky[1] while also recognising photography's reliance (in its digital and analogue forms) on material extraction and fossil fuel consumption, which equally contribute to environmental degradation. Even in its attempt to record planetary crises, photography becomes part of the problem.[2]

In my practice, I explore photographic methods that push the boundaries of what is usually understood as photography (involving cameras, lenses, light, representation, and so on).[3] It is a practice that involves enfolding various minerals and organic matter into experimental photochemical processes as a method to think *and practice* photography differently. Working directly with seaweeds and other plants directly in photochemical image-making also offers a correlation between image production and the site of production, which I use to facilitate conversations about the environmental and material histories that have shaped the ecologies of these locations. Recently, this has led me to investigate the photochemical capacities of seaweeds, creating strange hybrid *para*-photographic images that are generated not by light (as we might expect from photography) but produced instead through a chemical reaction taking place between the polyphenols (compounds produced by plants and algae) in seaweeds and the sensitised silver-halide crystals

1 For example, Edward Burtynsky's *Silver Lake Operations #15, Lake Lefroy, Western Australia, 2007*, www.edwardburtynsky.com/projects/photographs/mines.

2 T. J. Demos, "Photography in/of the Anthropocene", in *Widening the Lens: Photography, Ecology, and the Contemporary Landscape*, ed. Dan Leers (Carnegie Museum of Art, 2024).

3 By this, I produce images that resemble photographs but are made with non-standard photographic materials, such as salt, plants, soil, and algae, and created without light or cameras.

Seaweed as sensitised medium. Source: Image by author (2019).

Laying out seaweed samples in a photographic developing tray. Source: Image by author (2022).

Tiree, Scottish Hebrides. In Gallic, the island is known as *tìr bàrr fo thuinn*, "the island whose top lies below the waves", a name that conjures the image of a submerged land, made as much of water as it is of solid ground. Source: Image by author (2022).

My abode on Tiree is a traditional crofter's cottage. In the eighteenth century, many of the seasonal workers who came to harvest seaweed also lived in structures like these. Source: Image by author (2022).

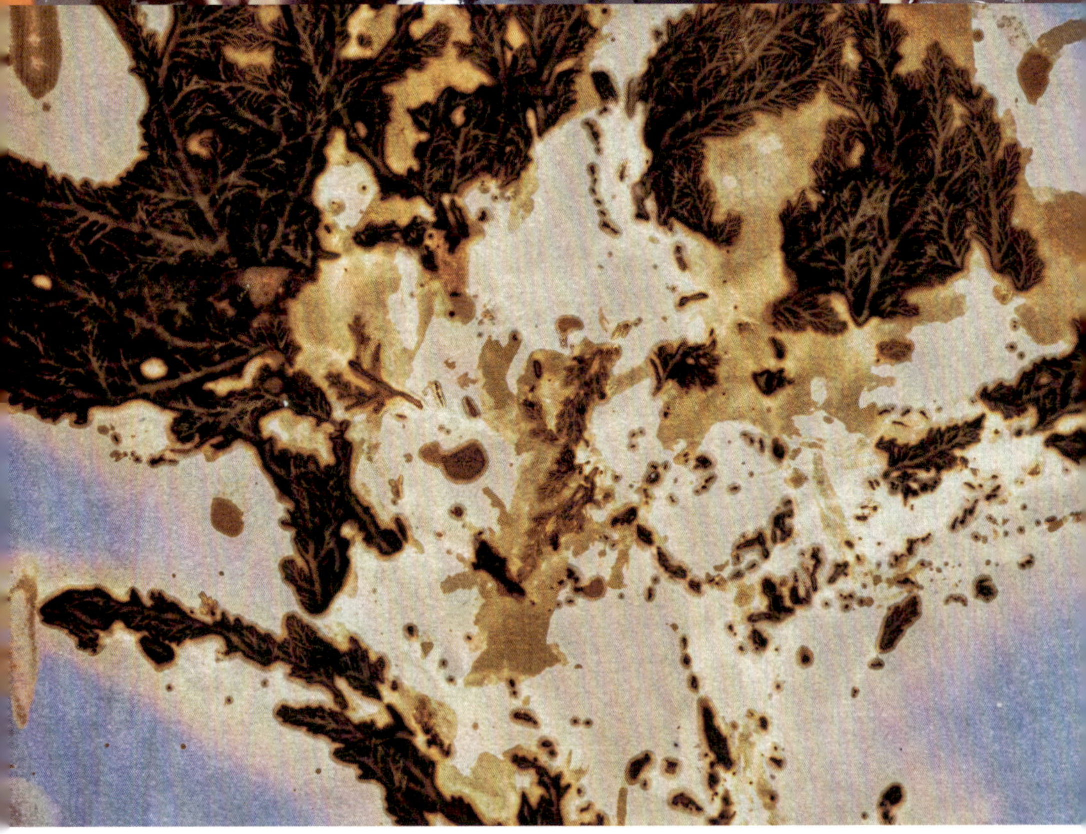

Washing sheets of photographic film. Source: Image by author (2022).
Para-photo-mancy (Ocean). Source: Image by author (2022).

held within black and white film emulsion. When combined in this way, the seaweed and film emulsion generate distinctive visual expressions. The primary site of this research is in the Scottish Hebrides, where I have been using *para-photo-mancy* to look at climate change, biodiversity, and the large-scale extraction of seaweeds that that are currently threatening the region, viewing these issues in tandem with the material history of seaweed harvesting that took place in the Hebrides during the eighteenth century and how chemicals derived from that industry, such as sodium carbonate and iodine, have been used in photochemistry.

Seaweed harvesting, known locally as kelping, began in the Hebrides during the eighteenth century.[4] The kelping industry provided employment to thousands of seasonal workers who came to harvest seaweed in the Hebrides each year. It was also a lucrative business for the landowners who benefited from selling this valuable resource to the chemical industry, where extracts from seaweeds were commonly used in manufacturing glass and detergents. The global demand for sodium carbonate drove much harvesting in the Hebrides: sodium carbonate can be obtained by burning seaweed (and certain other salt-tolerant plants) at high temperatures.[5] Workers waded through the ocean gathering seaweeds as they washed up on the shoreline—often having to carry it over long distances by horse and cart before the tangled web of algae was burnt in stone pits where it crystallised into a hard crystalline mass of sodium carbonate. However, in 1791, the chemist Nicolas Leblanc discovered a more cost-effective method to synthesise sodium carbonate from common salt.[6] This discovery essentially ended kelping on the islands, leading to the forced removal of workers in a brutal process known as the Highland Clearances, as croft owners cleared the land, turning it over to livestock grazing.[7] In the nineteenth century, there was a brief revival of harvesting activities when it was discovered that iodine could be extracted from seaweed. Both sodium carbonate and iodine have long been used as active agents in photochemistry, which continues today.[8]

As I researched and experimented with the chemical relationship between seaweeds, sodium carbonate, and photography, I started to learn about how changes in demand and the technology involved in seaweed harvesting are threatening marine environments in the Hebrides. Recently, there has been renewed interest in commercial seaweed harvesting in the region; on a local level, this tends to involve sustainable farming practices that encourage regrowth. However, more concerning are plans for larger-scale extraction that promise to provide a blue economy for the region. If such plans go ahead, the mechanical dredging equipment needed would far outstrip the methods employed during the eighteenth and nineteenth centuries. It signals a technological transformation that moves from harvesting done by hand, carefully attuned to seasons and species, to industrial extraction that will remove vast quantities of seaweeds and kelp

4 Kelp is a species of brown seaweed; however, in the context of *kelping* in the Hebrides, 'kelp' refers to a finished product.

5 Sodium carbonate is an alkali that takes the form of a hard crystalline mass derived from the drying and firing of several species of seaweed. J. Wisniak, "Sodium Carbonate - From Natural Resources to Leblanc and Back", *Indian Journal of Chemical Technology* 10, no. 1 (2003): 99–112.

6 Wisniak, "Sodium Carbonate".

7 For the history and context of The Highland Clearances, see Eric Richards, *History of the Highland Clearances: Agrarian Transformation and the Evictions, 1746-1886* (Routledge, 1982).

8 For example, Kodak D-19 black and white film developer uses sodium carbonate, as do many other photographic developers. Sodium carbonate is increasingly used in ecologically friendly homemade photographic developers, such as the caffenol process, which combines coffee, ascorbic acid, and sodium carbonate.

forests for use in bioremediation processes and as biofuel. Without sustainable management, such operations have the potential for over-extraction and deforestation, causing devastating effects on ocean biodiversity and contributing to coastal erosion on many islands.[9]

In the Hebrides, seaweeds' innate ability to sense, record, and modulate light guides and shapes my art-based research practice. Seaweeds' capacity for photosynthesis lends itself to thinking about seaweeds as not only sensory media but also operating as a hybrid photographic substrate. It is an analogy that media scholar Melody Jue makes when suggesting saturation is a precondition for both seaweeds and cyanotypes—a proto-photographic technique used by botanist Anna Atkins in the 1840s to make impressions of seaweeds and other flora.[10] Seaweeds and photographic images need light to exist—they modulate light for a particular outcome. Seaweeds thrive by drawing energy from light. A sensitised photographic surface literally draws an image out of light. However, it is not only the need for light that tangles seaweed and photography in the same media ecology; it is also how seaweed is chemically entangled in the history of photochemistry. The chemicals derived from seaweed "saturate"[11]—to use Jue's term—the material history of photochemistry: in photographic developing agents containing sodium carbonate, in Atkins' cyanotypes, and in Louis Daguerre's daguerreotypes—a precursor to modern photography—that involved using iodine vapours to generate photosensitive surfaces on sheets of silver-plated copper.

While on the island of Tiree, in the Hebrides, I worked from one of the old crofter's cottages, well placed next to the ruins of the former seaweed factory once used to process the sodium carbonate before being shipped. Each day, traversing the wind-blown island, I would gather seaweed, following in the footsteps of those who did this two hundred years ago. Like those before me, I searched for species—such as bladderwrack, sugar kelp, and dulse—which had been ripped from their holdfasts and left floating in the intertidal zone, or washed up onshore. Returning to the crofter's cottage, I followed a process of saturating the seaweed in a solution of ascorbic acid and seawater before laying the samples onto sheets of photographic film; the process of soaking initiates an alchemic fusion of alkaloids and acids that mimics the way traditional photochemical developers function.

Unlike regular photographs, which use light to inscribe images onto film emulsion, a cocktail of alkaloids and acids makes images visible through a molecular interaction between the polyphenols and silver-halide crystals in the photographic emulsion. The results resemble photographic images, however, they differ in that they emerge without optics or light; instead, the internal chemistry of seaweed generates a *para*-photographic image.

In the long walks along the shoreline, immersing my arms and hands in the freezing waters as I gathered seaweed, and later in the slow process-based work of *para-photo-mancy*, I was purposefully enacting some of the traditional practices of kelping that had once taken place on these islands. Coming to know seaweed on a chemical and material level, I discovered it is not only sodium carbonate that is crystallised but also stories of social and environmental change, such as the transformation from traditional harvesting practices to those of industrial-scale extraction of seaweeds. The *para-photo-mancy* images are not representational—

9 "Seaweed Harvesting", NatureScot, accessed 22 August 2024, www.nature.scot/professional-advice/land-and-sea-management/managing-coasts-and-seas/seaweed-harvesting.

10 Melody Jue, "The Media of Seaweeds: Between Kelp Forest and Archive", in *Saturation: An Elemental Politics*, ed. Melody Jue & Rafico Ruiz (Duke University Press, 2021), 185-204.

11 Jue, "The Media of Seaweeds".

in the way we typically think of a photographic image showing something that once sat before a camera—nor do they attend in any scientific way to the anthropogenic markers held within the seaweeds' morphological structure. Instead, *para-photo-mancy* images represent and mediate a process and an encounter in and with a particular environment involving various sensing bodies—human and more-than-human. Here, I want to think of Anna Tsing's description of "passionate immersion" in the lives of more-than-human beings and how the arts of sensing those lives can offer something new.[12] Perhaps this is the task of conjuring a different photographic imaginary to communicate the stories of planetary crises.

Interpreting the effects of a changing climate and anthropogenic activity traced in the morphology of seaweeds attends to the evidence-seeking demands of science, whereas attuning to the cultural histories associated with seaweed harvesting and use involves the work of environmental humanities. However, these disciplines are porous, crossing ecological, material, political, and aesthetic worlds. Drawing on knowledge from science and the humanities while combining (and often disrupting) it with art-based research and fieldwork is not only where my practice is situated; it is becoming increasingly essential to navigate, respond, and make sense of planetary crises outside of traditional representational modes.[13] Seaweeds can be considered 'media' because of their ability to register and store data about climatic and environmental events within their molecular structure. Enfolding seaweeds in the photographic processes involved in *para-photo-mancy* is a way to foreground their capacity to hold stories, histories, and speculations within them.

12 Anna Tsing, "Arts of Inclusion, or, How to Love a Mushroom", *Australian Humanities Review*, 50 (2011): 5–21.

13 For more on the role of art practice and art-based research in fieldwork, see Bridget Crone, Sam Nightingale, & Polly Stanton, eds, *Fieldwork for Future Ecologies: Radical Practice for Art and Art-Based Research* (Onomatopee, 2024).

WORKS CITED

Crone, Bridget, Sam Nightingale, & Polly Stanton, eds. *Fieldwork for Future Ecologies: Radical Practice for Art and Art-Based Research*. Onomatopee, 2024.

Demos, T. J. "Photography in/of the Anthropocene". In *Widening the Lens: Photography, Ecology, and the Contemporary Landscape*, edited by Dan Leers. Carnegie Museum of Art, 2024.

Jue, Melody. "The Media of Seaweeds: Between Kelp Forest and Archive". In *Saturation: An Elemental Politics*, edited by Melody Jue & Rafico Ruiz. Duke University Press, 2021.

NatureScot. "Seaweed Harvesting". Accessed 22 August 2024. www.nature.scot/professional-advice/land-and-sea-management/managing-coasts-and-seas/seaweed-harvesting.

Nightingale, Sam. "Seetang". *Zeitschrift für Medienwissenschaft* 16, no. 1 (2024): 103-106.

Richards, Eric. *History of the Highland Clearances: Agrarian Transformation and the Evictions, 1746-1886*. Routledge, 1982.

Tsing, Anna. "Arts of Inclusion, or, How to Love a Mushroom". *Australian Humanities Review*, 50 (2011): 5–21.

Wisniak, J. "Sodium Carbonate - From Natural Resources to Leblanc and Back". *Indian Journal of Chemical Technology* 10, no. 1 (2003): 99–112.

SENSING ECOLOGIES OF DISPOSSESSION

Al-Wah'at Collective

A large *sabr* (prickly pear cactus) hedge grows in the centre of Ein Qinya, Palestine. Source: Image by Gabriella Demczuk (2023).

AILO RIBAS The three of us met in 2021 at the Centre for Research Architecture (CRA) on the MA programme. We were all working with plants, and so we started spending multiple afternoons a week working on our projects, giving each other feedback and sharing ideas over food. While our work brought us together, it was our shared love of food and cooking—with our common Mediterranean heritage—that drew us closer. Cooking and sharing elaborate meals quickly became the singular focus of the time we spent together and, I would say, heavily influenced our practice.

AREEJ ASHHAB Gathering recipes and cooking was an important element of my dissertation project at the CRA, as I looked into the role of trees as political beings and storytellers in Palestine; a perspective that I sought to develop beyond the manufactured landscapes of the Jewish National Fund (JNF) forests that were planted to conceal Palestinian villages destroyed in 1948. These recipes provided new ways of engaging with the land and the trees planted to transform it, activating and centering local knowledge. Culinary relationships are often reflected in local names, such as *qreish*, meaning crunchy—the Arabic name for the Aleppo pine tree, which is frequently associated with the Zionist occupier due to its extensive use in JNF forests and whose seeds are used in the elaboration of a beloved Palestinian sweet, *malban*. Documenting these names and relationships becomes a challenging task in a world where scientific knowledge, often shaped by the extractive logics of colonialism and capitalism, tends to dominate the language used to describe the more-than-human.

GABRIELLA DEMCZUK The production and domination of scientific knowledge was the starting point of my research at the CRA, where I looked at proprietary modes of abstraction, specifically at the role of biological patents in reshaping the agricultural landscape. I came into this research concerned about the effects of climate change on food security, effects we are now seeing play out in real time.

I was critical of technological solutions that promise quick fixes, especially in the emerging field of genetic engineering, considering that these techno-fixes often come with property rights that restrict public access. Biological patents were an entry point for me to question how the physical world becomes property—the ways in which paperwork uses language and visuals to flatten biological life, converting it into information that the legal system can read, which ultimately creates a property structure around a living entity.

Gaza, lowland stronghold of the Philistines, from the southeast, Palestine. Underwood & Underwood, 1911. A stereoscope depicting a man looking out over agricultural fields in Gaza bordered by *sabr* hedges, stretching into the distance. Source: Library of Congress.

AR Similarly interested in property rights and issues of access, my research at the CRA sought to understand how our relationship to land and to the commons in the UK has been mediated through language—specifically, how the language of otherness has been weaponised to sever our relationships with other people (*witches*), plants (*weeds*), and land (*wastelands*), historically and to this day. Rooting my practice in the contemporary issue of unequal access to nature in the UK, especially in large metropolitan areas such as London, I questioned the inherited misinformation around urban plants, or weeds, and the ways in which urban ecologies have been targeted and villainised. Working closely with Phytology and the wider community of the Bethnal Green Nature Reserve, I organised a series of workshops exploring these issues together with fellow community gardener Chiara Famengo. While many plants growing wild in our cities are dismissed and even become the targets of vicious hate campaigns, many of them have long been sources of food, medicine, and valuable materials. Our generational loss of plant knowledge and land practices is the product of a long colonial and extractivist war on the working classes in the UK that has placed the majority of common land into private hands.

The work we do as a collective similarly straddles and moves between these worlds of people, plants, and land: worlds which inherently seep into and co-create one another, each presenting different modes of sensing what we call *ecologies of dispossession*, or in other words, the network of relations that emerges as living beings and the land itself witness, archive, and resist politics of dispossession.

AA The prickly pear cactus (comprising various species of *Opuntia*)—in Arabic called *sabr*, meaning patience—has been a key guide as we collectively trace

Black cochineal from Oaxaca, Mexico, at the KEW Economic Botany Collection. Source: Image by Gabriella Demczuk (2022).

these ecologies of dispossession across multiple temporalities and geographies: from Mexico where it originates, to Spain where it was capitalised, to Australia where it was villainised as feral and eradicated, and to Palestine where it has resisted multiple attempts at erasure.

Originally planted as hedges in Palestinian villages, used to demarcate property lines and agricultural fields, many of these cacti were uprooted during the Nakba of 1948, when villages across historic Palestine—now known as the 1948 lands—were destroyed and depopulated following a slew of massacres. Years later, these cacti hedges, rooted deep in the earth, have begun to grow back, retracing the boundaries of villages whose ruins have mostly either been removed or purposefully obscured by JNF afforestation. Having survived the massive destruction caused by Zionist militias in 1948, these cacti now face a new threat, that of the false carmine cochineal insect (*Dactylopius opuntiae*) which has recently spread across the Mediterranean. While living symbiotically with the cactus in Mexico, where they both originate, in the Mediterranean the insect has no natural predators, meaning it is left to fully drain the cactus of its water, eventually killing it. Yet, as they wither, these cacti leave material traces behind: their mesh-like fibres; the carminic acid produced by the cochineal insects as they feed on the cactus—the same Red Gold which compelled Spanish conquistadors to bring the cactus to Europe—painting the ground red; new growth emerging from desiccated pads.

GD Many countries are seeking biological controls or pesticides to manage the recent spread of the false carmine cochineal, which only compounds the damage to local ecosystems. Troubled by this, we want to challenge the idea of 'invasiveness', as well as colonial approaches to more-than-human species more broadly, by learning how local ecosystems repair and adapt to changes in their environments. Shifting our perspective and approach to the spread of the cochineal can open up new beneficial avenues for local communities. Travelling together around Palestine in early 2023, we witnessed the material possibilities of these insects and dried cactus fibres on a sensorial level through collecting, weaving, building, dyeing, printing, and cooking, which we brought together into three focused themes—fibres, pigments, and food—in our ongoing project *Wild Hedges*.

AR While the fruits of the cactus are prized in Palestine, the rest of the plant—its succulent pads, and the mesh-like carcasses it leaves behind when dried—as well as the cochineal that live on it are not traditionally used in the region. These practices—gathering dried pads for working with their fibres, harvesting fresh ones for cooking and extracting mucilage, and collecting cochineal for pigment-making—if widespread and sustained, not only present material opportunities for local communities but also help the cacti survive by keeping cochineal populations in check. Regular pruning to increase airflow and light to the cactus, as well as periodic removal of cochineal from its pads,

A tapestry experiment and modular prototype using dried cactus fibres held together with *ixtle* (agave fibres) to create the vertical structure (warp) and *carrizo* (cane) fibres for the horizontal structure (weft). Oaxaca, Mexico. Source: Image by Gabriella Demczuk (2024).

Skeins dyed with cochineal hang to dry on the terrace of Teñido a Mano, Oaxaca, Mexico. Source: Image by Gabriella Demczuk (2024).

Cochineal are cultivated on rows of hanging cactus pads at Artesanos Martinez Mendoza, Teotitlán del Valle, Oaxaca, Mexico. Source: Image by Gabriella Demczuk (2024).

are crucial ways of protecting the cactus and slowing the cochineal's spread without having to resort to more harmful forms of biological control—such as the introduction of natural enemies or the use of pesticides—that damage surrounding ecosystems.

AA In March 2024 we travelled to Oaxaca, the historical centre of cochineal production in Mexico, where we conducted extensive fieldwork and material experimentation to deepen our understanding of the region's traditional practices with both the insect and the cactus. By interweaving traditional basketry techniques using *carrizo* (cane) with cactus fibres, and through collectively experimenting with dyeing processes—particularly exploring the best methods for dyeing cotton with cochineal—we uncovered the material possibilities that could feed into our collective practices in rural Palestine. A cactus that originated in Mexico has become naturalised in the Mediterranean, where it is now a political symbol in Palestine, while it was eradicated as an invasive species in Australia. Similarly, an insect cherished in Mexico was used as a tool for eradication in Australia and is now viewed as a pest in the Mediterranean. As we navigate these disparate geographies, we encounter critical questions: how do species move between places? What forces drive their movement, and to what end? What do more-than-human beings reveal about preconceived notions of 'nativeness' and 'invasiveness'?

AR Instead of seeing the current spread of cochineal across the Mediterranean as a plague, as simply an ecological problem requiring an ecological solution—as many scientists, farmers and governments across the region view it—we want to draw attention to it being the direct result of colonial mechanisms and the ecologies of dispossession that emerge in their wake. As the product of what happens when states move botanical and animal species from one territory to another for economic gain, and later abandon or move to eradicate them once they no longer serve the state's interests, passing them off as 'invasive' in justification. It is not the plant, nor the insect, but rather the extractive actions of colonial states that are truly invasive.

AA With the ongoing genocide and ecocide in Gaza and Palestine, where lives, homes, and environments are violently torn apart, the forces of settler colonialism are laid bare—not just in the mass killing and displacement of human bodies, but in the dispossession and destruction of the land and its ecosystems. Yet, Palestinians continue to return to the land, its soil, seeds, and herbs for survival. They remind us of the importance of nurturing resilient ecologies and relationships, rooted in care and reciprocity, as acts of resistance against the colonial forces that seek to erase both human and more-than-human worlds.

GD In Palestine, with this in mind, we collected healthy *sabr* pads from destroyed and depopulated villages in 1948 lands, later planting them along the stone wall perimeter at Sakiya in Ein Qinya with the local community in hopes that they will grow into a strong hedge. This not only protects the site from settler raids but also serves as a living memorial to those who came before. These communal and collective practices that sustain the cactus, its surrounding ecology, and the local community–what we see as practices of care–counter and resist dispossession.

Participants gather for lunch before the start of an experimentation workshop using the sabr fibers and cochineal at Sakiya in Ein Qinya, Palestine. Source: Image by Yasmine Omari (2023).

Workshop participants plant *sabr* pads along the perimeter at Sakiya in Ein Qinya, Palestine. The pads will form a hedge to safeguard against Israeli settler attacks and memorialize the destroyed and depopulated Palestinian villages from which they were collected. Source: Image by Yasmine Omari (2023).

COUNTER-MAPPING AND ITS SHADOW

Naiza Khan

THE MAP IS LIKE THE X-RAY OF THE BODY

13 March 2013, Karachi, Pakistan: Perween Rahman, a social activist, architect, urban planner, and director of the Orangi Pilot Project - Research and Training Institute (OPP-RTI) was shot by four gunmen near her office.

The following reflections and fieldnotes are situated in the specific spatial and political geography of the Orangi Pilot Project (OPP) in Karachi, a cluster of low-income settlements with an estimated population of 2.4 million. The success of the OPP was realised by implementing five basic programs of low-cost sanitation, housing, health, education, and credit for microenterprises. The question of land security, belonging, and social justice—a basic human need—was at the heart of her killing.

For me, Rahman's work was positioned at the intersection of multiple forces; in particular, that of postcolonial feminist and environmental justice struggles. And so, I invoke her life and the work of OPP to raise a set of questions and open a dialogue with other transnational discourses which are crucially linked to social justice and Indigenous political organising and resistance within the Global South.

23 February 2013, Bangkok, Thailand: The last public address given by Perween Rahman at the Asian Coalition for Housing Rights regional gathering, just weeks before she was shot. I am interested in the language she uses and the way she migrates the terms of geographical mapping to a corporeal connection, one that is not easily translatable but is nonetheless rooted in her own experience. Her comparison of a map of the lanes of Orangi to an X-ray of a body creates frictions which intertwine the process of walking and the X-ray's primary functions of scanning and diagnosing. The metaphor of the X-ray renders visible something that cannot be seen, or that has been obscured. Through the act of making something perceptible it becomes a tool for change and transformation.

> *[W]ith the map we became visible, it made the government take us seriously. So that's the power of the map. The map is our eyes, it is like the X-ray, it tells us what to do, where to go, who to lobby.*[1]

Rahman has to physically walk the lanes of Orangi Town to understand her environment, as a way of sensing common and uncommon ground. She is drawing on paper as she goes along, involved in a process of embodied mapping to actually locate herself in the context of Orangi, because she is an outsider to that community. So there is a learning through the act of walking; something seen at

1 The last public address by Perween Rahman, at the Asian Coalition for Housing Rights (ACHR) regional gathering on the 23 February 2013 in Bangkok, Thailand. Perween Rahman, "We are all ninja turtles of mapping", Asian Coalition for Housing Rights (ACHR), February 2013, http://www.achr.net/upload/downloads/file_13122013114415.pdf.

Perween Rahman at a site meeting in Orangi with members of Sindh Katchi Abadi Authority (SKAA) and residents of the area in late 1990s. Source: Image courtesy of Arif Hasan.
View from the Madrassa on Sher Pahaar (Lion Hill), Muslim Nagar, Sector 14-G, Orangi Town, during a field trip after Covid-19 in 2021. Source: Image by author.

Perween Rahman at a site meeting in Orangi with members of Sindh Katchi Abadi Authority (SKAA) and residents of the area in late 1990s. Source: Image courtesy of Arif Hasan.

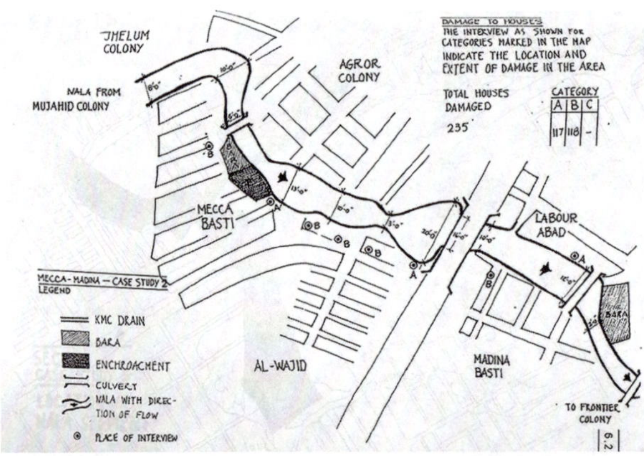

Low-Cost Sanitation Programme. Maintenance/ Rectification Report, OPP-RTI March 1991. Source: Image courtesy of Arif Hasan.

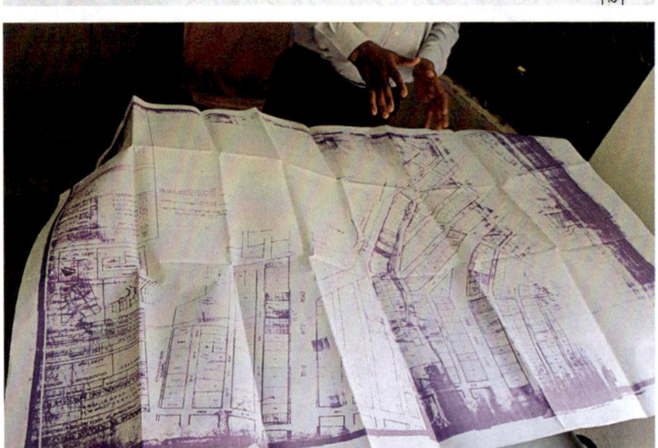

Muhammad Sirajuddin sharing the maps produced at the OPP-RTI office, Orangi Town, 2021. Source: Image by author.

Instruction Manual for Construction of Sewers, made by Ramzan Qureshi, Nadeem Usmani, Saleem Aleemuddin. Source: Images courtesy of Arif Hasan.

the level of the lane is documented and provides information that can be gathered only through intimate social interaction with the community, and which is different from the expediency that Google Maps offers, where communities can only be located at a distance.

The fact that the State does not map the informal settlements of Karachi is a clear political decision that becomes an obfuscation of knowledge as well as a passive form of slow violence, whereby basic infrastructures are withheld.[2] Rahman uses the analogy of the body to redress and resist the lack of political will in the governance system, "as if the State is conducting surgery on the body, without an X-ray".[3] The maps produced by the OPP-RTI[4] are 'counter' to the official maps; they are the means to collate data and reveal the gaps, as well as the true state of the settlement or body of land.

Within the traditional neighbourhoods of the settlement, Rahman's presence as a woman enabled her greater access to the domestic spaces within the community. As her mentor and colleague, architect Arif Hasan recounts, "she was able to befriend families rather than just individuals. She knew the social organisers, their families and children, meeting their wives, going to their homes. Wherever she worked there was a link with the house. All this brought a new dimension to the Orangi Pilot Project."[5]

The pedagogic dimension of Rahman's project is exemplified by the ways she had to learn and unlearn in order to establish trust with the community. In this way, the *walking map* is a method that produces a process of 'unlearning' the landscape, while at the same time reinscribing it with new potentialities. Geographer Tariq Jazeel suggests "that landscape conceived as a description of space bounds the concept to a specific spatiality, a spatiality that we suggest might in certain contexts need to be reconsidered or, 'unlearned' to include the views of other stakeholders, users, and communities."[6]

COUNTER-MAPPING AS A POLITICAL TOOL

In interviews with mentors and students who worked with OPP-RTI, there is an emphasis on participatory methods within the community, training the youth to map their settlements and encouraging the active participation of women through savings groups. They acknowledge the importance of the walking map, which functioned in multiple ways, and show the visible contribution of the community in building infrastructure in their neighbourhoods.[7]

At a certain point, the first generation of local community activists who had been working with Parveen and their children got involved. Parveen realised

2 See Rob Nixon. *Slow Violence and the Environmentalism of the Poor* (Harvard University Press, 2011).

3 Rahman, "We are all ninja turtles of mapping".

4 In 1987 OPP was divided into four sections. OPP Research and Training Institute (OPP-RTI), with Perween as its director, carried out Sanitation, Water, Mapping and Youth Training Programs.

5 Extract from an interview with Arif Hasan, architect, planner, activist, social researcher, writer, and chairperson of the Orangi Pilot Project-Research & Training Institute, Karachi. Arif Hasan, interview by Naiza Khan, December 2018, audio.

6 Daniel A. Friess and Tariq Jazeel, "Unlearning 'Landscape'", *Annals of the American Association of Geographers* 107, no. 1: 14–21.

7 Extract from interview with Professor Noman Ahmed, Chairperson of Department of Architecture and Planning at NED University, Karachi. Noman Ahmed, interview by Naiza Khan, 2020, online.

> *the best way of outreach and replication of knowledge through the mapping process being generated at the OPP-RTI was not to force architects from the outside to get involved, but create para-architects from within the community. These were the youth who were identified by the social activists and the social organisers of the OPP.*[8]

In the maps they created for the Low-Cost Sanitation Programme, a numerical marker in the corner pins the location of the interviews, which were a vital source for gathering data specific to the ground. This process of mapping became an urgent political tool and was the cornerstone that formed the participatory model of learning, mobilisation, and advocacy for the community.[9]

The role of women in mapping is further emphasised in Rahman's address at the conference in Bangkok. "She maps her villages in the flood-affected areas. All of us are a mixture of people living in the community, people [who] have community-based organisations, so the map helps us build up relationships."[10] Here, women and nature are seen as structurally and materially intertwined; the fact that women do most of the domestic work puts them in an integral relation with environmental questions of health, food, safety, and water quality.[11] The illustrations in the Manual for Sanitation produced by the OPP makes visible the important role of women in mobilising community within the urban settlement.

How can the process of counter-mapping become a way to redress the inequality and exclusionary policies of a colonial present? In her essay on counter–mapping forest territories in Kalimantan, Indonesia, in the 1990s, Nancy Peluso states that:

> *maps can be used to pose alternatives to the languages and images of power and become a medium of empowerment or protest... 'counter-maps' as I call them here, greatly increase the power of people living in a mapped area to control representations of themselves and their claims to resources... Counter-maps thus have the potential for challenging the omissions of human settlements from forest maps, for contesting the homogenization of space on political, zoning, or property maps, for altering the categories of land and forest management, and for expressing social relationships in space rather than depicting abstract space in itself.*[12]

A stronger coupling of research and activism over the last two decades has created solidarities between environmental defence and broader Indigenous counter-mapping, where human and land rights lawsuits have been woven together with participatory politics.[13] Here, it is useful to consider Abdul Maliq Simone's notion of *people as infrastructure*, and to repurpose this phrase to think about walking as the sharing of embodied knowledge; to see the passing of knowledge across generations as creating a very different kind of infrastructure, one built by the community's material and embodied contributions.

8 Extract from interview with Professor Asiya Sadiq Polack, architect-urbanist-academic, PhD Scholar and visiting professor at Faculty of Architecture, KU Leuven. Asiya Sadiq Polack, interview by Naiza Khan, 2020, online.

9 Audre Lorde, *The master's tools will never dismantle the master's house* (Penguin UK, 2018).

10 Rahman, "We are all ninja turtles of mapping".

11 Chitra Sankaran, "Place and Postcolonial Ecofeminism: Pakistani Women's Literary and Cinematic Fictions. By Shazia Rahman", *ISLE: Interdisciplinary Studies in Literature and Environment* 27, no. 2 (2020).

12 Nancy Lee Peluso, "Whose woods are these? Counter-mapping forest territories in Kalimantan, Indonesia", *Antipode* 27, no. 4 (1995): 383-406.

13 Ratna Kapur, "Damming Women's Rights: Gender and the Narmada Valley Projects", *Canadian Woman Studies* 13, no. 3 (1993).

WALKING IN COMMON

During the Covid-19 pandemic, my primary mode of research was a series of interviews I conducted as a means to get close to my fieldwork and field sites. It was also a way to understand the local, situated politics and the materiality of the place. These interviews were also a form of witnessing that sometimes referred to a specific violent act—a trauma, a memory—and as such, also offer testimonies in an attempt to understand and rebuild history.

I began to think about ways of expanding my research through a form of remote practice, which involved generating a set of guidelines for people that I felt were somehow connected to the work of Parveen. So I started storyboarding a chain of virtual encounters, or conversations, that linked time and space with artists, writers, and scholars in different locations. Mapping offered a way forward. I invited each participant to follow a loose set of walking guidelines, which were informed by an understanding of the map as the X-ray of the body. I thought about how each collaborator could move the frame of this storyboard forwards.

Eventually I found myself in the role of mediator within this field of documentation of multiple voices, creating a space for critical reflection between the shadow of my research and a new ambulatory walking practice conducted in common with others. Over a span of time, I received recorded sound moments from the Botanic Gardens in Port of Spain, Trinidad and Tobago; situated accounts and poetic spatialisations of Lahore city from the Lawrence Gardens; and a historical recount of the Po Hing Fong disaster of 1925, the scene of Hong Kong's worst landslide. Walking in common became a method of research that brought Rahman into dialogue with others. Thus, it was also an attempt to make work as an act of inheritance. To think about the ways in which Rahman's body of research could be reactivated through the creation of new forms of mobile knowledge and situated learning.

WORKS CITED

Friess, Daniel A., & Tariq Jazeel. "Unlearning 'landscape'". *Annals of the American Association of Geographers* 107, no. 1 (2017).

Kapur, Ratna. "Damming Women's Rights: Gender and the Narmada Valley Projects". *Canadian Woman Studies/les cahiers de la femme* (1993).

Lorde, Audre. *The master's tools will never dismantle the master's house.* Penguin UK, 2018.

Nixon, Rob. *Slow Violence and the Environmentalism of the Poor.* Harvard University Press, 2011.

Peluso, Nancy Lee. "Whose woods are these? Counter-mapping forest territories in Kalimantan, Indonesia". *Antipode* 27, no. 4 (1995).

Rahman, Perween. "We are all ninja turtles of mapping". *Asian Coalition for Housing Rights (ACHR)*, February 2013. http://www.achr.net/upload/downloads/file_13122013114415.pdf.

Rahman, Shazia. *Place and Postcolonial Ecofeminism: Pakistani Women's Literary and Cinematic Fictions.* University of Nebraska Press, 2019.

LEAD WHITE

Christina Varvia

1

Source: Image courtesy of the National Gallery.

Frederick Wiseman's film *The National Gallery*[1] depicts a scene in which a conservator explains his technical restoration work on a Rembrandt painting. Using a large-scale print of a composite X-radiograph of *Portrait of Frederick Rihel on Horseback* (circa 1663), he shows the original painting discernible in black and white, but also reveals a previous attempt which remains hidden beneath the surface. Art historians and conservators often investigate the materiality of a painting to analyse its production, in particular tracing the use of lead (Pb) in pigments. Lead white was one of the most essential colours for painters until its ban in the twentieth century.[2] Julio Montes-Santiago has researched claims that several successful artists suffered from lead poisoning, which some even assert is responsible for their eccen-

1 Frederick Wiseman, *National Gallery*, documentary (2014).

2 Laurence Lestel, 2 "The Banning of White Lead: French and International Regulations", in *Hazardous Chemicals*, ed. Ernst Homburg & Elisabeth Vaupel (Berghahn Books, 2022), 87–106.

tric temperament or madness.[3] Given that lead affects neurological and cognitive abilities, it might be fair to ask if the imaginations of artists such as Michelangelo Buonarroti, Francisco Goya, Vincent van Gogh, and Candido Portinari, were shaped by the influence of this toxic substance. While the effect of lead on Rembrandt's neurological and artistic capabilities cannot be determined, all matter he came into contact with would have played a part in his overall constitution: this is the real point of this art-historical anecdote. As Dorion Sagan highlights: "a body's capacities are literally the result of what it incorporates; the self is not only corporal but corporate", it consists of the agency of everything we ingest.[4]

Following lead particles allows me to consider a diverse range of images in which lead crucially features: from photographs, medical drawings, X-ray radiographs, microscopic sections of living cells, to GIS conglomerated data. Each imaging technique determines how lead contamination is evidenced across bodies. Each medium of inscription offers different focal points. Together, these images compose a biopolitical atlas tracing the exacerbation of a natural element by anthropogenic activities.

Lead has been mined, processed, and sold as part of 'necessary' products since antiquity. Its toxic properties have been discovered and forgotten multiple times throughout history. Its use has facilitated plumbing infrastructure for the creation of cities; the manufacturing of utensils, crockery and cookware; the sweetening and preservation of wine (*sapa*); the composition of paint, dyes, and make-up; the creation of batteries; the manufacturing of bullets and missiles; and, notably, as an additive in fuel.

In response to environmental degradation and adverse health effects, government agencies began regulating the distribution of lead and mitigating its corroding effects. Investigating lead contaminates and their proximity to different populations and ecologies allows me to read lead biopolitically. While lead is now understood as a toxic material and lead-contaminated lands are seen as unfit for habitation, racialised, marginalised, and impoverished bodies are still allowed, and often forced, to occupy toxic lands and other zones of precarity that sustain the comforts of a ruling class.

The following visual annotations offer some analytic windows into a chemical element that originates in subterranean landscapes, but which has been artificially propagated above the surface of the Earth and across bodies, disrupting life along the way. Breathing and consuming metals such as lead directly merges the geo- into our bio-, entangling and binding our fates to our landscapes. Lead particles are inhaled through the respiratory tract, ingested through the digestive system, and absorbed by skin.[5] Once inside the body, they can cause the death of cells (apoptosis) as they make red blood cells more brittle. Lead can bind to calcium receptors, forming bones. Displaced lead transforms body-scapes. Following Astrida Neimanis's hydrofeminist thinking, I follow metallic flows to observe how

3 Julio Montes-Santiago, "The Lead-Poisoned Genius", in *Progress in Brain Research*, vol. 203 (Elsevier, 2013), 223–40. See also Olga Khazan, "How Important Is Lead Poisoning to Becoming a Legendary Artist?", *The Atlantic*, 25 November 2013, accessed 16 December 2024, https://www.theatlantic.com/health/archive/2013/11/how-important-is-lead-poisoning-to-becoming-a-legendary-artist/281734/.

4 Dorion Sagan, "Metametazoa: Biology and Multiplicity", in *Incorporations*, ed. Jonathan Crary & Sanford Kwinter (Zone, 1992), 370.

5 Kathryn Yusoff, *A Billion Black Anthropocenes or None* (University of Minnesota Press, 2018), 9.

‘heavy’ metals interact with ‘soft’ organic cells.[6] Lead, unlike other metallic elements such as calcium, iron, zinc, potassium, and magnesium, offers no benefit to the human body—in fact, no concentration is safe for humans.[7] From a biological perspective, lead is a foreign body, yet it often features inside our bodily space, binding the terraforming of landscapes to the failure of vital functions.

Furthermore, lead acts as a neurotoxin, such that denizens of lead-contaminated sites not only suffer the health hazards of being intoxicated, but also undergo neurological alterations that affect cognitive abilities. If, as in the feminist tradition, we subscribe to the philosophy that rejects the harsh distinction between body and mind, nature and culture, then lead can help us understand how the very material processes of contamination influence the brain's ability to think thoughts, and imagine, perceive, and act on the world.

So how can we use these geo-bio-chemical images to reveal complex diagrams of power that do not only result in fast violence, murder, and war, but also in the slower types of violence that our era of environmental emergency entails?[8] Might these images be ‘charismatic’ enough, affective and actionable enough to evidence systemic environmental injustice as the uneven distribution of risk?[9]

2

This interactive map of the British Geological Survey (2011 to 2012) exists in virtual abstract space.[10] Its image canvas extends infinitely as one navigates and zooms in and out, determining points of focus. All perspective has been flattened as the Earth is unfolded in a Mercator projection, prioritising the accurate depiction of the United Kingdom. Although one can travel the globe on this platform, the dataset depicting the distribution of lead contaminates in soil only extends to the borders of England. Have there been no equivalent studies for Wales, Scotland, and Northern Ireland? The map itself is part of an open access project that utilises two datasets: the BGS G-BASE dataset on rural and urban topsoils, and the English National Soil Inventory dataset on topsoils. These involve sampling methods, laboratory analysis, as well as GIS technology. Samples were analysed by XRFS (X-ray fluorescence spectroscopy), a technique which registers X-ray reflectance to determine the presence of chemical elements such as metals. The result is a heatmap with a coarse resolution, but which allows us to have an overview of the soil contamination distribution

6 Astrida Neimanis, “Hydrofeminism: Or, on Becoming a Body of Water”, in *Undutiful Daughters: New Directions in Feminist Thought and Practice*, ed. Henriette Gunkel, Chrysanthi Nigianni, & Fanny Söderbäck (Palgrave Macmillan, 2012).

7 “Lead Poisoning”, World Health Organisation – The Global Health Observatory, 27 September 2024, accessed 16 December 2024, https://www.who.int/news-room/fact-sheets/detail/lead-poisoning-and-health.

8 Rob Nixon, *Slow Violence and the Environmentalism of the Poor* (Harvard University Press, 2011).

9 See Pine, Kathreen H. and Max Liboiron's conception of charismatic data: Kathleen H. Pine & Max Liboiron, “The Politics of Measurement and Action”, in *Proceedings of the 33rd Annual ACM Conference on Human Factors in Computing Systems* (CHI '15: CHI Conference on Human Factors in Computing Systems, Seoul Republic of Korea: ACM, 2015), 3147–56.

10 “Lead Contamination”, GeoIndex Onshore, British Geological Survey, accessed 18 November 2024, https://mapapps2.bgs.ac.uk/geoindex/home.html.

across the country.[11] Comparing the image of lead contamination distribution with the underlying distribution of minerals, we can clearly observe lead concentrations in urban areas as well as key sites that reveal mining and industrial processing. The fact that the two image patterns do not match demonstrates the difference between topsoil and subterranean material distribution, and confirms that lead distribution in topsoil is entirely anthropogenic. Lead has been intensively mined in Derbyshire and the Peak District since Roman Britain, which explains the excessive contamination of that site, however its urban density could allude to contamination from lead-infused petrol (scientists often observe higher concentrations of lead along highways), lead leakage from pipework, or lead paint on buildings. Scientists have also attributed anomalous lead levels in parts of London to the Blitz bombings.[12] Airdropped bombs added small metal compounds and distributed vast amounts of existing materials—calcium, zinc, and lead—as they pulverised buildings that also contained such elements. The fact that lead concentrations are not that high along the UK's southern shoreline, which was also intensely bombed during the Second World War, confirms that industrialisation was the most significant cause of pollution. Aerial bombing did not add significantly more metal to the landscape, however it did redistribute existing concentrations, transferring lead from within buildings into the ground.

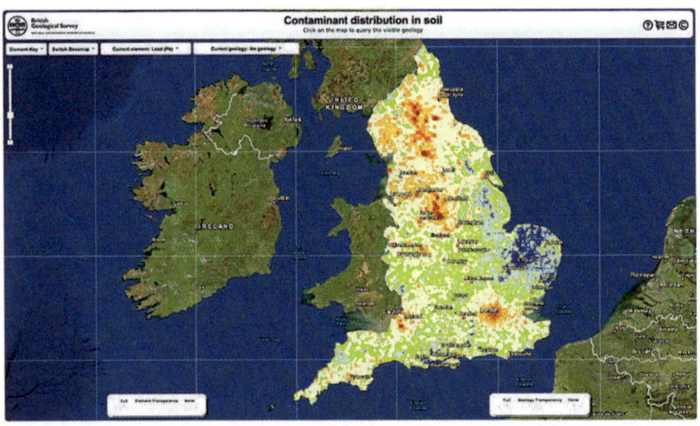

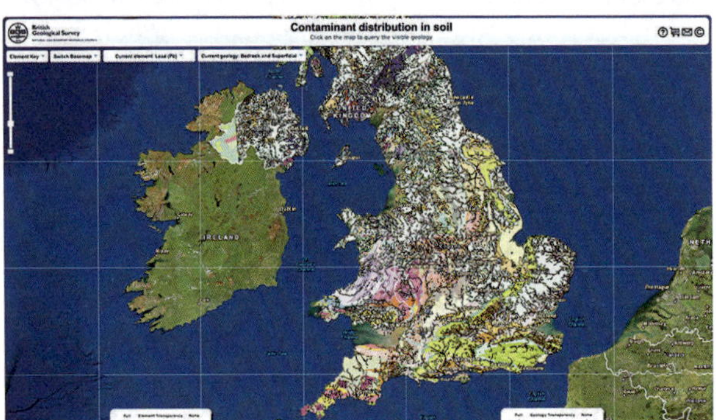

Source: British Geological Survey Materials
©UKRI, 2024.

11 The website informs us that "NSI samples cover all of England at a density of one site per 25 square kilometres. G-BASE samples are collected at a far higher density, urban samples at four sites per 1 square kilometres and rural samples at one site per 2 square kilometres. However, the G-BASE sample coverage (of analysed topsoils) is only for central and eastern England". https://mapapps2.bgs.ac.uk/geoindex/home.html.

12 J.D. Appleton & M.R. Cave, "Variation in Soil Chemistry Related to Different Classes and Eras of Urbanisation in the London Area", *Applied Geochemistry* 90 (March 2018): 13–24.

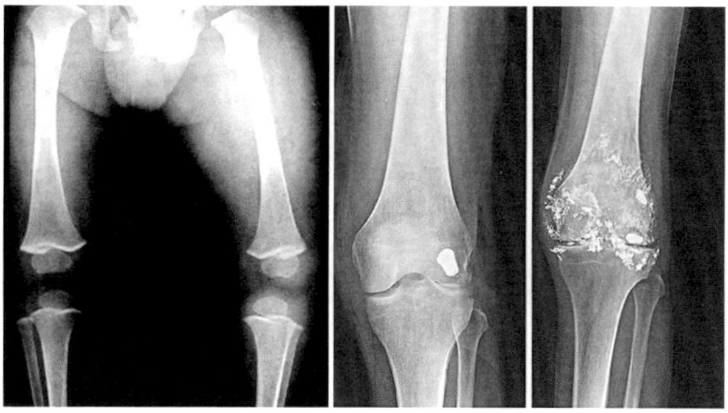

Source: Image courtesy of learningradiology.com.
Source: Image courtesy of Jose I. Marquez
& Michael A. Schindlbeck.

X-ray radiography is also used for the diagnosis of lead poisoning at the scale of a human body. In this image of a child's knees, dense metaphyseal bands indicate the presence of the heavy metal, as lead accumulates in bones, replacing calcium.[13] Since lead is denser (11.34 g/cm3) than calcium (1.55 g/cm3) it appears whiter and more solid in the X-ray image. This image not only captures the health condition of the body at the moment the radiograph is taken, but also gestures towards a longer temporality, as these metallic elements are slowly released over a person's lifetime. Once inside the body, lead moves easily across membranes, transgressing the blood-brain barrier and entering the amniotic sac during pregnancy. Its effects are physiological, causing illnesses from gout to anaemia and kidney failure, as well as neurological and cognitive, affecting attention, processing, speed, visuospatial abilities, working memory, and motor function.

Similar to the geological maps of lead distribution, close-up X-rays that capture the presence of lead in bodies could evidence faster forms of contamination. These twin images depict the knee of a fourty-six-year-old man who has sustained a gunshot wound. The bullet was not surgically removed, and fourteen years later, the patient returned to the hospital with worsening chronic knee pain. The bullet had fragmented, causing a series of conditions from anaemia to lower cognitive performance as lead was slowly released into the blood. This X-ray encapsulates both an incident of eruptive fast violence and a slower form of violence that is experienced through lead poisoning. The material disintegration of the bullet also highlights the transition from the insertion of a foreign object into the body, to its complete assimilation by the same body. The naturalisation of lead within a living organism transforms both the original object (the bullet) and the host organism.

13 William Herring, "Lead Poisoning (Plumbism)", *Learning Radiology*, accessed 18 November 2024, https://learningradiology.com/notes/bonenotes/leadpoisonpage.htm.

4

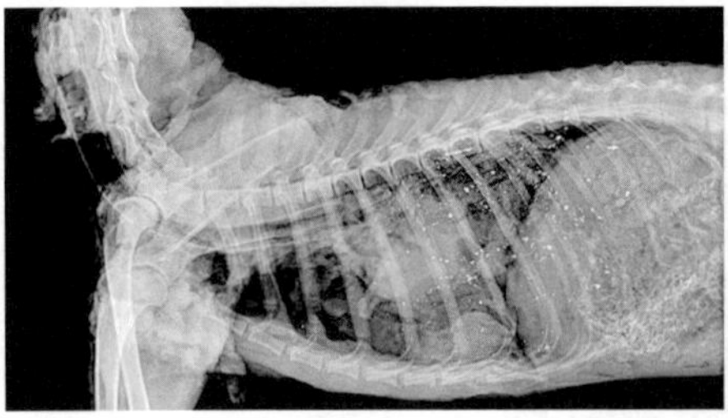

Source: Radiograph of a Dead Deer, USGS, image courtesy of the Peregrine Fund.

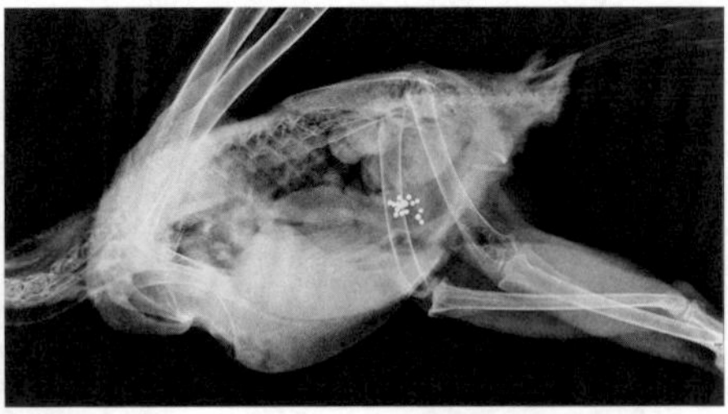

Source: X-ray of a bald eagle, USGS, image courtesy of the Raptor Center, Saint Paul, MN.

Lead bullets and pellets are found extensively in the bodies of animals across species. Environmental activist campaigns advocate against hunting with lead ammunition. Lead bullets not only cause the death of intended prey—such as the deer depicted in the image above—but also frequently of other animals as well; carrion birds, such as bald eagles, inadvertently ingest pellets embedded within the carcasses of animals that have been shot. Animals are also poisoned by drinking contaminated water, and from soils infiltrated by lead particles from spent ammunition. In 2023, the American Bird Conservancy estimated 16 million birds die each year in the US from lead poisoning.[14] Whether fragments of lead bullets are intended to kill the animal or not, the mere proliferation of lead ammunition and lead pollution at large has become an enormous hazard to wildlife worldwide.

5

The Wellcome Collection in London gathers all manner of materials relating to health. There, we can find images, hand drawings, scientific instruments and other artefacts from physicians who attempted to document and analyse various health conditions to aid their practices, as well as from artists who work around health issues. These two drawings of lead poisoning symptoms are attributed to Thomas Godart, a surgeon and anatomist who worked at St. Bartholomew's Hospital in London. Godart drew images both of living patients and of organs after autopsy. He also used early photographic methods to document patients' conditions. These images are not dated, but we can estimate that they are from the nineteenth century through association. The blackening of the gums and tongue, or 'Burton's line', is one of the few visible and distinguishable symptoms of chronic lead poisoning without the use of technology. Similar to X-ray images, these drawings do not offer a complete picture of the body that has been poisoned but rather capture partial views that expose only the areas of visible symptoms. This framing technique saves time for the artist/scientist, as well as provides anonymity for the patient.

Although we do not know what caused the lead intoxication of these anonymous patients, we can imagine a few possible causes, such as pica in children and occupational hazards in adults. Pica was (and still is in some parts of the world) a common way to ingest lead particles, especially for children who find lead-painted toys and paint chips peeling off lead-painted walls sweet. Children's health is much more heavily impacted by lead, as it attacks the development of the neurological system, which is fragile at young ages. Mel Y. Chen describes

14 "Conservation Impact Scorecard 2023", Annual Report, American Bird Conservancy (2023), 5, https://abcbirds.org/wp-content/uploads/2022/06/2021-Scorecard-1.pdf.

how panic during the late nineteenth and early twentieth centuries around white American children being poisoned from lead-painted toys manufactured in China gave lead a "tinge of racialisation", animating it as an Oriental biosecurity threat.[15] In this case, lead white and blackened gums point towards a racialised differential.

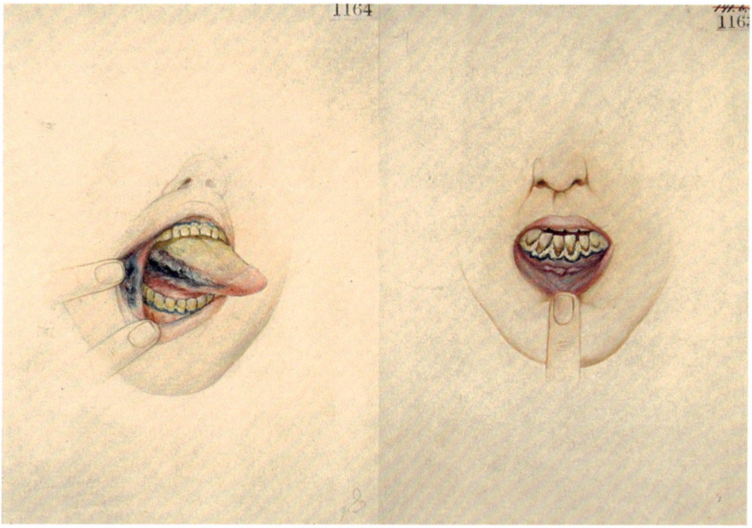

Source: Images courtesy of St Bartholomew's Hospital Archives & Museum, Wellcome Collection

6

These two images depict different types of paralysis of the ulnar and radial nerves of Hungarian potters poisoned by lead glazes. They feature in Joseph Rambousek's *Book of Industrial Poisoning*, published in 1913. Although some health regulations, like the banning of leaded paint or the development of leadless glazes, have improved conditions for workers exposed to lead intoxication, occupational exposure is still the predominant cause of lead poisoning. Today, it is the electronics market that is handling lead most closely. This is especially true for the manufacturing and recycling of rechargeable batteries. According to the United Nations Environment Programme: "approximately 86% of the total global consumption of lead is for the production of lead-acid batteries".[16] Recycling lead is both ubiquitous and profitable, meaning that little new lead is extracted from the ground.[17] However, studies have shown that recycling is happening mainly in the informal sector, for example in Bangladesh where more than 80 per cent of used lead-acid batteries are recycled.[18] Individuals often undertake the hazardous work of melting batteries to extract lead in their backyards, following

15 Mel Y. Chen, *Animacies: Biopolitics, Racial Mattering, and Queer Affect* (Duke University Press, 2012), 171.
16 UN Environment Programme, "Used Lead Acid Batteries (ULAB) - Waste Lead Acid Batteries (WLAB)", *UNEP.Org*, accessed 16 December 2024, https://www.unep.org/topics/chemicals-and-pollution-action/pollution-and-health/heavy-metals/used-lead-acid-batteries.
17 Fred Pearce, "Getting the Lead Out: Why Battery Recycling Is a Global Health Hazard", *Yale Environment 360*, 2 November 2020.
18 "Used Lead Acid Batteries (ULAB) - Waste Lead Acid Batteries (WLAB)", UN Environment Programme, accessed 18 December 2024, https://www.unep.org/topics/chemicals-and-pollution-action/pollution-and-health/heavy-metals/used-lead-acid-batteries.

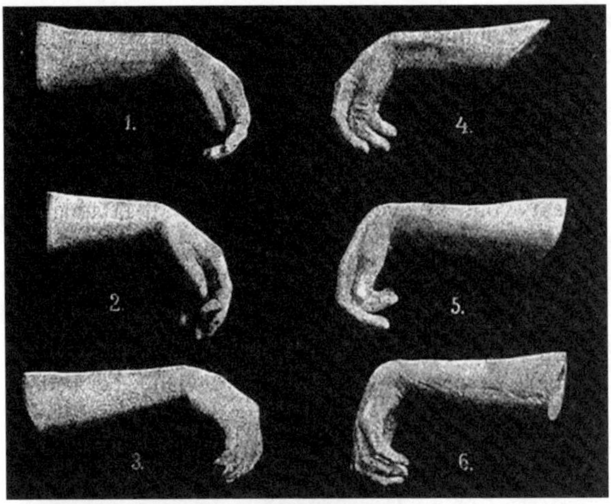

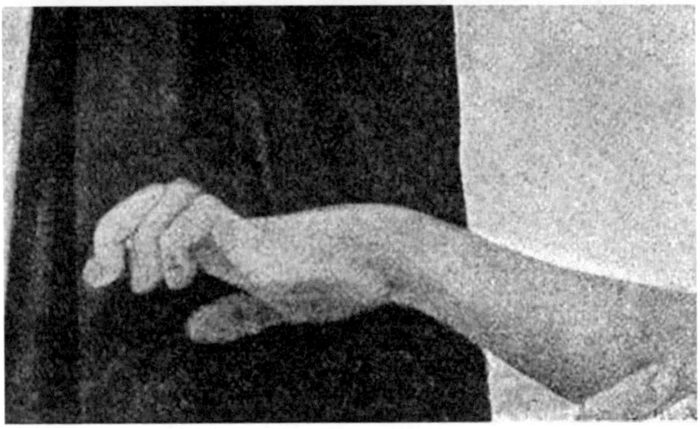

Source: *Les intoxications par le plomb se présent-ant dans la céramiquen en Hongrie*, image by Chyzer, 1908.

few safety measures and disposing of toxic waste directly into their surrounding environments. Green energy markets actively depend on cheap recycling options that take advantage of lax labour rights and allocate toxic risks to racialised communities that have historically been deprived of alternative options and guarantees. Lead's circulation is thus at the heart of today's green energy transition. Yet how can we promote clean energy without taking into consideration the dirty industry of metallic recycling? Which bodies are forced to bear the burden of this 'green revolution'?

By considering a series of images and techniques for discerning and detecting lead we begin to uncover an entangled material history of global inequality and neoliberal governance; one that begins with an intoxicated body and ends with a toxified Earth.

WORKS CITED

American Bird Conservancy. "Conservation Impact Scorecard 2023". Annual Report. American Bird Conservancy, 2023. Accessed 18 December 2024. https://abcbirds.org/wp-content/uploads/2022/06/2021-Scorecard-1.pdf.

Appleton, J.D., & M.R. Cave. "Variation in Soil Chemistry Related to Different Classes and Eras of Urbanisation in the London Area". *Applied Geochemistry* 90 (March 2018): 13–24.

Chen, Mel Y. *Animacies: Biopolitics, Racial Mattering, and Queer Affect.* Duke University Press, 2012.

Khazan, Olga. "How Important Is Lead Poisoning to Becoming a Legendary Artist?" *The Atlantic*, 25 November 2013. https://www.theatlantic.com/health/archive/2013/11/how-important-is-lead-poisoning-to-becoming-a-legendary-artist/281734/.

Lestel, Laurence. "2. The Banning of White Lead: French and International Regulations". In *Hazardous Chemicals*, edited by Ernst Homburg & Elisabeth Vaupel. Berghahn Books, 2022.

Montes-Santiago, Julio. "The Lead-Poisoned Genius". In *Progress in Brain Research*, 203. Elsevier, 2013.

Neimanis, Astrida. "Hydrofeminism: Or, on Becoming a Body of Water". In *Undutiful Daughters: New Directions in Feminist Thought and Practice*, edited by Henriette Gunkel, Chrysanthi Nigianni, & Fanny Söderbäck. Palgrave Macmillan, 2012.

Nixon, Rob. *Slow Violence and the Environmentalism of the Poor.* Harvard University Press, 2011.

Pearce, Fred. "Getting the Lead Out: Why Battery Recycling Is a Global Health Hazard". *Yale Environment 360*, 2 November 2020.

Pine, Kathleen H., & Max Liboiron. "The Politics of Measurement and Action". In *Proceedings of the 33rd Annual ACM Conference on Human Factors in Computing Systems.* ACM, 2015.

Rambousek, Josef. *Industrial Poisoning from Fumes, Gases and Poisons of Manufacturing Processes.* Outlook Verlag, 2023.

Sagan, Dorion. "Metametazoa: Biology and Multiplicity". In *Incorporations*, edited by Jonathan Crary and Sanford Kwinter. Zone, 1992.

UN Environment Programme. "Used Lead Acid Batteries (ULAB) - Waste Lead Acid Batteries (WLAB)". *UNEP.Org*, n.d. https://www.unep.org/topics/chemicals-and-pollution-action/pollution-and-health/heavy-metals/used-lead-acid-batteries.

Wiseman, Frederick. *National Gallery.* Documentary, 2014.

World Health Organisation – The Global Health Observatory. "Lead Poisoning", 27 September 2024. Accessed 18 December 2024. https://www.who.int/news-room/fact-sheets/detail/lead-poisoning-and-health.

Yusoff, Kathryn. *A Billion Black Anthropocenes or None.* University of Minnesota Press, 2018.

A CONVERSATION ON AIR AS TERRITORY AND ACOUSTIC RESISTANCE

Ariadna Serrahima

'The struggle for territory is inevitably
connected to the struggle for the word.'
—Nava and de Figuereido, 2022[1]

These field notes emerge from a conversation I recorded with Aldo Gonzalez on 23 November 2024 in La Sierra Norte, in a corner of the northern Zapotec mountain range of Oaxaca Valley. Aldo, who led the INI radio station XEGLO from 1990 to 1994, went on to become a member of the UNOSJO (Unión de Organizaciones de la Sierra Juárez de Oaxaca); currently, he is a teacher at the Universidad Autónoma Comunal de Oaxaca (UACO) in Guelatao.[2] In sharing fragments of our conversation I wish to reflect upon moments in which radio became a crucial sonic practice for the formation and expansion of a counter-hegemonic narrative across this region.

November marks a change of cycle. The rainy season finishes, daylight shifts the landscape towards a warmer spirit, and the humid and exuberant green of the Oaxaca Valley slowly transforms into a new breath. The skies are clear, the sun beats hard, and the intense yellow of the *yauhtli* flowers on the roadsides and the dried corn fields announce the harvest after *Muertos.*[3] Today, on 23 November in Guelatao, a small community of La Sierra Norte embraces the harvest by celebrating three fundamental axes of their communal life and daily resistance: the fourth anniversary of the Universidad Autónoma Comunal de Oaxaca; the corn fair of family producers;

1 Elena Nava & Guilherme Gitahy de Figuereido, *Tejiendo desde la contrahegemonía, medios, redes y TIC en América Latina* (UNAM, Instituto de Investigaciones Sociales, 2020).

2 The Instituto Nacional Indigenista (INI) was a public body of the Mexican government in charge of government policy for Indigenous people from 1948 to 2003. INI was a governmental institution created to support Indigenous peoples by providing them with infrastructure and promoting westernized development, thus introducing the values of modern life in the rural regions and particularly through radio, broadcasting their centralized political policies. UNOSJO (Unión de Organizaciones de la Sierra Juárez de Oaxaca) is a Zapotec organization, established in 1990 by the original people and campesinos in the region of La Sierra Norte, Oaxaca. UNOSJO fosters the local culture and defends the Indigenous rights in their territories. Aldo Gonzalez was also an advisor to the EZLN on Indigenous Rights and Culture in the San Andres Accords in 1996.

3 *Muertos* is translated as the Day of the Dead, a holiday traditionally celebrated on the 1 and 2 of November in Mexico. It originated as a syncretism between Catholic celebrations and Indigenous traditions to celebrate the deceased.

Acahual, Oaxaca. Source: Image by author (2024).

and the thirty-fourth anniversary of Radio XEGLO.[4] The dry season begins with festivities that remind them of their intrinsic relationship with agricultural rhythms and manifest the recognition of life that is lived at the margins of modern aspirations. These gatherings are part of efforts to celebrate their daily radical conviviality and the defence of their territory, which are central to the social and political organisation of communities in La Sierra Norte.

I met with Aldo in the headquarters of the UNOSJO, which was founded in 1994 as an organisational and economic commitment to improving the living conditions of the mountain communities of La Sierra Norte. Our conversation unfolds around how he subverted the institutional (INI) radio station in Guelatao, Radio XEGLO, which ran from 1990 to 1994, and how these experiences led him to participate in decisive moments of the subsequent autonomous media channels in Oaxaca. Since the late 1980s, the extraction of wood by national companies from monoculture tree plantations, the plunder of minerals by transnational concessions, and the abandonment of land due to local dispossession—all contributing to soil impoverishment and desertification—have continuously threatened the *buen vivir* (good living) of the original peoples in the region.[5] Resistance was imminent. A public sphere that represented all the communities, as well as a form of appearing that strengthened political cohesion, was needed.

Oral tradition is an essential dimension of daily conviviality in Oaxaca, and the many different ethnolinguistic groups that exist there combine to produce a powerful sonic vibration in the form of a collective body public. Radio, it seemed, was the medium the region was waiting for to get its voice on-air. In La Sierra Norte, 'territory' is a notion that has been resignified collectively by its own communities. Unlike the state's administrative divisions that convert land into private property, in the Zapotec mountains, 'territory' encompasses all spheres of communal life and its entanglements: the assembly, the *tequio,* the syncretic celebrations, the original languages, the subjectivation of non-human life, and the care of the *milpa*.[6] Here, communities become stewards of the land and decisions are consensual. The ancient paths of the mountains thus become a register of their collective

4 *Comunal* is a bounded term by a group of Indigenous thinkers that during the 1980s in La Sierra Norte de Juárez, throughout the defense of the territory, started a process of resignifying their own terminology to represent their own communities. *Comunal* is used to describe their community and collective forms of life. Radio XEGLO (La Voz de la Sierra Juárez or The Voice of the Sierra Juárez) is an Indigenous community radio station that broadcasts in Zapotec, Mixe, and Chinantec from Guelatao de Juárez in the Mexican state of Oaxaca. It is run by the Cultural Indigenist Broadcasting System (SRCI) under the direction of the National Indigenous Institute (INI).

5 *Buen vivir* is the way in which the communities of Abya Yala have named, through various different original languages, the space of conviviality, diversity, and reciprocity between the human and the more-than-human—the harmony between material life and spiritual life.

6 *Tequio* is a pre-Hispanic tradition of collective unpaid work for the collective good of the community in the native villages of Mexico. The *milpa* is a traditional agricultural system of pre-Hispanic origin that consists of growing maize, beans, squash and *quelites* (wild greens) in the same space and time. It is the basis of food sovereignty in many regions of Mexico.

knowledge. Elders, in particular, pass on stories that trace relationships between their spiritual life and their environment; a transgenerational orality that marks the territorial limits of each community. Without territory there is no communal life. As neoliberal economic forces began ravaging these mountain communities and their capacities for *buen vivir*, the air became a recognised part of their *defensa del territorio* (defence of the territory), along with water and land. Without air there is no "common breath".[7] During the early 1990s, the younger generation understood that the struggle had to be waged from within their own territories, and that the radical political compromise was to go back home to their ancestral lands. In other words, to forge a mode of resistance that operates by developing strategies that can create a local counter-power through different social mechanisms. Aldo was one of many young people who had been sent to study in Mexico City, with the promise of ensuring a future of national progress. Schooling and depopulating rural areas was part of a broader state strategy to dislocate Indigenous peoples, causing deep structural fissures and dissociating them from their identity. Aldo returned to Guelatao after his studies and took over the radiophonic field. Against the tide of neoliberal reforms, he used the transistor that INI had provided to create a counter-hegemonic medium that strengthened what was already in the air: the polyphonic voice of La Sierra Norte.

Collective map made by the students of the UACO, Guelatao during a session on territory. Source: Image by author (2024).

> ALDO: *I'm going to tell you a beautiful story. The radio started broadcasting on 21 March 1990, we had no facilities. We set up the transistor in the small room of the topiles [community guards]. The authorities of Guelatao lent it to us. Outside in the street, there was a big laurel tree. At that time, people were still growing a lot of corn in the village, and there were plenty of birds called zanates—which are very noisy—so, every day, when we opened the microphone to broadcast the radio programme, the first thing everyone could hear was the singing of the zanates. This is why we used to call the radio Radio Zanate instead of its official name.*
> *When I started working in the radio I was twenty-five years old, and I wanted to represent my people by giving them a 'space in the air', a space to tell their stories and broadcast their own music played in La Sierra Norte.*

Aldo's first radical gesture was to change the radio's official name from XEGLO to Zanate, giving agency and recognition to the more-than-human entities that make up an essential part of the acoustic day-to-day of the community. He turned what was a unidirectional transmission of centralised information by the state into a circular and polyphonic connector between the communities of the mountains.

7 The Indigenous anthropologist Jaime Martínez Luna describes in his last book, *Existimos Luego Pensamos* [We exist, then we think], "common breath", which I refer to as air, the common matter, that connects us and carries the vibrational voices of resistance in La Sierra Norte. Jaime Martínez Luna, *Existimos Luego Pensamos* (Honorable Cámara de Diputados, 2023).

The highway of information that was supposed to bring 'progress' deep into La Sierra Norte was being diverted; a radical radiophonic gesture that subverted the institutional media through what is now called "participatory communication".[8] The decentralisation of institutional media created a public sphere where the aural connected the diverse forms of life and struggles found within the same territory. Radio Zanate broadcast in the original languages of the people and projected their voices, concerns, urgencies, political issues, and local celebrations across the hills, connecting communities. Air became a substantial part of their daily resistance.

> ALDO: *I chose a group of young kids who mostly spoke at least one language of the region, because the station was going to broadcast in Zapoteco, Mixe and Chinanteco. It was complex, because Zapoteco in La Sierra Norte has four variants and Mixe has two variants. It would be the first time the radio was going to transmit in our own original languages to represent local life in our mountains.*
> *We also created the Radio Production Centres (CPR): we bought some very simple equipment such as a mixing console, cassette recorders, and microphones. We visited some communities that were interested in doing radio, because the idea was to strengthen the collective practice of listening, listening to the people of the communities on the radio... and there were some interesting experiences!*
> *For example, in Totontepec, in Tamazulapan, in San Juan Tabaá, and in Tanetze they ended up making their own radio stations. We taught them how to do manual editing because back then there were no computers, it was cut and paste, literally. We were very few people doing radio so we had to fake voices and do editing [he smiles].*
> *Working together with the jovenes radialistas* [young radio broadcasters], *we collected more than a thousand testimonies from different communities. At least there is a historical testimony of what the communities were like at the time, through these recordings.*

La Sierra Norte, view from Lachatao.
Source: Image by author (2023).

As our conversation continued, Aldo recalled that the distances between villages used to be very long, the roads narrow and unpaved. Even today some communities are hard to reach during the rainy season. To be able to record everyone who had a story to tell, they would have to stay in each community for at least five days. When they arrived at a village, old women, men, and children were already prepared to be recorded; they all had some gossip to unveil to the mountains. Aldo, in effect, collected the testimonial reverberations of

8 *Participatory communication* is a term widely used across Latin America in the context of community radios to refer to autonomous, self-organised and collective processes in which communities themselves, using different media, participate in creating information that represents them and circulates through their own independent channels. Voice is an essential element of these processes. See Griselda Sánchez, *Aire, no te vendas: La lucha por el territorio desde las ondas* (IWGIA, 2016).

the *buen vivir* in La Sierra Norte. The radio had become a key social actor—the messenger—connecting and transferring information through the air: stories and accounts that not only related to everyday life, but to the organisation and mobilisation of the people against external neoliberal policies and practices. Achieving autonomy of the radiophonic medium therefore felt like an indisputable requirement for defending the territory in the struggle for self-determination. What seemed to be only voices thrown into the air was in reality the enunciation of a historical paradigm shift: the Zapatista uprising in 1994.

> ALDO: *I didn't want to listen to Radio XEGLO after they fired me in 1994. [Aldo was dismissed because he was a member of the Indigenous Forums for the Autonomy of Indigenous Peoples, where he was elected to attend the National Democratic Convention convened by the EZLN in 1994] a member of various Indigenous Forums celebrated in Oaxaca and Chiapas.] It made me angry that all the work that had been done from 1990 to 1994 the new direction tore to pieces. The INI decided that the people should no longer be allowed to participate, they cut the budget, and the kids could no longer go out to the communities to record people. It was an INI radio station, in an Indigenous region, in 1994. They had to take control of the radio while the Indigenous peoples were rising up. [the Zapatista uprising took place in Chiapas in 1994] [...] One afternoon in 1995 I was in my house and, I don't know why, I turned on the radio: they were announcing the people invited to be advisors for the EZLN*[9] *in the San Andrés Accords and I heard my name! [Aldo was invited as a community radio communicator]*[10] *When we arrived in Chiapas, the Zapatistas had already designed the round tables for the forum. I wanted to be at the 'autonomy table', but they asked me to be at the 'communication table'. One of the agreements we specified was that all the INI radio stations that the state spread across the Indigenous territories had to be transferred to the communities and become autonomous. We wanted the autonomy of our community media. On the third anniversary of the Guelatao radio station, in 1993, we organised a big party for the Zapotec peoples, from the Istmo and La Sierra Sur, to Los Valles Centrales and La Sierra Norte. More than a thousand people came. That day, the director of the INI arrived at Guelatao, and asked: "what is this gathering about?"*

Encuentros Zapatistas de Resistencia y Rebeldía. 1 January 2025, Oventic, Chiapas. Source: Image by author. (January 1 2025)

9 EZLN, Ejercito Zapatista de Liberación Nacional is an armed group of insurgents created in 1984 that operated as guerrillas in the Lacandon jungle and led the Zapatista uprising on 1 January 1994. The EZLN is still operating today in all Zapatista autonomous zones of Chiapas.

10 The San Andrés Accords are agreements reached between the Zapatista Army of National Liberation (EZLN) and the Mexican government. The accords—signed in February 1996, in San Andrés Larráinzar, Chiapas—recognised the rights and cultures of the Indigenous population of Mexico and granted autonomy to these communities. The agreements were never accomplished by the government, but set a historical precedent in Latin America for Indigenous rights and recognition in constitutions.

Community radio Estereo Comunal, Guelatao, La Sierra Norte. Source: Image by author (2023).

And we told him that it was the anniversary of the radio station and that we wanted the radio station to be transferred to the communities and for them to have their autonomy. That is how the proposal was taken to the San Andrés Accords in 1996. It was not successful, though. The radio stations continue to belong to the federal government (today's INPI), although its transfer to the communities was reflected and agreed in the San Andrés Accords." [Gradually, autonomous community radio stations began to be set up throughout the region. Today, in Guelatao the autonomous radio station is Estereo Comunal.]

A decade after the Zapatista uprising, Oaxaca became *the* place to generate encounters and organise the insurrection against governmental oppression by taking control of state media and creating the APPO (Asamblea Popular de los Pueblos de Oaxaca). In 2006, the insurgent leadership of the popular uprising in Oaxaca city was mainly led by teachers (La Sección 22 del Sindicato Nacional de Trabajadores de la Educación, SNTE) and organised by clandestine radio stations set up on roofs across the city. These radio stations became the medium through which to circulate the ungraspable, once again: the voices of the people. Radio Plantón and Radio Universidad were crucial political actors during those months of uncertainty. Nahú Rodríguez, part of Radio Plantón, describes the autonomous radios as an open school:

> *The radio battle was very interesting because it allowed us to understand that this technology can be easily installed and reproduced. We played a lot with the state: we would put up a signal and then the state would block it, and then over and over again. We had to think carefully about the counter-insurgency strategy, so we turned on another transmitter to continue transmitting and gain territory from the state. 2006 was very important because the autonomous radio work was to bring people together, to make them feel that they were being listened to and that the movement was talking to them, organising with them. This is one of the most beautiful exercises that I have had the opportunity to accompany in the communication field.*[11]

Aldo also remembers those days as transcendental moments of encounter between the communities of La Sierra Norte and urban collectives and unions in Oaxaca city. Indigenous people in the rural areas have a lot of experience counter-organising their own community policies, in which listening practices are essential. He emphasises that their contribution to the APPO assemblies was about learning to listen to your comrades and create consensus.

> ALDO: *CORTEV was a state government radio station that was taken over by the women of the movement. I was walking with some comrades through*

11 Nahú Rodríguez is a sound artist and broadcaster. He is part of the emergence of autonomous community radio stations in Oaxaca during the 2006 social movement. This quote is part of a conversation we had together, which I recorded during a listening session of his personal archive of Radio Plantón during the civil uprising in 2006.

the centre of Oaxaca and someone came up to us and said: "hey, could you participate in some interviews on the radio?" We went to the radio station with some comrades from various communities of La Sierra Norte. They asked me to conduct the interviews, so we went in, did the interviews, and a little while later the people in charge of the radio station arrived and said to me: "can you keep coming to the radio station please? We really liked the way the programme turned out!" So, as we were organising the Foro Nacional Construyendo la Democracia y la Gobernabilidad en Oaxaca for 16 February together with the APPO, we used the radio to broadcast it and promote it. We did an Indigenous opening ceremony in the Plaza de la Danza and then we went to the Universidad Autónoma Benito Juárez de Oaxaca (UABJO) and that's where the forum was held. There should be a publication about that event. I think it was important that together with the APPO we made a collective effort to really go in search of deeper social change. This is how we contributed our communal knowledge to the urban media and modes of organisation.
In parallel, in the mountains, on 14 June, when the repression began in Oaxaca, we thought we couldn't just stand there as if nothing was happening. I spoke to Kendy, the director of Estéreo Comunal (the community radio of Guelatao), and told her: "it would be good if we could use the community radio station to transmit the conflict!" So we got on the radio and started talking about Oaxaca's movement. We opened up the microphones for people from all the communities to participate. We gave the microphone to everyone. [...] However, soon after we had to stop broadcasting due to various political threats, but thanks to the Guelatao community assembly we were able to take over the INI radio and recover the transmission of Oaxaca's uprising. Even the municipal president guarded the premises so that they wouldn't close the radio down... and so here I am again, after ten years, subverting the XEGLO radio. The police occupied Oaxaca city and all the radio stations that were in the hands of the comrades were taken away, so the only radio that could be heard in Oaxaca was XEGLO. We were the only ones who continued broadcasting, we were the last operational channel for listening to the struggle in 2006.

The air as a territory in itself, facilitating everyday oral and acoustic interdependencies, carries the resonances of a daily struggle. The air is where the voices, the storytelling, the whispers of the ancestors meet the radiophonic waves of the present to organise resistance in all spheres of life. For the past 500 years, communal life in La Sierra Norte has been shaped by a powerful communitarian commitment: to resignify the notion of territory and to recognise their own intrinsic forms of reciprocity and social organisation as fundamental values for surviving the threats of increasing neoliberal dispossession and individuation. Still as of today, radio is a fundamental agent of resistance; one that continues to challenge modes of representation as well as mechanisms of state assimilation and suppression of Indigenous resistance. The air is the zone where sonic togetherness enunciates itself, where transmissions move between the frictions and fissures of an alien world and our own.[12]

12 In UACO's autonomous learning framework, during the collective reflections, it is common to use the terms "alien world" to refer to the western ways of life and needs created by the capitalist system, and "own world" to refer to their community forms of integral life based on their ancestral cosmovision (from my notes during the sessions in the UACO, Guelatao).

UACO's encounter, Guelatao, La Sierra Norte.
Source: Image by author (2024).

I wish to express my gratitude to my colleagues at the UACO (Universidad Autónoma Comunal de Oaxaca): Aldo Gonzalez, Rosenda Wilde, and Fernando Ramos for sharing their experiences, knowledge, and concerns with me, and for our long conversations on autonomy and resistance. With special thanks to Aldo for his generosity in sharing the story of his life as it has intersected with the history of autonomous media in La Sierra Norte. Aldo's recording is part of the collection of stories Rosenda and I are compiling for a book on the beginnings of UACO. It is the testimony of an Indigenous autonomous project that focuses on learning as an essential axis for the construction of a critical collective view and a radical conviviality at the margins of hegemonic and oppressive forms of life.

WORKS CITED

Luna, Jaime Martínez. *Existimos Luego Pensamos.* Honorable Cámara de Diputados, 2023.

Nava, E. & Guilherme Gitahy de Figuereido. *Tejiendo desde la contrahegemonía, medios, redes y TIC en América Latina.* UNAM, Instituto de Investigaciones Sociales, 2020.

Sánchez, Griselda. *Aire, no te vendas: La lucha por el territorio desde las ondas.* IWGIA, 2016.

YOU WON'T SEE IT ABOVE GROUND

Jacob Bertilsson

It's a grey morning in late June, and my collaborator, fungal researcher Anders Dahlberg, has just sent me the latest update of the species dataset for our web application. This dataset now includes information on mycorrhizal fungi,[1] collected through DNA analysis of soil samples from 2,500 Swedish forests, gathered as part of the National Soil Inventory. The inventory collects minute sub-samples, which allows for good analysis of common fungi species but limits the representation of rarer fungi that are less likely to be detected in such focused samples. To create a more comprehensive and accessible tool for non-experts, we're supplementing the soil sample data with information on threatened and edible species, drawing on compiled knowledge from Anders and other mycologists, as well as citizen-submitted records of fruiting bodies in the national species database.

Our goal with this web tool is twofold. Firstly, we're communicating which mycorrhizal fungi may be present in different Swedish forests and how they are distributed in the soil, in order to foster an appreciation for their often-overlooked presence. Secondly, we're developing visualisations to illustrate how different forestry practices affect the species composition of mycorrhizal fungi. While the tool will be made publicly available, our primary audience is forest owners. Approximately half of Sweden's forests are owned and managed by just over 300,000 small private landowners.[2] Under the guiding principle known as *freedom with responsibility*, the management decisions of this group significantly impact the current and future state of forests and biodiversity across the whole country.

Back in 2022, prior to applying for financial support to visualise this data and information, Anders and I travelled to Dalagård in Dalarna—the Swedish lake district—to visit forest owner Leif Öster. Leif previously served as Head of Communications at the state-owned forestry company Sveaskog, but has since shifted his focus toward nature tourism and has become a vocal supporter of continuous cover forestry. This approach runs counter to the dominant clearcutting model in Swedish forestry, which involves cutting down all trees in a given area at once, similar to the harvesting of monocrops.

I'd met Leif once before, when I interviewed him back in 2021. During that initial visit, he explained some of the challenges in opposing the industry's preferred method of clearcutting. He shared how in theory, the Swedish model has a supposedly neutral expert authority who provides information and guidance

1 Mycorrhizal fungi form symbiotic form symbiotic relationships with plant roots, aiding nutrient absorption in exchange for sugars.

2 "Property and ownership statistics in forestry", The Swedish Forest Agency, accessed 4 December 2024, https://www.skogsstyrelsen.se/statistik/statistik-efter-amne/fastighets--och-agarstruktur-i-skogsbruk.

Torbjörn Nilsson from the National Soil Inventory showing soil samples at the National Soil Archive, where the samples are stored after analysis. Source: Image by author (September 9 2022).

This visualisation, created for the Skogssvamp.se web tool, illustrates the potential distribution of fungal species in fourty-one to ninety year-old pine forests in northern Sweden, where herbs thrive. Source: Image by author (2024).

Clearcut land with retention trees in northern Sweden.
Source: Image by author (2020).

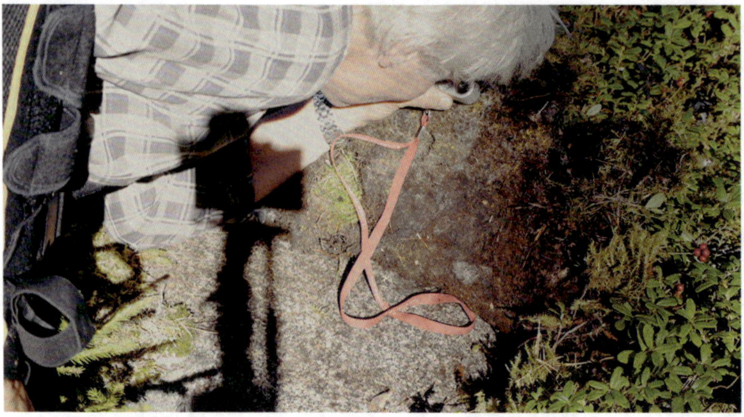

Using a magnifying glass, Anders Dahlberg inspects a mycelium hidden beneath the turned-over moss. Source: Image by author.

Image illustrating where mycelium (in pink and blue) survives along the edges of a clear-cut area and around groups of retention trees. Source: Image by author for a presentation by Anders Dahlberg.

This image highlights the mycelium distribution and the high diversity of fungi in the soil. Source: Image by author for a presentation by Anders Dahlberg.

in the shape of the Swedish Forest Agency.[3] In practice, however, the Agency has faced increasing budget cuts over the years; meanwhile, timber buyers—who profit from felling trees—have been gaining more influence. "The forest industry spends tremendous amounts on influencing forest owners to clearcut", he added.

Clearcutting thus remains the industry standard, so to speak, despite widespread critique from bodies such as the European Union, as well as the ecological and economic benefits that alternative forest management approaches present to small forest owners.[4]

During Anders' and I's visit to Dalagård in 2022, Leif lamented the forest industry's conflicting stance concerning public access to forest data. They are uncomfortable with the requirement to make plans for forest felling public, and have supported the termination and reversal of the inventory of key biodiversity areas that were previously registered in public records.[5] At the same time, the industry actively advocates for full public access to laser-scanned data of forests, which is highly beneficial for timber buyers, enabling them to identify areas with large timber reserves.

The topic of transparency is a central point of contention in the ongoing debate about the forest industry, especially as the sector increasingly incorporates digital tools into its practices. As part of this move, the industry has begun exploring *digital twins*[6] of forest environments, where high-resolution data is often masqueraded mistakenly as irrefutable evidence. One of the most striking claims I encountered during my research came from the CEO of a company providing below-canopy laser scanning services to the industry. He argued that besides producing more granular records of timber volumes, their LiDAR scans can verify the presence, or absence, of biodiversity values—such as fallen trees and other ecological indicators—which, in his words, would render greenwashing impossible, and thus unburden the industry from such critique.

There are obvious issues with the CEO's claims around the impact of their service on industry greenwashing practices. The idea that a LiDAR scan can sufficiently capture the complexity of biodiversity is misleading. While LiDAR can detect features like fallen trees, which is just one of many biodiversity indicators, it doesn't account for actual species. Obvious exclusions include birds, insects, and anything below ground, such as mushroom mycelium. These are biodiversity values that are often challenging to assess even in person, and to suggest that greenwashing becomes impossible through this technology only serves to suppress further debate.

If anything, digital tools such as laser scanning and digital twins—deployed alongside industry media rhetoric—risk creating a facade of transparency that obscures the continuation of destructive practices. The promise that increased digitisation in the forest sector will lead to more transparency could bring about

3 The Swedish Forest Agency is theoretically a neutral actor but it has often faced both internal and external critique for its connection to the industry. "About the Forest Agency's Products and services", The Swedish Forest Agency, accessed 4 December 2024, https://www.skogsstyrelsen.se/produkter-och-tjanster/om-skogsstyrelsens-produkter-och-tjanster/. https://www.dn.se/sverige/larm-inifran-skogsstyrelsen-svenskt-skogsbruk-definitivt-inte-hallbart/.

4 Leif Öster, interview by Jacob Bertilsson, 13 September 2021, audio.

5 Emma Ugge, "Massiv Kritik Mot Skogsstyrelsens Förslag Om Nyckelbiotoper" ["Massive Criticism of the Swedish Forest Agency's Proposal on Key Biotopes"], *Sveriges Natur*, December 10 2019, https://www.sverigesnatur.org/aktuellt/massiv-kritik-mot-skogsstyrelsens-forslag-om-nyckelbiotoper/.

6 Digital twins are virtual replicas of physical objects or environments, often promoted for precise monitoring and optimisation. The term originated in manufacturing and engineering but has recently expanded into fields like forestry.

a different type of 'washing', what law and technology scholar Monika Zalnieriute calls "transparency washing". This is when companies focus on showcasing their transparent procedures whilst avoiding any real scrutiny of the actual impact of their actions.[7]

Building upon Nicholas Bagley's critique of "procedural fetishism" in administrative law, Zalnieriute observes how regulations can become more concerned with whether processes are visible rather than whether they actually make a difference. This fixation on transparency in processes risks turning debates toward micro issues that, on their own, offer little promise of challenging the status quo.[8] In the context of forestry practices, the increased digitisation of the industry—often referred to as a turn towards precision forestry, where broad-stroke management is replaced by ideas of surgical interventions based on technological monitoring—further amplifies this risk.[9] Rather than addressing whether clearcutting should persist at all, the focus may shift to how well something is monitored, justifying ongoing practices through the illusion of precision and control, even if the underlying problems remain unchallenged.

Back at Leif's forest, Anders knelt down and reached his hand into the soil to turn over a bit of moss and forest mulch, revealing white and yellow thread-like fungal structures. "Some of the species you see here, like this yellow one, are among the most common mycorrhizal fungi in Sweden," he explained, pointing to *Piloderma fallax* (commonly known as *gultrådskinn* in Swedish, though it has no common name in English). "But it doesn't have visible fruiting bodies, so you won't see it above ground. In fact, most fungi live out of sight and aren't encountered on a typical walk. In a forest section like this, there could be up to 250 different species of mycorrhizal fungi."

"Incredible!" Leif marvelled.

"Few species are common and cover large parts of the forest, while many are rare and might only exist with a single mycelium in one spot. And just like the trees, they can be very old," Anders continued. "And then for some species, for example the mealy tooth, if you lift the moss covering it, you can see that it has a very thick, cotton-white mycelium. And if you continue to lift up the moss to follow it, you can see how far the mycelium reaches. Individuals are often around 10 square metres, but I've seen some as large as 50 to 75 square meters. In forestry, if you clearcut, these are almost guaranteed to die as they are dependent on the living trees. They would only survive on retention trees and along the edges of the clearing."[10]

About a third of all threatened species in Sweden, including flora, fauna, and fungi are directly impacted by the country's clearcutting industry.[11] This dynamic is well understood, particularly for mycorrhizal fungi, with clear indications that continuous cover forestry as an alternative to clearcutting benefits biodiversity. Through our app, we aim to foster an understanding of these forestry dynamics

7 Monika Zalnieriute, "'Transparency Washing' in the Digital Age: A Corporate Agenda of Procedural Fetishism", *Critical Analysis of Law* 8, no. 1, 2 April 2021: 139–53.

8 Zalnieriute, "Transparency Washing", 139-53.

9 Harsh Choudhry & Glen O'Kelly, "Precision Forestry: A Revolution in the Woods." *McKinsey & Company*, 25 June 2018, https://www.mckinsey.com/industries/packaging-and-paper/our-insights/precision-forestry-a-revolution-in-the-woods.

10 Anders Dahlberg, "A Visit to Leif Öster", interview by Jacob Bertilsson, 6 September 2022, audio.

11 Elisabet Ottosson, "Många Skogslevande Arter Hotas AV Trakthyggesbruk: SLU Artdatabanken" ["Many Forest-Dwelling Species Are Threatened by Clearcutting: SLU Species Data Bank"], *SLU.SE*, 21 February 2024, https://www.artdatabanken.se/arter-och-natur/Dagens-natur/manga-skogslevande-arter-hotas-av-trakthyggesbruk/.

and the often-overlooked diversity of fungi. It's a step towards incorporating biodiversity into the planning tools available to forest owners, as even the official tools from the Forest Agency lack such information. However, it's important to recognise that this isn't simply about layering new information on top of the old. What we provide differs significantly from the industry's approach—which often sees forests as simply collections of timber reserves—and deploys technology to reinforce that view. In contrast, while our approach is grounded in scientific analysis, it supports a broader, more imaginative engagement with forest ecosystems. By highlighting the hidden presence of fungi below the ground we hope to invite people to consider the lifeworlds that lie beyond what is immediately visible. This perspective opens the door to perceiving forests as dynamic, interconnected ecosystems—richer and more complex than what the forest manager's ledger could ever capture. In doing so, we aim to enrich public debate and expand the possibilities for how forests are understood and managed. We hope to encourage perspectives that go beyond reductive, profit-driven frameworks, fostering a deeper appreciation of forests as living systems, where even what is not visible may play a vital role.

WORKS CITED:

Choudhry, Harsh & Glen O'Kelly. "Precision Forestry: A Revolution in the Woods". *McKinsey & Company*, 25 June 2018. https://www.mckinsey.com/industries/packaging-and-paper/our-insights/precision-forestry-a-revolution-in-the-woods.

Ugge, Emma. "Massiv Kritik Mot Skogsstyrelsens Förslag Om Nyckelbiotoper" ["Massive Criticism of the Swedish Forest Agency's Proposal on Key Biotopes"]. *Sveriges Natur*, 10 December 2019. https://www.sverigesnatur.org/aktuellt/massiv-kritik-mot-skogsstyrelsens-forslag-om-nyckelbiotoper/.

Ottosson, Elisabet. "Många Skogslevande Arter Hotas AV Trakthyggesbruk: SLU Artdatabanken". *SLU.SE*, 21 February 2024. https://www.artdatabanken.se/arter-och-natur/Dagens-natur/manga-skogslevande-arter-hotas-av-trakthyggesbruk/.

Swedish Forest Agency. "About the Forest Agency's Products and services". Accessed 4 December. https://www.skogsstyrelsen.se/produkter-och-tjanster/om-skogsstyrelsens-produkter-och-tjanster/.

Swedish Forest Agency. "Property and ownership statistics in forestry". Accessed 4 December. https://www.skogsstyrelsen.se/statistik/statistik-efter-amne/fastighets--och-agarstruktur-i-skogsbruk.

Zalnieriute, Monika. "'Transparency Washing' in the Digital Age: A Corporate Agenda of Procedural Fetishism". *Critical Analysis of Law* 8, no. 1, 2 April 2021: 139–53.

FOLLOWING TIN IN THE AGE OF CRITICAL MINERALS

Adam Bobbette

Coast of Bangka Island, Indonesia, 2024
A tool larger than my body. The teeth bigger than my hands. I stretched my arms wide but they were still less than the diameter of the drill head. The ship rocked slowly and waves foamed up through the portal the drill would soon penetrate. I was wandering around and photographing the ship as the crew did some repairs—welding, sparks flying while straddling iron beams—reconnecting something to somewhere. Soon, they told me, the dredger would be ready to descend its tool into the water, then onto the ocean floor where it would spin a whorl of destruction; shattering coral, plants, fish, anything it encountered.

When the machine was turned on, the entire vessel vibrated and pumped black smoke into the air. The engines were so loud that you had to lean in and shout to communicate. I could feel the roar of the drill in my muscles. Often, the crew would run the dredger for six or seven hours at a time, pulling up the ocean floor through a pipe connected to the drill bit. Everything below the ship's trajectory would be spewed into a massive vat at the top of the vessel, nearly two storeys tall. A system of filters jittered, rocked, and swayed the material, separating the sediments according to their size, keeping only the finest at the bottom because they contained the material the boat was after: tin. Everything that was too large was expelled from the stern, leaving a smudge of chalk-white in the ocean. One of the crew members told me that when the global price of tin was up, they ran the dredger all day long. The global financial market was materialised right here, I could feel it on the deck and in the buzz of the machine that reverberated through my stomach as waste leaked from the ass-end of the ship.

Later that evening and back on dry land, I pulled into a dilapidating and vacant grand hotel for the night. The front courtyard was full of deserted tables and the remains of a wedding banquet. I was sitting for a while taking notes from the day's work when I was interrupted by the drone of engines. Behind a layer of trees there were tailings ponds where artisanal miners were dredging from ad hoc pontoons. One of the employees of the hotel told me that the sound was one of the reasons the hotel was empty, the hotel owner frequently called the police on the miners because the sound disrupted the guests. Not to mention, the mining was illegal. “Today,” the hotelier said, “it's not so bad because the price of tin is low. You should hear it when the price spikes, it's terrible”. Again, the local materialisation of the global, this time in the hum of two-stroke engines.

We now live in the age of critical minerals and tin is at the centre of it. Although the Anthropocene proposal was recently rejected by the Earth Science community as the name for our current geological epoch—and thus the fate of the term in the humanities and social sciences hangs in the balance—we might find a path forward for post-Anthropocene terminology in critical minerals. Developing its roots in the very same industrial processes of offshoring, the difference being that it occurred on Bangka during the height of the industrial revolution in the middle of the nineteenth century. In a disorienting loop, tin extraction is potentially returning to Cornwall, the very site that drove the intensification of mining in Bangka. Even more strangely, solar farms currently sit atop former tin mines in Cornwall, the panels of which are fabricated with solder made of tin that has been extracted from Bangka. How can we make sense of this strange recursivity, a kind of temporal whiplash in the age of critical minerals?

Tracing the routes of critical minerals offers a clue, I think, because they reveal the connected material histories, knowledges, and technologies of modern extractive capitalism. Most critical minerals are recent inventions—many of them only isolated in the late eighteenth century, including the rare earth elements, germanium, tantalum, platinum, and niobium. These materials became newly visible because of the recent intersections between the science of mineralogy and chemistry, which gave birth to entirely new material worlds that defined the first and second industrial revolutions. Steel in trains and buildings, aluminium for everything from airplanes and typewriters to food containers and electric heating, germanium laced weapons, antimony in nuclear bombs, mica and tin in nearly all forms of radio communication (including the internet). Lewis Mumford called this new material world the "neotechnic" phase of technological evolution, presciently understanding how it remade global geopolitics seeing as Western states could no longer rely on materials within their own borders, such as wood, water, coal, limestone, etc. Instead, "they must either organise and safeguard and conserve a worldwide basis of supply, or run the risk of going destitute and relapse into a lower and cruder technology. The basis of the material elements in the new industry is neither national nor continental but planetary."[4]

The age of critical minerals is planetary in another sense, too. The sciences that helped identify the new materials of the industrial revolution were also engaged in redefining the history of the Earth. Platinum in South Africa is a good example. The Bushveld Igneous Complex that cuts across the north of the country was defined in the early twentieth century by colonial geologists and is now a textbook study in geology classes of *ophiolite genesis*, ancient bits of the ocean floor that instead of subducting beneath continental masses *ob*duct and are raised up onto continents. The scientists who explained this process in the Bushveld were early adopters of theories of continental drift, long before it became the standard narrative of Earth's evolutionary structure in the 1960s. What was key to the theory of obduction was an explanation of how precious minerals, such as platinum, were produced in deep mantle processes. The Bushveld was a kind of snapshot of what was happening down below, and the science of the Bushveld revealed that it was one of the largest deposits of platinum on Earth. Geological interest there, in part, gave rise to the Anglo American mining company and Johnson Matthey chemicals company, both headquartered in Britain. Johnson Matthey is now a major producer of catalytic converters, which try to reduce the pollution of automobile emissions. Both Anglo American and Johnson Matthey made huge profits from the apartheid regime, and their mines are at the centre of what Gabrielle Hecht has called "residual governance", the production of wasted environments and populations that need to live with them for untold generations.[5] Destitution and racialised violence seeps through the towns and camps that line the edges of Anglo American and Johnson Matthey platinum mines.

4 Lewis Mumford, *Technics and Civilization* (Harcourt, Brace and Co., 1934), 232.
5 Gabrielle Hecht, *Residual Governance: How South Africa Foretells Planetary Futures* (Duke University Press, 2023).

sensing practices around materials such as tin might also help us make 'sense' of what it means to live in a time of radical transitions.

We know that humans move more earth sediments around than all natural processes combined. It is also becoming clear that the decarbonisation of energy systems may well require more mining than ever before in human history. The energy transition is mineral intensive. Lists of exotic sounding materials such as manganese, germanium, ytterbium, and tantalum are being published by major world powers and defined as 'critical' because they play essential roles in the creation of renewable energy technologies. More familiar minerals are also on these lists: tin, copper, platinum, cobalt, lithium. Another reason that some minerals are defined as critical is that the extraction of the mineral is highly concentrated in a few places. South Africa, for instance, produces nearly seventy percent of the world's total volume of platinum, which means that the global production of catalytic converters, electronics, highly specialised medical technologies, even cosmetics, would all come to a halt if South Africa closed its mines. State risk assessments generate the category of criticality, and it is unsurprising, then, that many critical minerals are mined in the Global South in former colonies and imperial possessions of European and North American states. Such lists, including the *EU Critical Raw Materials Act of 2024,* can be read as deeply encumbered documents that negotiate legacies of colonialism, contemporary liberal narratives of the energy transition as an opportunity for progress, and fears of the return of the repressed—extensive new mines on European soil. A mineral is critical, then, for geopolitical reasons.

Defining a mineral as critical generates a narrative of scarcity, which in turn sends prospectors prospecting and speculators speculating. India, for instance, has recently announced the discovery of a huge deposit of lithium in Jammu and Kashmir, a region that New Delhi took imperial possession of in 2022 after nearly seventy-four years of autonomy. Silicon Valley start-ups such as KoBold Metals, funded by Jeff Bezos and Bill Gates, are currently prospecting Greenland for rare-earth elements as glacial retreat, spurred by climate change, is beginning to reveal rocks long-hidden below. Protests over lithium prospecting have flared up in Portugal, Wales, and in Cornwall, England, where the mining company Cornish Tin is considering reopening tin mines that were closed in the late nineteenth century.

One of the reasons that I was on the dredger was to trace the particular path of tin along its complicated and sprawling extractivist routes. The modern story begins—or at least one of its many strands begins—in the hollowing out of the tin deposits in Britain in the late nineteenth century. At the time, tin was mostly used in plating and canning. As a material for wrapping and preserving, the globalisation of food would have been impossible without tin cans, and so it also became essential in provisioning armies on the move. When Cornish tin was largely exhausted, the British and Dutch governments looked to Southeast Asia to replace it with one of the largest concentrations of tin on earth. The Southeast Asian tin belt runs from Burma to Indonesia and was formed by ancient volcanic activity in a region of intense tectonic friction. On the very southern tip of the tin ore body is the Indonesian island of Bangka, about 350 kilometres from Singapore, and nearly the size of Greater London. The dredger I was on while it was doing its destructive work was a few kilometres off the coast of Bangka. The Southeast Asian tin belt has been harvested for millennia, and was long connected to extended trade networks throughout the Indian Ocean world. But when the British and Dutch colonial governments set their sights on it, extraction began at an unprecedented scale and intensity.

The British consolidated their colonial holdings in the Malay peninsula at Singapore, Penang, Dinding, and Malacca, which formed, roughly, the current

The tailings ponds on Bangka are too acidic for plants or animals to establish themselves there. Source: Image by author (August 2024)

Abandoned tin sluice boxes, traces of artisanal mining, litter the landscape of Bangka. Source: Image by author (August 2024)

Tin mine tailings and tailings ponds, Bangka. The environmental damages and losses caused by PT Timah between 2015 and 2022 is estimated to have cost the state a staggering $19 billion USD. Source: Image by author (August 2024)

territorial boundaries of peninsular Malaysia and Singapore, to control the extraction of tin. The mines drew in migrants fleeing a crumbling Qing dynasty, and in the two years between 1899 and 1900 nearly 100,000 Chinese men entered the Malay states. Thirteen years later, over 200,000 male labourers were recorded as working in the Malaysian tin mines. An additional 200,000 Chinese women were later permitted to join family members or to work in the mines.[1] In competition with British operations in Malaysia, the Dutch intensified extraction of their colonial holdings on Bangka.

The early years of the twentieth century were violent, with often grotesque transformations of the tin belt. Extraction was transformed from an almost entirely manual process racked by labour disputes between organised Chinese and Malay labourers and armed European mine owners, to mechanisation through the arrival of dredgers. The first one landed in Perak in 1912; seventeen years later 105 of them ravaged the landscape.[2] European dredgers, the size of apartment blocks—built in docks in Rotterdam, Leeds, and Glasgow—were operated by small teams that hauled the equivalent of 6,000 labourers' work in one month.[3] The dredgers eviscerated any of the miners' powers over extraction.

The tin fields, though, had already been damaged by the manual labourers even before the dredgers arrived. Strip mining, using a method of blasting jets of water on the landscape to create a slurry, had rendered vast regions into deserts. The monsoon season started creating floods in central Malaysia largely because of the erosion caused by mining. Whole villages were swallowed in mud. Tropical forests were terraformed into hardpacked white sand dunes and tailings ponds of clear blue water so acidic that plants and animals could not live in them. When the dredgers arrived, miners were already combing through tailings ponds looking for more tin and digging ever-deeper tunnels for underground extraction. The dredgers dialled up the scale of destruction, rendering areas the size of small towns barren, reshaping rivers, and expanding operations off the coast into the ocean floor. As the national mining company PT Timah's slogan puts it, "go offshore, go deeper".

When I arrived in July 2024, I happened to meet Dedi, an artisanal miner. He was working at a checkpoint, charging people to enter a local park. We struck up a conversation and I told him that I was trying to get access to the mining areas because I wanted to see how the process worked. He was passionate about mining, and angry with PT Timah. Dedi proudly called himself an "illegal miner", an insult that the authorities, and often PT Timah, directed at small scale miners. At the time, PT Timah was involved in one of the largest corruption scandals in Indonesian history. The cost to the state of the environmental damages caused by the company have recently been estimated at nearly US $19 billion by Bambang Hero Saharjo, an environmental economist at the Institut Pertanian Bogor University. PT Timah have often tried to foist the blame for the devastation they have caused onto people like Dedi. He was keen to show me around, explaining how the corruption operated, how the company knowingly cooked their books, participated in smuggling, and paid off police and government officials. He was telling me all of this, in part, as a tiny fuck you to PT Timah.

The next day, Dedi and I were walking through abandoned white desert tailings ponds in the baking sun when I noticed shards of nineteenth century clay

1 Nim Chee Siew, *Labour and Tin Mining in Malaya,* Cornell University Department of Far Eastern Studies, Southeast Asia Program, Data Paper Number 7, February (1953): 3.
2 Siew, *Labour and Tin Mining in Malaya*, 7.
3 Cory Ross, "The Tin Frontier: Mining, Empire, and Environment in Southeast Asia, 1870s—1930s", *Environmental History* 19, no. 3 (July 2014): 466-465.

pipes embedded in the ground around me. [fig 5] Originally, the pipes were used by those early Chinese and Malay labourers to blast water at the ground and filter out the tin from the streams they created. By now, the earth had been extracted and turned over so many times that contemporary miners were extracting from their own predecessors' waste, trying to squeeze out any last bit of tin that may have been missed. The devastated fields spread to the horizon; some miners had moved onto other parts of the island, or offshore entirely. Scattered around us were other ruins of these operations, such as sluice boxes made with cheap lumber and felled sticks crudely fastened together [fig 6]. The bottoms of the sluice boxes were lined with automobile mats—those plastic, thickly woven things that lie on the front seat floors of cars to catch dirt from shoes. The miners would pour a slurry of water and sand pumped from the bottom of tailings ponds over the mats in the sluice box, and the tin would get caught in the mesh of the car mat. Now, some of those mats hung, dishevelled, off the scaffolding of the abandoned boxes. In the distance, we could hear the faint sound of an active mining area.

PT Timah was founded during the wave of post-colonial nationalisation of industry that was typical after the Second World War. Since then, the company has persisted with as ruthless a drive for total environmental devastation as during the colonial period. Artisanal miners like Dedi have been made into a disposable class of people by the mining company to keep profits up and tin prices low. Miners die every year on Bangka, some of them by drowning at the bottom of tailings ponds or in the ocean while diving to dredge tin. In other areas of the island, miners are buried under collapsing tunnels. PT Timah regularly sets a low price for the tin they buy off the miners, yet the pay is higher than the wages for their own employees, driving state workers to mine off the books on their own time. I met one such miner on the beach. He had just descended from a day's work on a sketchy pontoon where he was working 'illegally' because the price he would make selling the tin—to his own employer—was higher than his wage [fig 7]. He was even still wearing a company uniform. He told me that tin mixed with other critical minerals—such as zircon (which is used in mobile phones)—was regularly smuggled out of the country to old pirate islands in the nearby Riau Archipelago, off the coast of Singapore, where it was then filtered into the global market [fig 8]. Because PT Timah sets the local price of tin, they can buy tin at an extremely low price from artisanal miners and sell high on global markets. This strategy has kept miners extremely poor, while creating extreme wealth for the managers of PT Timah, ensconcing them in the oligarchic class of Indonesia where they document their extravagant weddings, parties, and private jets on their Instagram accounts. On the ground, Bangka is a catastrophe of extractive capitalism, a material testament to the violence and trauma that is enacted on both the landscape and the people who live there.

One afternoon, I visited a reclamation project of PT Timah to ground-truth the company's many claims of rehabilitating former mining areas. What I found was a palm oil plantation, the same kind that has brought devastation to vast areas of Malaysia and Indonesia, a monocrop that is destroying ecologies in the region to produce cooking oil, cosmetics, and junk food. The plantation, now operating on top of the former mine, encapsulates the brutalised landscape of Bangka since the late nineteenth century.

The dark and often confusing reality of mining has been invisible to many in the Global North for nearly half a century. Neo-liberal reforms, many of which were responses to the strength of labour movements, drove the extractive industries to the Global South in the 1970s and 1980s. The 'offshoring' of the extractive industries coincided with the acceleration of climate breakdown through the intensification of fossil fuel mining in the neo-liberal period. Mining in Bangka has

An artisanal tin miner on the northwest coast of Bangka, Indonesia. This miner is performing a third or fourth order of extraction of the tin slurry. The first extraction is out of the frame and created a tailings pond at an unknown date. The second order of extraction is the current dredger, out of the frame, situated in the tailings pond and producing the slurry seen in the image. The sluice box is removing tin, the miner in the photo is trying to catch any remains of tin after the sluice box. I say third or perhaps fourth-order extraction because it is unclear how many times the tailings pond has been extracted. I did not get the miner's name. Source: Image by author (August 2024)

The dredging pontoon in the tailings pond producing the slurry seen in figure 1. Three miners operate a water pump fixed to a bore which they drive into the bottom of the pond by repeatedly jumping onto the bore. The borehole technology was introduced by Chinese migrant labourers in the eighteenth century to prospect for tin and was only more recently modified into a suction device. Source: Image by author (August 2024)

Today, the rush for critical minerals is driving an expansion of interest among economic geologists in highly complex computer-generated modelling of mantle processes to better prospect ophiolites in other places. The new material worlds created by critical minerals, then, should not be separated from the emergence of new ways of thinking about, and mapping, the Earth. Similarly, understanding the age of critical minerals means grappling with the histories of calculating and cataloguing world mineral reserves and their rates of depletion. How, for instance, did colonial geological surveys become folded into contemporary monitoring technologies to provide a picture of all of Earth's minerals? Through what methods do geologists calculate the volume of a mineral in the ground, and how much is needed for the future? Crucially, what are the blind spots in these methods, what do they *not* know?

One of the key challenges facing any ethical energy transition is the unfamiliarity of the materials that are driving it. Critical minerals are so diffuse, ubiquitous, and invisible that it is extremely difficult to narrate their agency in shaping the modern world. Rare earths, for instance, are in phone screens, lasers, and wind turbines. Making sense of rare earths' role in the contemporary conjuncture requires a new kind of Mumfordian taxonomy (Eotechnic, Paleotechnic, and Neotechnic) that can describe the material worlds we inhabit in a time of transitions. Mineral pathways bring us into contact with the sites and people who have also otherwise been made invisible to the Global North by the offshoring of extraction in the past half-century. But the goal of this is not only to make the unseen visible, but to imagine and build new forms of solidarity in which minerals and their global pathways can become connective materials. In other words, to generate *geosolidarities* and a *geocommons.* I am interested in experimenting with how energy transition minerals can operate as sites that connect people not only across distance but also to the deep history of the Earth itself. If the energy transition is mineral intensive, then a new mineral ethics and sensory commons needs to be developed which is up to the task of decarbonisation.

WORKS CITED

Hecht, Gabrielle. *Residual Governance: How South Africa Foretells Planetary Futures.* Duke University Press, 2023.

Mumford, Lewis. *Technics and Civilization.* Harcourt, Brace and Co., 1934.

Ross, Cory. "The Tin Frontier: Mining, Empire, and Environment in Southeast Asia, 1870s—1930s". *Environmental History* 19, no. 3 (July 2014): 466-465.

Siew, Nim Chee. *Labour and Tin Mining in Malaya,* Cornell University Department of Far Eastern Studies, Southeast Asia Program, Data Paper Number 7, February (1953): 3.

A POSTSCRIPT ON REHEARSING JUSTICE FROM WITHIN THE COMMONS

SHELA SHEIKH

On 16 November 2023, I joined the Centre for Research Architecture (CRA)'s second Roundtable seminar of the academic year, having been invited to lead the morning's discussion. The seminar was aimed at PhD students and there also were numerous MA students in attendance, as well as the Centre's faculty and James Parker, a legal scholar visiting from Melbourne who presented later that day on the relations between law, sound, and listening. In the spirit of the Roundtable as a pedagogical and experimental space that I had been welcomed into over the ten years prior, I chose to foreground the practice of *rehearsal* and to invite those present to think with me about what rehearsal, as a generative mode of thinking and acting, might open up for us all in our respective studies and quotidian practices.

While I spoke about my own current work, which takes rehearsal as a catalyst, the session was intended more as a space to prompt discussions of method and approach that might translate across subjects. I had asked that participants prepare by reading an interview with Michi Saagiig Nishnaabeg scholar, writer and artist Leanne Betasamosake Simpson, and Black feminist scholar Robyn Maynard about their 2022 book *Rehearsals for Living*, in which they map various senses in which the term 'rehearsal' might be understood according to an array of thinkers such as Ruth Wilson Gilmore, Ariella Azoulay, and Fred Moten and Stefano Harney.[1] During the seminar, I suggested that we also hold in the back of our minds geographer and prison abolitionist Wilson Gilmore's proposition that "abolition is life in rehearsal"[2] since, while I have long been captivated by the potentialities of abolitionism vis-à-vis the promise of justice that punitive legal systems seem to foreclose, this was all the more prescient given the climate in which our discussion was taking place: the near six weeks since 7 October already seemed like an eternity and by this point I, for one, as per many others, was experiencing intense disillusionment regarding the possibilities of international law and its institutions.[3]

In introducing the discussion of rehearsal that took place, I would also like to qualify the discussion on that day as rehearsal, and to take up the honour of closing this publication on common sensing by proposing that we think of the CRA Roundtable itself as a scene of rehearsal. In the context of my own research trajectory, the invitations both to lead the Roundtable that day and to write this postscript have solidified for me the manners in which my current work—on peoples' tribunals as spaces of rehearsal; on modalities of testimony,

1 Leanne Betasamosake Simpson, Christopher Griffin, Robyn Maynard & Hannah Voegeele, "Every Day We Must Get Up and Relearn the World: An Interview with Robyn Maynard and Leanne Betasamosake Simpson" (2021), https://hcommons.org/deposits/item/hc:51211/.

2 Ruth Wilson Gilmore, "Foreword: Spectacles", in Robyn Maynard & Leanne Betasamosake Simpson, *Rehearsals for Living* (Haymarket Books, 2022).

3 On the relationship between law and justice, see Nadine El-Anany, "Race, Law, and the Air that we Breathe", in *Border Environments*, ed. Riccardo Badano, Tomas Percival & Susan Schuppli (Spector Books, 2023), 95–109. Regarding abolition and Palestine, see Nadine Naber, "When Abolitionists Say 'Free Them All,' We Mean Palestine Too", *Truthout*, 29 December 2023, https://truthout.org/articles/when-abolitionists-say-free-them-all-we-mean-palestine-too/. On the tactical use of international law in the struggle for justice in Palestine, see Afeef Nessouli, "The Limits of the Law: An interview with legal scholar and activist, Noura Erakat", Acacia 2 (2024), https://www.acaciamag.com/issue-02/the-limits-of-the-law.

truthmaking, and collective knowledge production across the more-than-human spectrum; and on the relationship between law and justice--owes so much to reflections accumulated over the course of the past twelve years, either literally around the CRA Roundtable or within its conceptual vicinity.[4] Here it is useful to think of rehearsal, understood in the sense given to it by playwright Bertolt Brecht, as a pedagogical strategy. This is not about rehearsal as 'repetition of the same' or a learning by rote to the point of 'perfection' or arrival at a predetermined goal that is scripted in advance,[5] but rather, in the words of legal scholars Christine Schwöbel-Patel and Wouter Werner, "is about creativity, collaboration, surprise, refusal, critique and reflection".[6] Where Schwöbel-Patel and Werner's work takes Brechtian rehearsal to inform an experimental and progressive practice of mooting ('acting out' or rehearsing as legal pedagogy), I propose that we conceive of the CRA Roundtable—as a singular pedagogical and interdisciplinary space of critical encounter ("a generative assembly" in the words of this book series' editors)[7]—as a forum of rehearsal.

Central to the work of Forensic Architecture, which emerged from the CRA's research and pedagogy, is the relation between "the two constitutive sites of forensics--namely fields and forums". In other words, to put it straightforwardly, the field as "the site of investigation and the forum [as] the place in which the results of an investigation are presented and contested".[8] Where forums include legal trials, press conferences, exhibitions, public hearings, and other forms of assembly, the space of the CRA Roundtable has always been a constitutive forum (a semi-public gathering) in which to test out—to *rehearse*—the manners in which 'evidence' from the field is attended to and animated, and in particular the manners in which law, rather than being a stable set of tools to be called upon, must be endlessly questioned and, often, employed tactically. (Indeed, where Director of Forensic Architecture and former Director of the CRA, Eyal Weizman, writes that "[t]he field is not only a neutral, abstract grid on which traces of a crime can be plotted out, but itself a dynamic and elastic territory, a force field that is shaped by but also shapes conflict",[9] we can conceive of 'law' in similar ways.)[10]

4 In 2013 to 2014, while Publications Coordinator and Research Associate with Forensic Architecture, I took part in a number of Roundtables at a moment when PhD research was integral to the investigative work of Forensic Architecture. I have had the pleasure of participating in several PhD Roundtables and MA 'crits' sessions over the years since.

5 It is worth noting that in French (a language that I now often work in), the word *répetition* signifies both 'repetition' and 'rehearsal'. The rehearsal that I am emphasizing entails repetition but with difference, and as open-ended, entailing no defined blueprint.

6 Christine Schwöbel-Patel & Wouter Werner, "A Brechtian Way of Mooting", EJIL: Talk!, 24 October 2022, https://www.ejiltalk.org/a-brechtian-way-of-mooting/. See also Wouter Werner, *Repetition and International Law* (Cambridge University Press, 2022).

7 Editors' Introduction in Badano, Percival & Schuppli, eds., *Border Environments*, 6.

8 Eyal Weizman, "Introduction: Forensis" in Forensic Architecture, ed., *Forensis: The Architecture of Public Truth* (Sternberg Press, 2014), 9.

9 Weizman, "Introduction: Forensis", 9.

10 I place the singular noun 'law' in quotation marks here since to speak of 'the law' is problematic and overlooks the manifold attempts to pluralise law and adapt it to situated contexts, for instance from feminist and Indigenous perspectives, not to mention the many varieties of law. When I speak of law in the singular, it is to evoke hegemonic forms of law, based in Western epistemologies and histories of colonialism, that have served to uphold the interests of the 'West' and its economies. On this, see in particular the work of Third World Approaches to International Law (TWAIL) scholars, https://twailr.com/about/founding-statement/.

Besides this, we can also think of publishing practices as a particular kind of calling-into-being of forums and 'making public' ('to publish' from publicare). In the context of the present publication, which is part of the CRA's *Pedagogy, Politics, and Practices* book series, looking back across the contributions there is a rich range of community-based 'common sensing' projects in a variety of locales that we might at least schematically designate as 'fields' (I say schematically since the distinction is not rigid). For all its significance, I suggest that we compliment this by recalling the importance of both fields and forums. At this moment of heightened political instability in which alternative political imaginaries and languages of reason or common sense are increasingly foreclosed, it seems crucial to place an emphasis on forums as spaces in which local activities 'on the ground' intersect with broader campaigns for justice, as these converge with legal struggles. In this sense, what follows is an attempt to signal one possible avenue for opening up insights from within the common ground of this publication, in particular in the knowledge that this is in all likelihood the final volume in this publishing series. Integral to this opening up is the notion of rehearsal that we discussed at the CRA Roundtable.

Δ Δ Δ

One particularly generative kind of forum that sits in parallel to community-based sensing practices is that of peoples' tribunals, which, given the problematics of the current legal and political frameworks that foreclose social and environmental justice, seek, through necessity, to rehearse an alternative justice-to-come. Recent years have seen a marked increase in peoples' tribunals, with topics addressed ranging from the rights of nature,[11] crimes against humanity in Rojava,[12] environmental violence in West Papua,[13] to police killings,[14] not to mention the Russell Tribunal on Palestine founded in 2009.[15] In my own work, forums have always been of interest—as tense but often productive spaces of testimony, negotiations, mistranslations, and *différends*—and in recent years I have been increasingly drawn to spaces of tribunals. Indeed, the broader research project that informed our seminar discussion around the CRA Roundtable is a monograph I am currently working on, *Rehearsing Environmental Justice: People's Tribunals, Staged Hearings, Potential Histories*, which argues for the importance of peoples' tribunals in the present moment.

In 1948, the United Nations General Assembly recognised genocide as a crime under international law. In 2021, an independent expert panel drafted a legal definition of ecocide (the mass damage and destruction of the natural living world—literally 'killing one's home') that could be used were it to be ratified as an independent crime within the Rome Statute of the International

11 See for instance the International Rights of Nature Tribunal, https://www.rightsofnaturetribunal.org/; and Wild Legal France, https://www.wildlegal.eu.

12 See "Statement of the PPT Panel of Judges Following the 54° Session on Rojava vs Turkey", *Permanent Peoples' Tribunal*, 7 February 2025, https://permanentpeoplestribunal.org/statement-of-the-ppt-panel-of-judges-following-the-54-session-on-rojava-vs-turkey/?lang=en.

13 See "Permanent Peoples' Tribunal on West Papua – Centre for Climate Crime and Climate Justice", 27 June 2024, https://ccccjustice.org/2024/06/27/elementor-2823/.

14 See "The People's Tribunal on Police Killings", 24 November 2024, https://peoples-tribunal.org/.

15 https://www.russelltribunalonpalestine.com/en/index.html.

Criminal Court (ICC).[16] How might ecocide be established as an international crime with similar standing and evidential grounding to genocide? Calls have been made since 2008 for the establishment of an international court for the environment and a global Climate Justice Tribunal.[17] Given that the campaign for ecocide to be adopted by the ICC is gaining traction,[18] a speculative question arises as to what an eventual legally binding ecocide tribunal at the ICC might look like and whether this would be capable of offering environmental justice. *Rehearsing Environmental Justice* looks specifically to the role of (international or local) peoples' tribunals as privileged spaces for responding to such questions. Where 'the environment' remains politically and ontologically contested within international environmental law, with its origins in a Western epistemology,[19] I argue that the performative deployment of the tribunal form allows for the (re)constitution of the 'subject' of human and non-human rights. These discursive spaces nurture and consolidate the ongoing transformation of understanding of human life, emphasising how it is inseparable from its material, planetary means of sustenance and reproduction (its 'home'). They also provide forums for reconfiguring established theories of justice to encompass the environment. In its academic remit, the project contributes to the 'decolonising' of the humanities, social sciences, and international law by privileging 'southern' approaches—including grassroots minority and Indigenous representation—that propose alternative epistemologies and imaginaries of environmental justice, and that recast testimony and evidence between the human and non-human.

Peoples' tribunals have a long history, beginning notably with the 1966 Russell-Sartre International War Crimes Tribunal for Vietnam, which gave birth to the Permanent Peoples' Tribunal (an umbrella organisation for many contemporary tribunals founded in Bologna in 1979).[20] In recent years these have increasingly responded to issues of environmental justice, a movement that began in the 1970s in the wake of the US civil rights movement and responds to unequal distribution to environmental harm along lines of race, gender, and class, seeking equitable participation and governance in matters relating to a healthy environment. Rooted in local struggles, environmental justice is now embraced by global political institutions such as the UN Development Program.[21] At a grassroots level, it underlies transnational campaigns against ecocidal activities of multinational corporations such as Monsanto, now Bayer. Guided by the thematic of this book, this postscript foregrounds peoples' tribunals as forums instigated from the ground up by affected communities and activists, following a logic of *common sense* that seeks exposure of and redress for injustices.

16 "Legal Definition of Ecocide Drafted by Independent Expert Panel", Stop Ecocide International, https://www.stopecocide.earth/legal-definition. Crimes against nature were discussed in the Forensic Architecture research seminar, "'The 5th Geneva Convention': Nature, Conflict and International Law in the Anthropocene" on 25–26 January 2013 at the London School of Economics.

17 Polly Higgins, *Eradicating Ecocide* (Shepheard-Walwyn, 2015), 156–59.

18 For updates on ecocide legislation in multiple nations worldwide, see https://www.stopecocide.earth.

19 See Usha Natarajan & Julie Dehm, "Where is the Environment? Locating Nature in International Law", *TWAILR: Reflections* 3 (2019).

20 To date, the Tribunal has held more than 50 sessions worldwide. See https://permanentpeoplestribunal.org/?lang=en.

21 Francine Pickup, "Five steps to environmental justice", United Nations Development Programme blog, 23 June 2022, https://www.undp.org/blog/five-steps-environmental-justice.

Through close readings of a global selection of case studies, *Rehearsing Environmental Justice* asks how international law and its forums might need to be reconfigured to account for violations of both human and non-human rights. With these enormous questions on the horizon, I explore the potential of peoples' tribunals that question the legitimacy and efficacy of existing legal forums and rehearse legal frameworks to-come. Furthermore, I propose that much is to be learned by looking to speculative practices such as theatrical hearings and staged, fictional, or mock trials that, functioning in an experimental and propositional rather than merely representational mode, recast the tribunal form. Some examples include Indian theatre director Zuleikha Chaudhari's staged hearings, *Landscape as Evidence: Artist as Witness* (2017) and *In the Matter Re: Rights of Nature* (2023), Abbderrahmane Sissako's film, *Bamako* (2006), and Jonas Staal and Radha D'Souza's Court for Intergenerational Climate Crimes (2021).

For many international legal theorists, peoples' tribunals, which are not established by states or state-backed institutions, lack the legitimacy and authority to enact justice. They have received fairly scant attention within mainstream international justice scholarship and their contributions to international law are largely ignored.[22] Likewise, scholars of law, politics, and culture have, by and large, overlooked the performativity and theatricality of law that tribunals bring to the fore.[23] My project offers a corrective to this from the perspective of critical legal studies, which emphasises law's role in constructing and upholding race, gender, coloniality, as well as established categories of humanity and personhood (i.e. who counts, and how, as a legal subject). Taking a selection of theatrical staged hearings as a starting point allows me to bring to light the dimensions of rehearsal and performativity already at work within the law and to consider how rehearsal within law and politics might be practiced not as mere rote or repetition but, to recall the Brechtian sense evoked above, as an open-ended form of experimentation. If for Brecht rehearsal is about collectively discovering what making theatre entails, I argue that rehearsal within peoples' tribunals enables a questioning of what it is to make law and to strive towards justice, with justice understood as something that cannot be predefined or fully attained but that must be constantly *rehearsed*.[24] Peoples' tribunals tend to be set up by civil society *after* unsuccessful recourse to state-led legal forums, or when it is states themselves that have committed violations. They seek to enact sovereignty and highlight the (neo-colonial) illegitimacy of existing laws, often functioning as "counter-hearings".[25] But some peoples' tribunals have an even more future-oriented

22 Aldo Zammit Borda & Stefan Mandelbaum, "'If I Would Stay Alive, I Would Be Their Voice': On the Legitimacy of International People's Tribunals", *The Modern Law Review* 86, no. 1 (2022): 72.

23 Henning Grunwald, "Justice as ›performance‹? The Historiography of Legal Procedure and Political Criminal Justice in Weimar Germany", *InterDisciplines. Journal of History and Sociology* 3, no. 2 (17 December 2012): 46–78, at 46. A notable exception here is CRA faculty member Başak Ertür. See Başak Ertür, *Spectacles and Specters: A Performative Theory of Political Trials* (Fordham University Press, 2022). See also the work of Julie Stone Peters, Danish Sheikh, and Wouter Werner.

24 See Jacques Derrida, "Force of Law: The 'Mystical Foundation of Authority'", in Drucilla Cornell, Michel Rosenfeld, & David Gray Carlson, eds., *Deconstruction and the Possibility of Justice* (Routledge, 1992), 3–67.

25 Chowra Makaremi & Pardis Shafafi, "Introduction: Desire for Justice, Desire for Law: An Ethnography of Peoples' Tribunals", *PoLAR: Political and Legal Anthropology Review* 42, no. 2 (2019). See also Ertür's forthcoming *Just Publics: Counter-claims to Public Truth and Justice.*

remit: to rehearse legal rulings to-come. For instance, the International Monsanto Tribunal that took place in the Hague in 2016 to 2017 entailed promoting the legal concept of ecocide, advocating for its use in future legal proceedings, and consolidating relevant legal expert networks.[26] And the findings of the Airspace Tribunal, informed by artist Shona Illingworth's *Topologies of Air* installation (2021) and established by Illingworth and human rights lawyer Nick Grief, have led to the proposal for a new human right to protect the freedom to live without physical or psychological threat from above.[27] While there are a multitude of actions globally that are challenging and reconfiguring relations between law and the environment (for instance, protest, class action, Earth summits, citizens' assemblies), I privilege peoples' tribunals insofar as they "place the forms of legal process, and the standards of law, at the centre of their activities".[28] Creative staged hearings take this one step further, providing space and attention to also interrogate the aesthetics and ontological premises of environmental justice.

With regards to the temporality of bringing jurisprudence into being, I draw from scholars such as Amy Cohen and Bronwen Morgan, who speak of "prefigurative legality".[29] But in speaking of future-oriented rehearsals, as is the case for contemporary social justice movements, it is crucial to not lose sight of lessons from the past, especially earlier movements that did not benefit from wide (social) media coverage or are simply overlooked by younger generations of scholars and activists. In this sense, rehearsal, as a repetition-with-difference of past initiatives, is also a form of recitation, part of a broader practice of citation politics. Here, Ariella Aïsha Azoulay's notion of "potential history", of that which *could have* taken place, is generative. (This "potential history" resonates with Wilson Gilmore's notion of rehearsal as "a historical geography of the future". As she writes: "the purpose isn't to document that a specific thing happened, but rather to offer thickly analytical, detailed descriptions of many different ways people arrive at arranging themselves into a social force".)[30] For instance, although not discussed in the framework of environmental justice, the 1966 Russell Tribunal for Vietnam included discussion of the use of rainbow pesticides, most notably agent orange by the US military, and is thus an important backdrop for current discussions around ecocide including those of the 2016 International Monsanto Tribunal.[31] Thus, we might think of the Vietnam Russell Tribunal as a *proto-environmental tribunal*, an anticipatory rehearsal, *avant la lettre*, for more explicitly environmentally-oriented peoples' tribunals of recent years that would emerge

26 Giovanni Prete & Christel Cournil, "Staging International Environmental Justice: The International Monsanto Tribunal", *PoLAR: Political and Legal Anthropology Review* 42, no. 2 (2019): 192.

27 https://airspacetribunal.org.

28 Andrew Byrnes & Gabrielle Simm, "Introduction" in *People's Tribunals and International Law*, eds. Andrew Byrnes & Gabrielle Simm (Cambridge University Press, 2018), 3.

29 Amy J. Cohen & Bronwen Morgan, "Prefigurative Legality", *Law & Social Inquiry* 48, no. 3 (August 2023): 1053–82. The authors speak of the prefigurative legality of peoples' tribunals, in particular rights of nature tribunals.

30 Ruth Wilson Gilmore, "Foreword: Spectacles".

31 See David Zierler, *The Invention of Ecocide: Agent Orange, Vietnam, and the Scientists Who Changed the Way We Think about the Environment* (University of Georgia Press, 2011), esp. 21–22.

from its potentiality[32]—from its "rehearsal" in "nonimperial thinking", to borrow Azoulay's terms.[33]

Rehearsing a history of peoples' tribunals from the 1960s onwards allows one to trace the shift from Third World, anti-imperial and anti-colonial internationalism and 'worldmaking' as emancipatory frameworks to the neoliberal language of international law and rights. In the context of climate justice and the failure of international conventions such as the COP gatherings to offer viable long-term 'solutions', let alone necessary reparations,[34] the critique offered of the International Monetary Fund and the World Bank in the fictive trial of the film Bamako is particularly prescient. In retrospect, we see how the actions and interventions of these international bodies have helped neither the economic, nor the ecological, situation, let alone the self-determination of countries worst affected by climate change.[35] Thus, when we read a more recent, 'real' peoples' tribunal such as the International Monsanto Tribunal back through the *potential history* of this fictitious work, we catch sight of a necessary anti-capitalist and third-world perspective that is lacking in contemporary debates on the legal framework of ecocide.[36]

To use the formulation of Leah Bassel, who worked with the Permanent Peoples' Tribunal on the Hostile Environment in London in 2018, "the power of [peoples' tribunals] lies in *the promise to listen*" (emphasis added).[37] In other words, thinking of the various sensing practices progressed through this volume, forums such as peoples' tribunals are also important spaces for reorganising forms of sensing, expression, and reception, in particular in regards to unconventional forms of testimony that may not be allowed, let alone registered, in traditional legal settings. (Here, the untranslated sung lament of the griot Zegué Bamba in Sissako's film *Bamako* is exemplary, as are rights of nature tribunals that welcome Indigenous testimony based on non-Western cosmologies.)[38] For instance, current work in environmental justice

32 I thank my longstanding interlocutor Ros Gray for responding to my thinking here with the term *proto-environmental tribunals.* Regarding the "anticipatory", see Gray's discussion of "the radical moment" and its afterlives in her *Cinemas of the Mozambican Revolution: Anti-Colonialism, Independence and Internationalism in Filmmaking, 1968-1991* (Boydell and Brewer, 2020), esp. 4, 12, 13. See also the discussion of Brecht on 161–62.

33 Ariella Aïsha Azoulay, *Potential History: Unlearning Imperialism* (Verso, 2019).

34 See Olúfhemi O. Táíwò, *Reconsidering Reparations* (Oxford University Press, 2022).

35 See Keston K. Perry, "The IMF and the World Bank Must Be Abolished to Save the Planet", *Al Jazeera*, 26 November 2024, https://www.aljazeera.com/opinions/2024/11/24/the-imf-and-the-world-bank-must-be-abolished-to-save-the-planet.

36 See, for instance, Eliana Cusato & Emily Jones, "The 'Imbroglio' of Ecocide: A Political Economic Analysis", *Leiden Journal of International Law* 37, no. 1 (March 2024): 42–61; and David Whyte, *Ecocide: Kill the Corporation Before It Kills Us* (Manchester University Press, 2020).

37 Leah Bassel, "A Promise of Listening: Migrant Justice and the London Permanent Peoples' Tribunal", *Race & Class 63*, no. 4 (2022): 43. See the indictment submitted to the Permanent Peoples' Tribunal for the "Hostile Environment on Trial" London hearing (November 2018), https://permanentpeoplestribunal.org/wp-content/uploads/2018/01/Indictment_final.docx.pdf.

38 For a reading of Bamba's testimony as subaltern speech, see Gayatri Chakravorty Spivak, "Rethinking Comparativism" in *An Aesthetic Education in the Era of Globalization* (Harvard University Press, 2012), 467–83; and Stephen Morton, "The Wageless Life of the Subaltern", Cultural Studies 30, no. 5 (2016): 754–73. Regarding 'untranslatable' or 'incomputable' testimony in truth and reconciliation commissions, another generative kind of forum, see Susan Schuppli, "Computing the Law: Searching for Justice", in *Former West: Art and the Contemporary after 1989*, ed. Maria Hlavajova & Simon Sheikh (BAK, basis voor actuele kunst; MIT Press, 2017), 535–49.

studies stresses that responding to environmental racism and environmental injustice is not simply a matter of working with data that reveals discrimination; rather, "they are forms of state and institutional violence that perpetrate direct, immediate, and long-term physical, emotional, and spiritual harms that lead to suffering and premature death for the denizens of affected communities".[39] Here we can highlight "emotional, and spiritual harms": peoples' tribunals and their staged counterparts allow for an expression of these, of "emotional and cultural violence, and forms of trauma and grief that are not simply reparable through material solutions",[40] thus pushing beyond traditional Western notions of environmental harms that do not sufficiently capture how communities, particularly Indigenous or subaltern, are impacted by forms of environmental violence "through different ontologies of health and the impacts on traditions and cultural practices".[41]

For Dianne Otto, who served as an Expert Panellist at the Asia-Pacific Regional Women's Hearing on Gender-Based Violence in Conflict, held in October 2012 in Phnom Penh, peoples' tribunals demonstrate the potential to not only challenge "the inadequacies of the existing law and its institutions by invoking a collective responsibility" but also "to see that justice is also done 'beyond the law',"[42] entailing "a broader extra-legal responsibility that enjoins us all"[43] insofar as extra-legal justice "requires challenging the structures of economic and military power, which institutionalise impunity in a larger sense".[44] For the purposes of this volume, we can say that key to this "justice beyond the law" is the idea of common sensing. Firstly, the claims and complaints addressed by peoples' tribunals are, simply put, matters of common sense insofar as various violations, be they of human and/or non-human rights, need to be accounted for and adequate legal regimes are required to do so. In this sense, peoples' tribunals are everyday practices organised on ad hoc, grassroots, 'bottom-up' bases by non-state actors that put forward common-sense responses towards urgent conditions, either on a local level or in the context of international peoples' tribunals that address, cumulatively, the local effects of the actions of transnational actors, namely corporations. (A prime example here is the International Monsanto Tribunal, which gathered plaintiffs and experts from around the world to testify against Monsanto's actions.) Here we might recall the Permanent Peoples' Tribunal, which aims to "restore the authority of the people when states and international organisations have failed to protect the rights of peoples",[45] and indeed, in the longer term,

39 Erik Kojola & David N. Pellow, "New Directions in Environmental Justice Studies: Examining the State and Violence", *Environmental Politics* 30, no. 1–2 (2021): 101. See also pp. 108–9 regarding the place of emotions and grief in environmental justice studies.

40 Kojola & Pellow, "New Directions in Environmental Justice Studies", 103.

41 Jamie Vickery & Lori M. Hunter, "Native Americans: Where in Environmental Justice Research?" *Society & Natural Resources* 29, no. 1 (2016): 36–52, referenced in Kojola & Pellow, "New Directions in Environmental Justice Studies," 108–09.

42 Dianne Otto, "Impunity in a Different Register: People's Tribunals and Questions of Judgment, Law, and Responsibility", in *Anti-Impunity and the Human Rights Agenda*, ed. D. M. Davis, Karen Engle, & Zinaida Miller (Cambridge University Press, 2016), 292.

43 Otto, "Impunity in a Different Register", 291–92.

44 Dianne Otto, "Beyond Legal Justice: Some Personal Reflections on People's Tribunals, Listening and Responsibility", *London Review of International Law* 5, no. 2 (2017): 229.

45 Cited in Gabrielle Lefèvre, "Les tribunaux citoyens réinventent la justice", *Plein droit* 118, no. 3 (2018): 3–6.

to see "the people" as protagonists and potential authors of law and justice. Such demands are made from the perspective of local, place-based issues, thus pushing against the often-times universalising drive of international law, the origins of which lie in Western epistemologies.

While peoples' tribunals follow legal formats, which some might view as paradoxical given the friction they enact with national and international law, the actions of peoples' tribunals go beyond written, legal outcomes and include "publicising information, supporting campaigns, providing a corrective, mobilising public opinion, collecting primary and secondary material for formal inquiries, catalysing networks to recognise the suffering of victims and survivors, and memorialising 'historical' wrongs".[46] As Bassel writes, echoing the framing of the Permanent Peoples' Tribunal, "[w]hile enthusiastic about the power of international law to redress wrongs, '[a]t the same time, proponents of peoples' tribunals recognise that international law embodies and perpetuates historical and current structures of power that underpin such violations and that international law also needs to be remade in the interests of peoples and not just nation-states'."[47] Peoples' tribunals can thus also be understood as laboratories—at once experimental and based on everyday common sense—for rehearsing potential strategies of "legal rupture". Here I refer to lawyer Jacques Vergès's "rupture defence [*defense de rupture or procès de rupture*]", which sought to reveal the colonial criminal system as itself criminal.[48] This was the subject of a Roundtable discussion at the Centre in 2013[49] that responded to what Brenna Bhandar calls the "primary and inescapable question" of how one might "utilise the law without re-inscribing the very colonial legal order that one is attempting to break down".[50]

∆ ∆ ∆

To return to the space of the CRA, I had asked that participants of the November 2023 Roundtable prepare by also watching the video documentation of *Performing Environmental Justice: Staged Reflections*, a 'rehearsal' exploring epistemological and aesthetic frameworks for considering environmental harm, conceived by theatre director Zuleikha Chaudhari and I, and performed at the Haus der Kulturen der Welt in Berlin in 2022.[51] Taking Brecht's theoretical, unfinished text *The Messingkauf Dialogues* from the 1930s/40s as a proposal for a mutual learning encounter, Chaudhari and I invited interlocutors to select roles best suited to their own practice to replace the original characters of

46 Bassel, "A Promise of Listening", 43.

47 Andrew Byrnes & Gabrielle Simm, "Reflections on the International Peoples' Tribunals", in *People's Tribunals and International Law* (Cambridge University Press: 2017), 273, cited in Bassel, "A Promise of Listening", 44.

48 Jacques Vergès, *De la stratégie judiciaire* (Éditions de Minuit, 1968).

49 "Devil's Advocate" PhD Roundtable seminar at the Centre for Research Architecture, 1–2 March 2013. Guest speakers included Michael Sfard, Brenna Bhandar, Eitan Diamond, and Nicola Perugini.

50 Brenna Bhandar, "Strategies of Legal Rupture: The Politics of Judgment", *Windsor Yearbook of Access to Justice* 30, no. 2 (2012): 66. For discussions of legal ruptures in the context of peoples' tribunals, see Tor Krever, "From Vietnam to Palestine: Peoples' Tribunals and the Juridification of Resistance", in *Making Endless War: The Vietnam and Arab-Israeli Conflicts and the Remaking of International Law. Law, Meaning, and Violence*, ed. Brian Cuddy & Victor Kattan (University of Michigan Press, 2023), 233–61; and Bassel, "A Promise of Listening", 46–7.

51 https://archiv.hkw.de/en/programm/projekte/veranstaltung/p_195960.php.

Brecht's play with their own reflections.[52] In the performance, Chaudhari and I discussed our understanding of rehearsal, and legal scholar and now CRA staff member Başak Ertür amplified this by outlining the relationship between law, performance/performativity, and theatricality. During the CRA Roundtable, we paid particular attention to Ertür's choice, in our Berlin rehearsal, to present herself not as a lawyer or activist, but as a gleaner.

To quote:

> I write and I teach with the bits and pieces I glean from across disciplines. A while ago, I took a few wrong turns, and I came upon the field of law. At first it was hard going, there is much toxicity in the soil, and I didn't know how to glean for sustenance without getting poisoned. I have survived so far, with some bouts of nausea and chronic headaches. And I've been learning to get by thanks to friends and comrades who've been teaching me to *use my senses*: when you are gleaning, they say, you must look, touch, smell, taste: *trust your senses*, they say (emphasis added).

Ertür's contribution raised much for our Roundtable discussion, and likewise for the purposes of closing this postscript. For a start, the necessity for sensing, while navigating the terrain of law and politics, and its potential to open up the field of dispute and debate to other practices such as art, theatre, and performance. Speaking for myself, my research is inherently 'interdisciplinary', to use the institutionalised term, borrowing from multiple fields and practices without ever fully being 'at home' in any of them. This practice of gleaning—with all the chance finds, connections, and unexpected perspectives it can entail—would not have been possible without the nurturing and intellectual fodder provided by a pedagogical environment such as that of the CRA, which, as per so many academic centres, lives under the menace of institutional cuts and restructures, not to mention the threats of redundancy for the figures who animate it, who prompt and guide the rehearsals that it sets in place.

While those leading and participating in the CRA and Forensic Architecture Roundtables over the years perhaps did not have this vocabulary in mind, I suggest that we retroactively inflect the Roundtable through the notion of rehearsal which, as Chaudhari proposed in Berlin, can be conceived of as "the untidy process of thought and consideration with its related notions of version, repetition, and failure" and as "a series of tentative moves towards framing and reframing discourse".

And in the spirit of abolitionism, rather than a mode of deferral, rehearsal entails a learning-through-doing and attending to the unexpected in the present moment. Rehearsal can be understood and practiced as "an operating strategy", again to borrow Chaudhari's words, "[to foreground] that which takes place on the periphery and that which may be obscured by the presentation of a polished and final piece". In the context of this publication as well as the Roundtables of which it is a residue, this can also be understood, in the words of the Centre's director Susan Schuppli, as "a method for establishing arguments, forging solidarities, making political claims, etc. [...] and for creating spaces of active rehearsal for a more just future". Building upon the common sensing practices

52 Where Brecht's principal characters are The Philosopher, The Actor, The Actress, The Dramaturg, and The Electrician, our rehearsal was comprised of The Director (Zuleikha Chaudhari), The Performer (Shweta Bhattad), The Lawyer (Emilie Gaillard), The Gleaner (Başak Ertür), The Activist (Radha D'Souza), and The Critic (Shela Sheikh).

contained herein and gesturing beyond the pages of this publication, I end by recalling the urgency of making and maintaining spaces for research that cultivate a reciprocal relation with society: research that opens back out into and aids in narrating the everyday, common-sense practices of resistance and rehearsing justice that animate and nourish the university as a community, a commons, and a communal political project.

WORKS CITED

Azoulay, Ariella Aïsha. *Potential History: Unlearning Imperialism*. Verso, 2019.

Badano, Riccardo, Tomas Percival & Susan Schuppli. "Editor's Introduction". In *Border Environments*, edited by Badano, Percival & Schuppli. Spector Books, 2023.

Bassel, Leah. "A Promise of Listening: Migrant Justice and the London Permanent Peoples' Tribunal". *Race & Class* 63, no. 4 (2022): 35–55.

Bhandar, Brenna. "Strategies of Legal Rupture: The Politics of Judgment". *Windsor Yearbook of Access to Justice* 30, no. 2 (2012): 59–78.

Borda, Aldo Zammit, & Stefan Mandelbaum. "'If I Would Stay Alive, I Would Be Their Voice': On the Legitimacy of International People's Tribunals". *The Modern Law Review* 86, no. 1 (2022): 67–84.

Byrnes, Andrew, & Gabrielle Simm. "Introduction". In *People's Tribunals and International Law*, edited by Byrnes & Simm. Cambridge University Press, 2018.

Byrnes, Andrew, & Gabrielle Simm, "Reflections on the International Peoples' Tribunals". In *People's Tribunals and International Law*, edited by Byrnes & Simm. Cambridge University Press, 2018.

Cohen, Amy J., & Bronwen Morgan. "Prefigurative Legality". *Law & Social Inquiry* 48, no. 3 (August 2023): 1053–82.

Gilmore, Ruth Wilson. "Foreword: Spectacles". In Robyn Maynard & Leanne Betasamosake Simpson, *Rehearsals for Living*. Haymarket Books, 2022.

Grunwald, Henning. "Justice as ›performance‹? The Historiography of Legal Procedure and Political Criminal Justice in Weimar Germany". *InterDisciplines. Journal of History and Sociology* 3, no. 2 (17 December 2012): 46–78.

Higgins, Polly. *Eradicating Ecocide*. Shepheard-Walwyn, 2015.

Kojola, Erik, & David N. Pellow. "New Directions in Environmental Justice Studies: Examining the State and Violence". *Environmental Politics* 30, no. 1–2 (2021): 100–118.

Lefèvre, Gabrielle. "Les tribunaux citoyens réinventent la justice". *Plein droit* 118, no. 3 (2018): 3–6.

Makaremi, Chowra, & Pardis Shafafi. "Introduction: Desire for Justice, Desire for Law: An Ethnography of Peoples' Tribunals". *PoLAR: Political and Legal Anthropology Review* 42, no. 2 (2019).

Otto, Dianne. "Impunity in a Different Register: People's Tribunals and Questions of Judgment, Law, and Responsibility". In *Anti-Impunity and the Human Rights Agenda*, edited by D. M. Davis, Karen Engle, & Zinaida Miller. Cambridge University Press, 2016.

Otto, Dianne. "Beyond Legal Justice: Some Personal Reflections on People's Tribunals, Listening and Responsibility". *London Review of International Law* 5, no. 2 (2017): 225–49.

Pickup, Francine. "Five steps to environmental justice". United Nations Development Programme blog, 23 June 2022. https://www.undp.org/blog/five-steps-environmental-justice.

Prete, Giovanni, & Christel Cournil. "Staging International Environmental Justice: The International Monsanto Tribunal". *PoLAR: Political and Legal Anthropology Review* 42, no. 2 (2019): 191–209.

Schwöbel-Patel, Christine, & Wouter Werner. "A Brechtian Way of Mooting". *EJIL: Talk!*, 24 October 2022. https://www.ejiltalk.org/a-brechtian-way-of-mooting/.

Simpson, Leanne Betasamosake, Christopher Griffin, Robyn Maynard, & Hannah Voegeele. " Every Day We Must Get Up and Relearn the World: An Interview with Robyn Maynard and Leanne Betasamosake Simpson". 2021. https://hcommons.org/deposits/item/hc:51211/.

Stop Ecocide International. "Legal Definition of Ecocide Drafted by Independent Expert Panel". https://www.stopecocide.earth/legal-definition.

Vergès, Jacques. *De la stratégie judiciaire*. Éditions de Minuit, 1968.

Vickery, Jamie, & Lori M. Hunter. "Native Americans: Where in Environmental Justice Research?". *Society & Natural Resources* 29, no. 1 (2016): 36–52.

Weizman, Eyal. "Introduction: Forensis". In *Forensis: The Architecture of Public Truth*, edited by Forensic Architecture. Sternberg Press, 2014.

BIOGRAPHIES

AL-WAH'AT is an artist-research collective formed by Ailo Ribas, Gabriella Demczuk, and Areej Ashhab at the Centre for Research Architecture. The collective is committed to growing communal practices in ecologies typically regarded as hostile and lifeless and to countering anthropocentric and colonial narratives about arid lands and futures. Al-Wah'at experiments with archival research, on-the-ground fieldwork, material experimentation, and image-making through practices of care and knowledge exchange across the human and the more-than-human.

RICCARDO BADANO is an architect, researcher, and editor working at the intersection of migration circulations and critical ecologies. He is currently a Tutor on the MA City Design programme at the Royal College of Art. Badano completed his MA at the Centre for Research Architecture, where he is currently undertaking his PhD.

JACOB BERTILSSON is an artist and researcher working between the UK and Sweden. His practice integrates video, web-based code, and 3D visualisations to examine the intersection of technology, aesthetics, and ecosystem governance, with a particular focus on digital representations of forest environments. He holds an MA from the Centre for Research Architecture. He currently co-leads Mushroom Forest, a science communication project in collaboration with fungal researcher Anders Dahlberg at the Swedish University of Agricultural Sciences.

ADAM BOBBETTE is a geographer and Lecturer in Political Geology at the University of Glasgow. His books include *The Pulse of the Earth: Political Geology in Java* (2023). His current project, Earthworks: Political Geology in the Age of Critical Minerals, will soon be published by Verso.

COOKING SECTIONS examines the systems that shape the planet through food, tracing the spatial, ecological, and political legacies of extractivism. Cooking Sections was founded in London in 2013 by Daniel Fernández Pascual and Alon Schwabe, graduates of the Centre for Research Architecture. Their practice operates at the intersection of art, architecture, ecology, and geopolitics. Their work has been exhibited at Tate Britain, Serpentine Galleries, SALT, Carnegie Museum of Art, and the Venice, Istanbul, and Sharjah Biennials, among others. Since 2015, they have led CLIMAVORE, a platform examining how to metabolise climate breakdown. They are Readers in Architecture and Spatial Practice at the Royal College of Art and are Fellows at the Canadian Institute for Advanced Research.

IFOR DUNCAN is a Postdoctoral Researcher on the EcoViolence ERC project at Utrecht University. His interdisciplinary research and art practice focuses on political violence in the contexts of devastated river systems and dispossessed communities. He approaches the weaponisation of rivers as borders, mega-dams, and as the mediums and dynamic archives of genocide through cultural memory and an audio-visual practice that involves submerged methods. Ifor has a PhD from the Centre for Research Architecture, Goldsmiths, where he was also a Lecturer, and has been Postdoctoral Fellow in Environmental Humanities at NICHE, Ca' Foscari, University of Venice.

JENNIFER GABRYS is Chair in Media, Culture and Environment in the Department of Sociology at the University of Cambridge. She leads the Planetary Praxis research group and is Principal Investigator on the ERC-funded project, Smart Forests: Transforming Environments into Social-

Political Technologies. Her publications include *Citizens of Worlds* (2022), *How to Do Things with Sensors* (2019), *Program Earth* (2016), and *Digital Rubbish* (2011). Her work can be found at planetarypraxis.org and jennifergabrys.net.

NAIZA KHAN is a visual artist with a multidisciplinary practice built on critical research, documentation, and mapping-based exploration. She trained at the Ruskin School of Art, University of Oxford, and completed her MA at the Centre for Research Architecture in 2020. Her work examines geography as a heterogeneous assemblage of power, colonial history, and collective memory. Her practice raises questions about optics, erasure, and frictions between old and new infrastructures. She works between Karachi and London.

HANNAH MESZAROS MARTIN is an artist, filmmaker, and writer. She is currently a Postdoctoral Researcher working on the NSF-funded project 'Aquifers, Science and Responsibility' at the University of Southern California. She is also a Research Fellow at Forensic Architecture, which she has been a member of since 2012. She holds a PhD from the Center for Research Architecture.

MARGARIDA MENDES is a researcher and curator. Her research explores the overlap between infrastructure, ecology, experimental film, and sound practices, investigating environmental transformations and their impact on societal structures and cultural production. She is interested in exploring alternative modes of education and political resilience through her curatorial practice and activism. She completed her PhD at the Center for Research Architecture.

ENRICO MILAZZO is a Research Associate at CLIMAVORE x Jameel at the Royal College of Art, where he leads Monoculture Meltdown, a project examining the socio-ecological impacts of intensive farming in periods of drought. He holds a PhD in Anthropology from Ca' Foscari University of Venice, the University of Verona, and the University of Padua. A founding member of Epidemia Collective, he investigates the legacies of Xylella fastidiosa, a pathogen that has devastated olive monocultures in Southern Italy. His ethnographic research in Sicily and Apulia focuses on agroecology movements in the climate crisis.

SAM NIGHTINGALE is an artist-researcher working within environmental media. Nightingale is involved in various interdisciplinary projects, including conducting field-labs and collaborating with rural communities, geographers and social scientists in Europe, Africa and Australia. He is co-editor of the book *Fieldwork for Future Ecologies* (2022/24). He teaches at the Royal College of Art and is completing a PhD at Goldsmiths, University of London.

TOMAS PERCIVAL is an artist, researcher, and writer. His work critically investigates the intersections of space and (in)security. He completed his PhD at the Centre for Research Architecture, where he was also a Lecturer. Percival is currently an Affiliated Fellow at the ICI Berlin Institute for Cultural Inquiry.

GODOFREDO ENES PEREIRA is an architect and researcher. He is the Head of the MA Environmental Architecture programme at the Royal College of Art. For the past decade, he has been conducting research, publishing, and exhibiting on environmental architecture and collective politics. His doctoral research, The Underground Frontier: Technoscience and Collective Politics, conducted at the Centre for Research Architecture, investigated political and territorial conflicts within the planetary race for underground resources.

GEORGE RIDGWAY is an artist, researcher and ecological surveyor. His practice engages with questions of ecological justice and restoration, the political production of natures, and architectures of listening. He currently tutors in the MA Environmental Architecture programme at the Royal College of Art. He completed his MA from the Centre for Research Architecture.

JOÃO PRATES RUIVO is an architect whose research focuses on the technical transformations of soils after the Second World War, specifically the relation between colonisation and irrigation. A PhD graduate from the Centre for Research Architecture, where he is currently an Associate Lecturer, his dissertation 'Soil Politics' investigates the role of scientific soil surveys in the anti-colonial struggles in Angola, and the relation between counterinsurgency and present-day environmental disputes in Alentejo, in the South of Portugal. Together with George Ridgway, he leads the Alentejo Research Unit at the Royal College of Art.

SUSAN SCHUPPLI is an artist-researcher whose work examines material evidence from war and conflict to environmental disasters and climate change. Her current work is focused on Learning from Ice and is the subject of numerous documentary films. Schuppli is the author of *Material Witness* (2020) and is Professor and Director of the Centre for Research Architecture, as well as the Board Chair of Forensic Architecture.

ARIADNA SERRAHIMA is a publisher, researcher, and graphic designer. Her research explores struggles in relation to autonomous spaces, the circulation of critical knowledge, and the production of collective insurgent learning. Serrahima co-founded the graphic design studio Oficina de Disseny. She is part of L'Automàtica cooperative print shop in Barcelona and co-founder of I.F Publications. She completed her MA in Research Architecture and is a PhD candidate in Visual Cultures at Goldsmiths.

SHELA SHEIKH is Senior Lecturer in International Politics at the University of London Institute in Paris (ULIP). Her research spans post/decolonial cultural studies, environmental humanities, and global arts. She is also committed to editorial practices; she was co-director (with Malcom Ferdinand) of issue *ONE of Plurivers: revue d'écologies décoloniales*, a plurilingual open-access journal edited by the Observatoire Terre-Monde; and is co-editor (with Ros Gray and Jennifer Gabrys) of the *Planetarities series* (Goldsmiths/MIT Press). At Goldsmiths, she convened the MA Postcolonial Culture and Global Policy (2014–22) and was Research Associate and Publications Coordinator with Forensic Architecture (2013–14).

PAULO TAVARES is an architect, author, and educator. His practice dwells at the frontiers between architecture, visual cultures, and advocacy. Operating through multiple media, Tavares's projects have been featured in various exhibitions worldwide, including the Oslo Architecture Triennial, Istanbul Design Biennale, São Paulo Art Biennial, and Venice Biennale. He is the author of several books questioning the colonial legacies of modernity, including *Des-Habitat* (2019), *Lucio Costa era Racista?* (2022), and *Derechos No-Humanos* (2022). He holds a PhD from the Centre for Research Architecture.

ASLI ULUDAĞ is an artist and researcher. Her work examines environmental governance and extractivism, with a focus on watery environments and the subsurface. She employs historical, material, and spatial analysis to investigate the scientific, architectural, and legal structures that shape environmental disputes, and explores the local practices, narratives, and environmental relations that reveal areas for intervention. She is a tutor in the MA Environmental Architecture programme at the Royal College of Art. Uludağ is a PhD candidate at the Centre for Research Architecture.

CHRISTINA VARVIA is a Lecturer at the Centre for Research Architecture. She has been a member of the Forensic Architecture agency since 2014 and formerly acted as its Deputy Director. Currently, she is completing her PhD a t Aarhus University, where her research focuses on feminist notions of the human body within the context of investigative practice. She is a founding member and the chair of the board of Forensis e.V., and the co-founder and co-director of the Forensic Architecture Initiative Athens (FAIĀ).

A Centre for Research Architecture series exploring pedagogy, politics, and practices

Series Editors:
Riccardo Badano
Tomas Percival
Susan Schuppli
Ariadna Serrahima

Common Sensing

Editors:
Riccardo Badano
Tomas Percival
Susan Schuppli

Associate Editor: Aslı Uludağ

Graphic Design: Ariadna Serrahima

Copy Editor: Ailo Ribas Goody

Image Correction: Xavier Tulleuda

Printed in the EU

Published by:
Spector Books Verlagsgesellschaft mbH
Harkortstrasse 10
04107 Leipzig
www.spectorbooks.com

The publication has been made possible through the generous support of the Graham Foundation for Advanced Studies in the Fine Arts and the Departments of Visual Cultures and Art at Goldsmiths, University of London.

Distribution:
- Germany, Austria:
  GVA, Gemeinsame Verlagsauslieferung Gottingen GmbH & Co. KG, www.gva-verlage.de
- Switzerland:
  AVA Verlagsauslieferung AG, www.ava.ch
- France, Belgium:
  Interart Paris, www.interart.fr
- UK:
  Central Books Ltd, www.centralbooks.com
- USA, Canada, Central and South America, Africa:
  ARTBOOK / D.A.P., www.artbook.com
- South Korea:
  The Book Society, www.thebooksociety.org
- Japan:
  twelvebooks, www.twelve-books.com
- Australia, New Zealand:
  Perimeter Distribution, www.perimeterdistribution.com

First edition: 2025

ISBN: 978-3-95905-688-5

Additional Image Sources:
Araucaria tree with destroyed bark. Source: Jennifer Gabrys, 2023. (p. 20)
A *bocachico* fish caught in the reservoir near the flooded town of Barbacoas. Source: Ifor Duncan, 2024. (p. 32)
The Pedoteca underneath the Instituto Superior de Agronomia, Lisbon. Source: João Prates Ruivo, 2016 (p. 52)
Fieldwork photograph in the Lower Mississippi River journey. Source: Margarida Mendes, 2019. (p. 74)
CLIMAVORE Assembly at Museo delle Civiltà, Rome. Source: Cooking Sections and Enrico Milazzo, 2023. (p. 90)

Graham Foundation